The Ernst & Young Guide to

PERFORMANCE MEASUREMENT FOR FINANCIAL INSTITUTIONS

Methods for Managing Business Results

REVISED EDITION

MCGRAW-HILL

NEW YORK   SAN FRANCISCO   WASHINGTON, D.C.   AUCKLAND   BOGOTA
CARACAS   LISBON   LONDON   MADRID   MEXICO CITY   MILAN
MONTREAL   NEW DELHI   SAN JUAN   SINGAPORE   SYDNEY   TOKYO   TORONTO

McGraw-Hill

A Division of The **McGraw·Hill** Companies

ISBN 1-55738-737-0

Printed in the United States of America

BB

    5 6 7 8 9 0

CB/BJS

Table of Contents

PART IV—Implementation Issues Related to
Performance Measurement

List of Figures

Acknowledgments

A book of this scope is the product of cooperation and a tireless effort among many people. Kenneth J. Bozzi, Jeffry W. Calotta, Patrick E. Garrett, John Karr, Kevin W. Link, Mike McGrath, Douglas W. Meyer, James H. Morgan, Brendan O'Sullivan, Mason E. Snyder, Stephen R. Robinson, and Deborah Wilson contributed greatly to the direction and analysis of the content. Many others at Ernst & Young LLP contributed time and energy to further this work. In all respects, this book is the product of Ernst & Young LLP's Financial Services Industries Consulting Practice.

Ernst & Young LLP Financial Services Industries Consulting Practice

The Financial Services Industries Consulting Practice mission is to add value for its clients by designing and implementing business solutions that result in improved growth and profitability. Our consultants work with leading financial institutions on large-scale reengineering, organizational change and information technology initiatives. These efforts are resulting in dramatic cost savings, cycle-time reductions, knowledge base development and customer service innovations for clients.

Ernst & Young LLP financial management consulting is differentiated by its proven ability to design and implement large-scale business change initiatives that deliver measurable results for clients, as well as by a focus on solutions that integrate people, processes and technology. The practice is also at the forefront of the industry in investments in developing new ideas and approaches.

PART I

Introduction to Performance Measurement

CHAPTER 1

The Changing State of Banking

In the past several years since the first edition of this book was published, the financial services industry has undergone more change than in the previous decades since World War II. The environment in which commercial bankers operate has never been more competitive.

Until the 1960s, commercial banks operated in a highly regulated environment, featuring low interest rates, regulated rates for deposits, and a relatively predictable yield curve. Substantial interest spreads were common, which meant that profits were virtually guaranteed. There was little need for cost control, and little incentive for improving productivity.

Performance measurement was seldom needed because product offerings were limited and prices were set either by government or by competition. External financial statements and regulatory reports sufficed for banks to manage their business profitably.

Deregulation in the banking industry, which began in the 1960s and has continued apace for nearly 30 years, did more than merely reduce spreads. Its greatest effect was to increase competition. Commercial banks both broadened their product offerings and their geographic reach. And, a host of traditionally nonfinancial companies entered the financial services industry.

It became increasingly important for financial institutions to measure their profitability in as many ways as possible: by product, customer relationship, branch, etc.

Further complicating matters in the early years of deregulation, both deposit maturities and interest rates began to vary. When rates began rising in the late 1960s, many banks were caught with portfolios of earning assets that did not begin to match the maturity and interest-rate structure of the liabilities funding them.

By the 1980s, consumers could obtain financial services products from a host of sources: from a universal credit card through a retail company (the Sears Discover card) to a home mortgage through a car company (GM Credit). Moving into the 1990s, interstate banking proliferated, and Americans held more money than ever before in money market mutual funds offered by mutual fund companies and brokerage houses.

In today's environment of "hypercompetition," it no longer is enough to measure performance "by the numbers." The competitive landscape is changing too quickly; today's profitable product can turn into tomorrow's obsolete product almost overnight. With the proliferation of competitors, both traditional and nontraditional financial service companies, banks must focus ever more on the satisfaction customers derive from each banking transaction.

Increasingly customers are determining their banking relationship not merely by the price of product, but by the speed with which loan applications are processed and how quickly deposits are processed from a lockbox. Banks, like many other businesses and industries, are "reengineering" processes to provide more effective, efficient service for customers. They are reducing their cost structure while maintaining a level of customer service that garners high customer satisfaction.

$$\text{Reduced time + increased service + lower cost clearly}$$
$$\text{= enhanced profitability.}$$

It is obvious that yesterday's profitability measurement has become today's performance measurement. Yesterday's focus on reducing unit cost (often through simply reducing head count and all of the fixed costs that it implies) has become today's focus on removing "non-value-added" steps from processes, often through process reengineering and subsequent automation.

The amount of information needed to measure performance is greater than the amount needed simply to measure profitability. But today's information systems are up to the task—both in terms of the central processes capacity of today's hardware, and the tools and techniques used by the best of today's systems development experts.

While the nomenclature may be different today than a decade ago—while the customer may drive the process instead of the bottom line—the management process for performance measurement is the same as that for profitability measurement:

- Establish organizational objectives.

- Prompt decisions and actions designed to achieve those objectives.

- Monitor, through performance measurement systems, the success of those decisions and actions in achieving the objectives.

CHAPTER 2

How to Use This Guide

The *Ernst & Young Guide to Performance Measurement* has been developed to assist financial institutions with the design, implementation, and management of performance information. It is intended to explain the latest strategies and practices in performance measurement, drawing the experiences of many of the top commercial, retail, and wholesale banks, investment companies, and mutual fund businesses. As no single formula exists for measuring performance, this book provides a set of guidelines that can be tailored to any organization.

This guide is organized according to the way the process of creating performance measures evolves within many institutions, as shown in Figure 2-1. First comes the strategic development phase, which focuses on developing an information management system that can evaluate the institution's current and future viability. This strategy evolves into a conceptual design phase centered on addressing the overall design and reporting of the information. Next comes implementation of the conceptual design. Finally, the institution must decide how to use the information being produced.

Figure 2-1—Stages of Performance Measurement

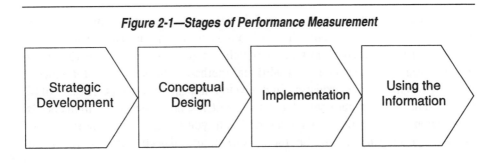

This guide covers these phases in five sections, each made up of several chapters. Each chapter covers specific subject matter in depth, discussing issues and potential solutions. The sections are:

1. **Introduction to Performance Measurement**—Defining an institution's true information needs can be as significant an exercise as the implementation itself. The first section of this guide provides the framework for successful performance measurement system designs.

2. **Income Statement Components of Performance Measurement**—Bottom-line profits represent the single most important element in most measurement systems. Included in this section are the many issues related to the design theory, design implementation, and reporting of income-statement items.

3. **Balance Sheet Components of Performance Measurement**—No performance measurement system is complete without addressing the balance sheet, which ultimately drives the income statement. This section addresses the issues inherent in the design and reporting of the balance sheet.

4. **Implementation Issues Related to Performance Measurement**—A detailed conceptual design is vital to the timely and accurate implementation of a performance measurement system. This section discusses the elements of conceptual design and presents alternatives for implementation. Included are two chapters reviewing emerging technology issues related to measurement systems.

5. **Using Performance Measurement Information**—The final test of an effective system is knowing how to use the information. This section suggests many applications for using this information in day-to-day management decisions.

As competition heats up and financial institutions offer more similar products and services, managing the bottom line through performance measurement systems will become increasingly important. To remain competitive, financial services institutions need to look beyond the traditional method of measuring performance— tracking revenue against expense—and develop new measurements. These will include product development, service enhancement, responsiveness to customer needs, and customer satisfaction. This guide will help you think beyond the traditional methods, develop new approaches for measurement, and begin implementing them.

CHAPTER 3

Strategic Performance Measures

OVERVIEW

While institutions deploy significant resources in the design and development of comprehensive systems to measure and report financial performance, few devote similar resources in deciding whether those systems encompass the right measures. Too often, they use the typical financial-driven measures that have long served as the foundation for performance measurement systems for many years.

With increased pressures on the industry, financial institutions are beginning to question whether these financial measures are indeed the best indicators of health, stability, and even viability. Today's financial executives are faced with ever-increasing challenges to their institutions, from more demanding customers at the smallest branches to intense global competition. They need an appropriate set of tools to manage those challenges. More and more, executives are adding to their repertoire of profitability measures a group of nonfinancial measures.

"During the 1980s, many executives saw their companies' strong financial records deteriorate because of unnoticed declines in quality or customer satisfaction or because global competitors ate into their market share," wrote the Harvard Business School professor Robert Eccles in "The Performance Measurement Manifesto," published in the January-February 1991 *Harvard Business Review*. These declines go unnoticed simply because they are not routinely measured and managed. Understanding your customer's satisfaction level and your share of the market will ultimately lead to results on your income statement.

Knowing these nonfinancial measures therefore has a significant strategic value in managing the institution. As Eccles writes, "Tracking these measures is one thing.

But giving them equal (or even greater) status in determining strategy, promotions, bonuses and other rewards is another."

Profitability measures assess only the relationships among different components of an institution's profitability statements, and provide a common basis for evaluating financial performance across the business. They emphasize the profitability of an activity as measured by the performance of the organizations, its products, and its customers.

Performance measures, on the other hand, are a quantitative assessment of progress toward achieving a particular goal or objective, be it financial or qualitative. Within the performance measurement system are many profitability measures, such as return on equity (ROE) and return on assets (ROA). Also included are a number of nonfinancial performance measures, such as customer satisfaction as measured by the quality of service levels, cycle time (e.g., loan processing time), and product variation or differentiation.

Linking these performance measures to strategy is a process known as "strategic performance measurement." A simple example is an institution that places heavy emphasis on selling relationships and measures the number of new customers who purchase multiple products as a percentage of total new customers.

"A new vision is emerging which better aligns measurements with objectives, and which looks beyond historical indicators. The vision is primarily concerned with strategic linkages, but its premises can be generalized throughout the organization and used to reshape tactical measures as well," wrote Ernst & Young partner John Karr in "Performance Measurement in Banking, Beyond ROE," published in *Bank Cost and Management Accounting* (v.6, n.1, Spring 1993).

It is important to remember that success in reaching the goals and gauged objectives measured by nonfinancial measurements will almost surely translate to bottom-line results. And if the goals and objectives are closely linked to an institution's long-term vision, those results should endure.

"Building a strategic measurement system involves more than merely collecting non-financial data," wrote Mike Vitale, Mark Hauser, and Sarah Mavinac of the Ernst & Young Center for Information Technology and Strategy in their 1993 working paper "Measuring Strategic Performance." Thought must go into the type of data to be collected, the source of the data, its uses, and ultimately the value of knowing it.

Four guiding principles need to be considered when developing appropriate measures. These four M's (M^4 Principles) ask whether each measure is:

Meaningful   Will knowing the measure provide insight into the current health, stability, and viability of the institution? Measures provided to management must aid in decision making.

Measurable   The measure must be quantifiable. Measures must be developed that are indeed measurable.

| **Manageable** | Does it take significant manual effort or programming to measure the results? This can outweigh any benefit of knowing the measure. Also, can you reasonably manage the data required to calculate the measure? |
| **Material** | Is the measure material to the overall organization? Will a significant improvement in the measure provide material results? |

Strategic performance measurement is often described as the intersection between three dimensions as shown in Figure 3-1. Thus, it provides executives with multiple views of their institutions.

Internal	The Internal view provides measures about the institution based on internal operations and financial results.
Market/ Industry	The Market/Industry view provides measures relative to such external indicators as industry trends and norms and the market.
Customer	The Customer view provides measures that continually view the organization through the eyes of the customer.

Balanced Strategic Performance Measures

Strategic performance measurement provides the vital link between the institution's strategy and the evaluation process, and seeks to determine whether the business activities are executing the strategy. Developing the strategic performance measure-

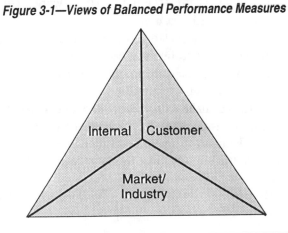

Figure 3-1—Views of Balanced Performance Measures

ment system not only means creating the right measures, but also striking the right balance of internal, customer, and market/industry measures. Understanding the relationships between the measures and the interdependencies is also vital in helping to map the defined measures against the three dimensions.

Most institutions find a map of their current measurement set to be heavily weighted to the internal measures of profitability. A strategic performance measurement set that truly does its job in today's environment gives a more even weight to the three dimensions.

Developing a More Balanced Strategic Performance Measurement Set

Establishing a balanced strategic measurement set is a process, not an event. It takes disciplined and dedicated effort by an institution's top executives. But while there is no one simple methodology, there are several important steps that should be addressed in developing the measures.

First, the institution's strategic objectives must be well defined. For strategic objective, critical success factors need to be identified.

Second, the institution must define the necessary views of its business (i.e., internal, customer, and market/industry). Other views might be focused on regulatory requirements or on a particular business process such as product delivery. Institutions should keep in mind that too many views will dilute the importance of any one view, and too few views will provide little direction in terms of balance.

Third, once the critical success factors (CSFs) have been defined, measures can be developed that provide quantitative results for each CSF. For instance, with a CSF focused on customer satisfaction levels, an institution might develop a measure of ATM up time or loan approval turn-around time, both of which point toward more overall customer satisfaction. Figure 3-2 provides a framework for determining critical success factors and associated measures.

Fourth, once the CSFs and associated measures are defined and adopted, they should be mapped against the institution's views of internal, customer, or market/industry, as discussed above. This mapping provides immediate focus on whether the measures give a balanced look at the institution.

Fifth, the measures need to be refined to create a more balanced approach. It is helpful to evaluate each measure as to whether another measure is needed to keep it balanced. For instance, knowing that your institution increased market share by 10 percent is important internal information. But knowing that the market grew at 8 percent adds context to that information.

The sixth step is to look at all existing measures in place today and map them on top of the new measures defined in each of the business views. This mapping exercise

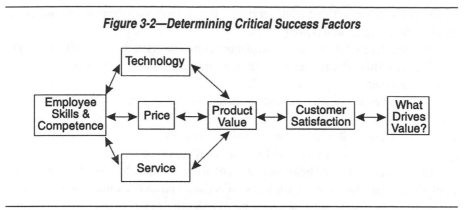

Figure 3-2—Determining Critical Success Factors

will again highlight overlap and conflicts, and will provide you with some comfort that you are measuring the right things.

A final step is filtering out the measures to provide the right balance. Each measure should be evaluated to ensure that it:

- Provides a link to strategy.

- Complements the measures in other business views.

- Does not conflict with any other measure.

- Follows the four M principles.

The most common internal performance measures are the financially driven measures that institutions have always used. But even in the area of financial measures, current thinking is driving management to a broader vision than that measured under traditional systems.

Contemporary Financial Measures

With the onset of activity in the competition for banking customers, banks started to compete not only with each other, but also with nonfinancial institutions. They found themselves competing not only for deposits and loans but for the full spectrum of financial services, to bolster overall fee income. Spreads on loans continue narrowing, and account for less and less of the overall income statement equation.

With narrower spreads, volume becomes important to sustained income. To quickly add volume, financial institutions have gone into the market and acquired funds—typically through negotiable-rate CDs, competitive savings rates, and money market funds. Another approach has been to shift from spread-based income to fee-based income generated from services such as cash management, commercial paper issuance, trust, and custody.

As a result, institutions now control more components of their overall return. To accommodate this increased control, they have begun to look to new financial performance measures.

On the revenue side, these measures include such ratios as fees to total assets and interest earned to total assets. Such ratios are excellent indicators of an institution's direction. In Figure 3-3, two commercial banks with comparable return on asset figures are shown to vary widely with regard to these other ratios.

The variance may well be an indication of different strategic directions. Management should consider the institution's objectives before deciding which of these indicators to use in measuring performance. On the expense side, contemporary measures include such ratios as interest expense to total assets, efficiency ratio, and noninterest expense to total assets. Again, the institution's performance should be reflected in these measures, as shown in Figure 3-4.

Other ratios used for performance measurement combine expense and revenue components. One such ratio is loan loss provision to interest margin, which reflects the institution's risk/return posture. If, for example, a commercial bank has a high loan loss percentage, it should be coupled with a higher interest margin. Management can use this measure to determine whether it is pricing its risk appropriately.

Figure 3-3 —Comparison of Performance Measures

	Bank A	Bank B
Key Financial Data		
Total Assets	$124,916	$18,245,587
Interest Income	12,816	1,563,649
Fee Income	300	82,105
Net Income	$ 1,421	$ 217,122
Capital	$ 9,473	$ 1,277,188
Key Financial Ratios		
Return on Assets	1.14%	1.19%
Return on Equity	15%	17%
Interest Income/Total Assets	10.26%	5.07%
Fee Income/Total Assets	.24%	.45%
Efficiency Ratio	54%	51%

With management's increased control of the components of return on assets, its use as a performance measure is more valid. The same can be said of return on equity, although the controllability of leverage has been restricted by regulatory capital adequacy constraints.

In general, the post deregulation changes that have taken place in the use of performance measures have been appropriate, but it is doubtful that the evolution of these measures is complete. Several key questions remain:

- How should off-balance-sheet transactions be incorporated into performance measures?

- With transfer pricing systems, should managers be looking at return on liabilities? In general, how should profitability be viewed at each level of the organization; product, customer, delivery channel, etc.?

Effect of Capital Ratios on Performance Measurement

Leverage (assets to shareholder equity) was a commercial bank's least controllable profit component under regulation, and it is the one component whose controllability has been further reduced under deregulation. As commercial bank capital ratios

Figure 3-4—Comparison of Performance Measures

	Bank A	Bank B
Key Financial Data		
Total Assets	$124,916	$18,245,587
Interest Expense	7,545	925,051
Noninterest Expense	3,885	397,754
Net Income	$ 1,421	$ 217,122
Equity	$ 9,473	$ 1,277,188
Key Financial Ratios		
Return on Assets	1.14%	1.19%
Return on Equity	15%	17%
Interest Expense/Total Assets	6.04%	5.07%
Noninterest Expense/Total Assets	3.11%	2.18%

varied, institutions that focused on return on equity tended to "lever up" or increase the level of assets supported by shareholder equity. That practice recognized the significant influence that leverage has on ROE.

For example, if Bank A and Bank B have identical returns on assets of .8 percent, but Bank A has a 6 percent capital ratio and Bank B has a four percent capital ratio, then Bank A's ROE is 13.3 percent, while Bank B's is 20 percent. Figure 3-5 illustrates this calculation. Institutions with low minimum capital requirement thus can increase their ROE by increasing leverage. However, the performance improvement depends on the institution's risk/return profile.

One pitfall of such traditional measures as ROA is that they are not universal measures across all businesses. Deposit or fee-based business has no assets, requires capital but cannot be measured accurately in terms of ROA. A logical step in addressing this issue is to calculate the ROE for business units, products, or customers (more likely customer groups). In taking this step, however, management must devise an approach of allocating equity so that a return may be computed. (See the discussion of techniques for capital allocation in Chapter 12, Capital Issues.)

Once the allocation is made, stakeholders can compare ROE to returns gained from other investments and weigh the institution's risks. A financial institution's risk is essentially the risk of loss associated with its businesses, products, and customers. In a sense, the institution needs equity to offset the possibility of losses. If an institution allocates equity by asset percentage, it ignores its components of that risk, unless, coincidentally, there is equal risk with all assets.

Figure 3-5—Effect of Capital Ratio on Performance Measurement

	Bank A	Bank B
Key Financial Data		
Average Assets	$150,000	$900,000
Average Equity	$ 9,000	$ 36,000
Net Income	$ 1,200	$ 7,200
Key Financial Ratios		
ROA	0.8%	0.8%
Capital Ratio	6.0%	4.0%
ROE	13.3%	20.0%
(ROA × 1/Capital Ratio)		

This idea can be demonstrated by the use of ROE to evaluate product perform-ance. For example, if we assume that losses are greater for credit card loans than for other types of consumer loans, then the allocation of shareholder equity needed to protect against that risk should be greater for the credit card loans as well. But if management allocates shareholder equity strictly by asset percentage, it overstates the ROE for credit card loans and understates the other types of consumer loans. Similar examples could be drawn for business units and customer relationships.

Return on Assets

When regulatory capital is inadequate, leverage management is reduced to monitor-ing the equity mix to insure that the institution is at least at the required capital level. Management effort is therefore shifted to ROA. With a similar leverage, ROA rankings of institutions would closely match ROE rankings. It is not clear, however, that ROA is the better measure of performance. Granted, with ROA there is no equity allocation issue, but assets need to be allocated to the measured business unit, product, or customer relationship.

For example, what happens when ROA is used as a measure for product profit-ability. At first it does not appear to pose a problem, because assets can be related to products rather easily. The return or revenue component cannot be dismissed as quickly because not all return is attributable to assets. In fact, with appropriate transfer pricing, return is attributed to assets and to liabilities.

Because deposits are a liability, one must determine how to measure a return. Should a return on liabilities be computed? Even if management can allocate income to assets and liabilities, and can calculate an appropriate return, where should such off-balance-sheet items such as letters of credit or foreign exchange positions be considered? Furthermore, where should the return on interest rate positions be assigned? Money desk return would be calculated on a zero-asset base—an untenable solution.

This is a further problem with compensating balances versus fees. If ROA is the chosen performance measurement, a deposit manager will attempt to have customers pay fees instead of keeping a compensating balance. Figure 3-6 illustrates the situ-ation. Given that the services delivered are the same for both institutions, Account B fares far better on a return basis, because it pays in fees and has far fewer deposits.

Product Profitability Financial Measures

One of the most significant moves in the industry was the unbundling of products. Institutions that previously sold "relationships" found customers price-shopping for products. It is therefore not uncommon now for a company to have its cash management performed by one institution, its financing through another, and its trust activity through a third. In this environment, product profitability information is essential—for product pricing, development, and termination.

This information can be obtained using several nonbottom-line profitability measures. One is a product's contribution margin, which is its price less its variable per-unit costs. If a manager knows this number and the annual fixed costs associated with the product, he can calculate the break-even volume. Figure 3-7 illustrates this concept.

The manager can also make product introduction and termination decisions based on the product's contribution and expected volume. Contribution margin can be beneficial in pricing as well. Management can use the contribution margin to perform "what if" analyses on price, associated volume, and the effects of both on profitability.

Another nonbottom-line profitability measure is a product's return on sales (ROS). This measure is most useful in evaluating noncredit products similar to nonfinancial service industries. It is calculated by dividing a product's profit or loss before tax by its fee revenue. Although ROS contains allocated costs, it enables management to judge the percentage of revenues that flow through to bottom-line profits with the current volume. Again, "what if" analysis can be used to see how changes in volume affect ROS.

Figure 3-6—Effect of Different Performance Measures on Profitability Measurement

		Account A	Account B
A.	Compensating Balance (Investable Funds)	$5,000,000	$500,000
B.	Fee Revenue	$ 10,000	$370,000
C.	Income Earned on Compensating Balance	$ 400,000	$ 40,000
D.	Total Income (B + C)	$ 410,000	$410,000
E.	Return (D/A)	8.2%	82.0%

Assumption:
8% credit for compensating balances.

Figure 3-7—Determining Variances for Performance Measurement

Area:	Data Processing
Activity:	Loans Processed
Standard Charge:	$1,000.00
Volume:	500
Unit Standard Cost:	$2.00
Actual Cost:	$900.00
Favorable/(Unfavorable) Variance	$100.00

To help in selecting new products or evaluating expenditures for fixed assets, management might use net present value analysis. Net present value addresses timing of relevant cash flows.

Net present value and contribution margin both help assess a product's future performance, while ROS can help assess current performance. A fourth measure that can be helpful in deciding whether to discontinue a product is overall contribution (contribution margin times volume) less the fixed costs that can be reduced by terminating the product. Simply stated, if the measure is positive, then the product should be retained; if negative, the product should be dropped, reengineered, or reevaluated. Management should keep in mind that the volume number should be the expected volume over a particular period of time. In addition, it is important to consider how the elimination of the product will affect other products.

Earlier in this chapter, we stated that ROE below the organizational level has many limitations. One area where it may be useful, however, is in viewing products as net users or suppliers of shareholder equity. With a regulatory capital adequacy ratio, financial institutions must maintain a certain level of equity financing. The degree to which a product uses shareholder equity may be useful in measuring its success at financing its own growth.

Business Unit/Organizational Financial Measures

A business unit can be defined as a group of products that make up a so-called business or self-sufficient unit. It also can be defined as a portion of an institution that, because of function or geography, has been classified as a separate unit. This section considers business units as the latter, since product performance has already been discussed.

Depending on management's objectives and the business unit's function, many different performance measures may be used. Two specific yet broad types of business units are back-office support centers and marketing centers.

Back-Office Support Center Financial Measures

A back-office support center is a cost center that provides operational support for the delivery of products to customers. Typically, back-office support centers in financial institutions include bookkeeping, item processing, and the central computer operations input area for loan processing. These areas have little, if any, direct control over either the revenue stream for products or the volume of work actually processed. Generally, their objective is to minimize the per-unit cost of supporting transactions without causing a decrease in overall service quality.

Because support centers are part of the product delivery mechanism, delivery costs must be monitored on a per-unit and volume-related basis. Looking solely at expenses reported for line items within financial or profitability statements, without considering volume relationships, might be misleading and result in poor decisions. If an aggregated increase in actual salary dollars and equipment costs for a product-support center is accompanied by large volume increases, for example, an investment in qualified people and additional resources might actually lead to reduced per-unit operating costs.

Performance in back-office support centers should be measured according to whether certain cost-per-volume and quality control objectives are reached. The volume objectives could be in the form of per-unit standards for costs within the center's control. For example, added volume may require a cost-center manager to add another employee. The manager cannot control volume, but he can control aspects of hiring, salary, and workflow that may affect per-unit costs.

If an institution uses standard cost as its cost accounting method, it could look at the rate variances in support centers to see how efficiently managers are using their resources.

Assume, for example, that an institution is using a standard cost of $2 for each loan processed in its operations area, with a volume of 500 loans. Further assume that these 500 loans actually cost the operations area $900. As Figure 3-8 shows, $1,000 in standard cost is passed on to the loan area. The $100 favorable variance between what it actually costs to process the loans and what is charged to the loan area remains as a $100 favorable variance in operations.

Viewed another way, the operations area "earned" $100 due to the efficient use of its resources. Management must be careful, though, in judging support centers by variances without looking at other performance measures, such as the level of quality. If quality did not matter, institutions would find it relatively easy to reduce costs.

Quality does matter. As a result, quality control performance measures are needed. Examples of such measures are errors per 100 transactions, or such subjective readings of customer satisfaction as customer wait time or complaints per 100 customers.

Figure 3-8—Determining Variances for Performance Measurement

Area: Loan Operations

Activity: Loans Processed

Standard Charge		$1,000.00
Volume:	500	
Unit Standard Cost:	$2.00	
Actual Cost		900.00
Favorable /(Unfavorable) Variance		$ 100.00

Appropriate quality control standards are based on management's decisions regarding the quality of service it seeks to establish to remain consistent with its goals and strategies. Quality has a cost, however, and it is important for management to determine when the cost of additional quality outweighs the benefits.

SYNOPSIS

The nature and role of measurement systems have significantly changed over the last several years, given industry changes and new competitive factors. Strategy plays a key role in defining what is measured and how the measures are used. Historically, financial measures drove systems, but today other nonfinancial measures are gaining increased attention.

This chapter reviewed the steps needed to develop a measurement tool that can be used to quantify an institution's success in executing its business strategy. Additionally, several traditional and alternative measures were presented for various cuts of profitability.

CHAPTER 4

The Changing Evolution of Management Information

OVERVIEW

Traditionally, financial institutions have had a limited number of alternatives for changing bottom-line results; namely, increasing net interest margins, raising fees, or reducing operating expenses. However, these tools are becoming less viable as market rates inevitably change and greater competition limits the extent to which institutions can alter fee structures.

Not only is competition arising from industry consolidation, as illustrated by the emergence of several "super-regionals" in the early 1990s, but also from the entry of unconventional players into the banking market, for instance, diversified financial and nonfinancial corporations.

Adding to the difficulty of relying exclusively on traditional methods for improving bank profits are such dynamics as volatile interest rates; rapid technology based innovations in products and delivery systems (electronic funds transfer (EFT), point-of-sale (POS) terminals, smart cards, etc.); reduction or elimination of geographic barriers; and the widespread diversification of banks into fee-based services. Also, the legislative, regulatory, and Financial Accounting Standards Board (FASB) responses to the changing shape of the industry are impossible to fully anticipate.

All of this, and the ever-increasing demand by stakeholders to improve returns on their capital contributions, has forced institutions to evaluate the drivers of real value rather than thinking solely in terms of direct revenue increases and expense reductions as ways to improve the bottom line. The drivers of real value are the profits generated by products, product lines, business segments, and customers. Information is needed on the performance of each of these components of the institution's total profits so that tactical or strategic actions can be taken to ensure that each contributes to shareholder value.

This chapter shows how the evolution of performance measurement has paralleled changes in the environment in which financial institutions operate. The need for greater flexibility, detail, and speed in determining how the institution is performing have forced many managers to reevaluate their performance measurement systems. Many banks have found that ever-increasing information needs have forced them finally to develop such a system.

The Evolution of Management Accounting

During the 1970s and 1980s, changes in the financial industry significantly altered the way executives viewed financial information. Historically, financial standards such as Generally Accepted Accounting Principles (GAAP) and regulatory requirements defined the accounting information produced. Reporting took place along "legal entity" lines to comply with these rules. More recently, executives have been exploring alternatives to the external accounting framework for reporting financial data.

As competitive pressures mounted in the industry and stakeholder demands for performance became more difficult to meet, financial institution managers were forced to search for ways to organize existing financial data in a way that would enhance their decision-making capabilities. Such a thought process led to the dissection of bank-wide performance into product, product line, segment, and customer views. While financial accounting informed stakeholders and regulators of organization-wide performance via public statements, management accounting data improved management's understanding of the components of bottom-line profits or losses through internal reporting.

Although management accounting data is used primarily for internal purposes, this information does have external value. Securities analysts and regulators, for instance, have a growing need and desire for data on line-of-business or strategic business unit (SBU) performance. Whether management accounting information is financial or nonfinancial, historic or projected, precise or estimated, it can be useful outside the organization, provided it is based on careful analysis and detailed reporting.

Two management accounting conventions make the practice far more controversial than simple financial accounting. One is the subjectivity of the various cost/revenue allocations. The other is the fact that no formal regulatory infrastructure exists to guide the internal management accounting discipline.

In the banking industry, difficulties arise in the determination of how joint costs should be distributed among the products or centers supported, as in the case of operations or information systems departments. Also, for product or organizational performance measurement, the decision as to how net interest margins should be split between funds suppliers and users can have a dramatic impact on performance results.

The evolution of managerial accounting from its financial accounting origin has coincided with the gradual adaptation of financial systems to accommodate the management accounting information requirements of bank managers. Since financial systems were originally designed to perform external reporting for regulators and shareholders, they capture data primarily by legal entity. For example, deposit and loan data is typically tracked by branch, and accounting subsystems such as payroll and fixed assets generally record only direct costs by organizational unit.

In recent years, many institutions have reconfigured their financial systems to look across legal entities so as to facilitate reporting performance by business line, product, or customer. This progression typically has involved moving beyond use of the general ledger to generate performance information, as the general ledger is most helpful in reporting organizational performance.

Product and product-line performance analysis may place demands on the general ledger for which it was not intended. This necessitates the use of allocation software and extract tools that can be programmed to pull the data needed to perform the allocations off of such bank applications as loan or demand deposit account systems. Vendors have been responsive to these changes in the system requirements of management accountants, developing numerous alternative software programs to perform cost allocations, funds-transfer pricing, and performance measurement reporting.

Impact of Performance Measurement on Culture

An important aspect of the implementation of a performance measurement system is its potential impact on an institution's culture. In other words, how will performance measurement information be viewed by managers?

Any uncertainty that exists about the effect on culture can and should be managed. Executives need to take steps to insure that performance measurement is not construed by managers as a scheme to measure them in areas they may consider beyond their control. Education of managers is important, as is the integration of the performance measurement system implementation with other performance measurement initiatives.

Possibly the most effective means of minimizing any potential adverse effects on culture is to involve those measured by the system in its development. Efforts to design, populate, and roll out the system without input from management will likely meet with resistance once reporting begins. Cost allocations, accounting theories, and system methodologies will be scrutinized and may be questioned, diminishing the credibility of results. But with management involvement these negative results can be avoided.

Defining the Drivers of Performance Measurement Information

Developing performance measurement data can be an expensive and lengthy undertaking. To prove valuable and cost effective, the reporting system must be capable of providing management with timely and actionable information. Reports must include sufficient detail and the revenue and expense data necessary to develop (with a reasonable amount of analysis) an improvement agenda of action steps to take with respect to products, customer services, or market segments. Additionally, performance results should help executives measure progress toward strategic goals they set for the institution.

More specifically, the data should provide adequate information to guide decisions made by managers in the areas listed below, and these decisions should have an impact on bottom-line profits at least as great as the system implementation cost:

- Pricing products/services

- Deploying marketing dollars

- Increasing asset profitability

- Reducing funding costs

- Eliminating of marginal or unprofitable products/services

- Reducing operating costs

- Product and service mix/packaging

- Identifying loss leaders

Developing Information from a Business Perspective

Historically, management accounting information has been developed from a customer-support perspective rather than from a business-management perspective. The typical demand deposit account (DDA) system, for example, carefully records transaction and balance activity rather than account profitability information. (Account analysis systems that interface with DDA systems provide some—albeit incomplete—profitability analysis.) Commercial loan systems, although they compute interest income, primarily record customer loan activity, not loan profitability.

The new challenge facing those responsible for management accounting is to provide the information necessary to measure performance. This can be accomplished by carrying out a combination of the following activities (and addressing some related questions):

- Identifying the performance information that is needed. (What are the products? What cost allocations are necessary? What level of detail is appropriate?)

- Determining how to obtain the information. (Which application systems are relevant?)

- Analyzing and reporting the information. (What is the reporting frequency? How are reports to be formatted? Who receives the information?)

Performance Information Development: A Continuum

The financial services industry consists of institutions that differ in size; in diversity; in the skill, experience, and philosophy of management; in information requirements and information-producing capabilities; and in staff and dollar resources available to devote to developing performance measurement information. Some institutions have years of cost accounting experience, while others have little or none. Some have sophisticated budgeting systems and others do not. Some have some form of product performance measurement information and others have none.

Due to these differences, institutions have varying needs for performance measurement information. This range of needs, from the simplest to the most complex, can be seen as an evolutionary continuum because financial institutions tend to evolve through a series of distinct but related phases. This continuum is shown in Figure 4-1.

The phases are not necessarily sequential, and the precise method of passing through them varies by institution, as do the end results. In general, however, the phases are closely related to the development of the institution's management decisions, and to the growing need for information to make those decisions. Each phase can be viewed as an indication of the organization's level of skill in developing such information. Figure 4-1 illustrates the continuum concept, moving from simple management information needs on the left to more sophisticated needs on the right. The vertical axis depicts information systems requirements, which become more complicated as the information needs become more sophisticated.

The continuum, which provides a framework for studying performance information, may be broken down into 11 distinct phases.

Phase 1—Budgeting and Responsibility Reporting

In this phase, management seeks to control noninterest expenses and to assign responsibility for those expenses to individual managers. Typical management information at this stage includes budget reports and comparisons of actual expenses, budgeted expenses, and prior year actual expenses. Variance reports for executive management are also characteristic of this phase, as are goals for revenues, profits, and growth.

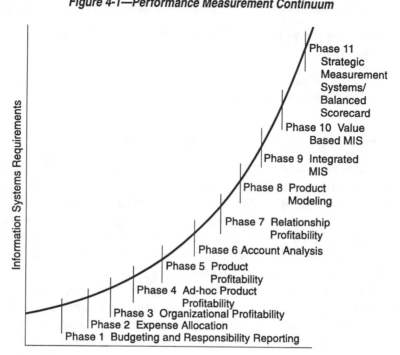

Figure 4-1—Performance Measurement Continuum

Phase 2—Allocations

In this phase, management seeks to identify sources of revenues and expenses for many of the institution's responsibility centers. Typical activities include the development of a charge-back system for allocating information technology and operations expenses, and the allocations of space and premises costs and expenses such as those incurred for personnel, mail, and other office services.

In this phase, an institution dedicates staff to cost accounting, a step that represents the organization's first formalization of the cost accounting function. The cost accounting skills are typically learned "on the job," and results are usually rudimentary. The comparatively simple allocations performed by the staff are done manually or with personal computers.

Phase 3—Organizational Profitability

With some responsibility reporting and expense allocations in place, management directs its attention toward assessing the profitability of organizational entities. A primary objective is to establish a basis for assigning manager accountability and for measuring manager performance. When the institution can accurately measure the profitability of a unit, that measure can be used to assist in the evaluation of unit managers, branch performance, cost efficiencies, etc.

This phase is characterized by the addition of a transfer-pricing mechanism for funds, and by an emphasis on correcting allocation method deficiencies and improving the detail in the allocation bases to achieve greater overall understanding and buy-in. Because funds management is generally considered to require specialized skills, the transfer pricing function is often segregated from the cost accounting function.

Phase 4—Ad Hoc Product Profitability

Phases 1 through 3 for the most part focus on profitability information from an organizational perspective. In Phase 4, management seeks to determine which products contribute to overall profitability and which do not. Product costs necessary for this analysis typically are developed on an ad hoc basis as opposed to systematically, regularly, or consistently among various products. Frequently, an institution uses these product costs to price and unbundle services. For example, it might break a major service area into distinct parts and charge separately for each part.

In Phase 4, product costs are developed as extensions of existing cost allocations. The amount of information requested in this phase is greater than in Phases 1 through 3, however, and a typically limited cost accounting staff often is unable to respond to all requests. As a result, independent costing analyses are performed throughout the institution.

The increase in the number of organizational areas actively seeking profitability information can be positive. But inconsistencies can arise among the various analyses, and that can lead to time wasted on arguments over "different" costs. It also can weaken the credibility of all profitability information to the extent that much of the information is disregarded.

Phase 5—Product Profitability

In this phase, use of emerging technologies provides management with ongoing product profitability information. The information is comprehensive, rather than for selected products only, and is produced in a systematic, often automated fashion. Objectives include eliminating the credibility problems associated with ad hoc product profitability, and assuring that reliable, accurate, and timely information is integrated into the decision-making process.

Phase 5 requires a much more substantial cost accounting staff than do Phases 2 through 4, necessitating a greater investment of resources.

Phase 6—Account Analysis

Here management recognizes the need to go beyond organizational and product profitability by collecting customer information, especially about commercial customers. Product costs for DDA, cash management, and other services are developed—typically on an ad hoc basis, using available allocations. These costs then are pulled together in a typical (commercial) account analysis.

Although costing in this phase amounts to little more than detailed allocations of expenses to selected services, several significant elements are present. First, periodic cost updates are performed. Second, cost information typically is automated in the account analysis process. Third, the institution begins to routinely collect and report nonfinancial information (e.g., the number of lockbox items processed).

Phase 7—Relationship (or Customer) Profitability

In this phase, management seeks information on the "true" profitability of the institution's customers. This pursuit addresses the entire relationship with the customer—not just deposit and loan activity, but also trust services used, specialized cash management services purchased, and so forth.

For several reasons, the results obtained here supersede those obtained in the previous account-analysis phase. First, this phase allows management to determine which entities of a "customer" are included in a "relationship." By expanding the definitions of these terms, relationship profitability provides management with more reporting flexibility than does Phase 6. Also, it permits greater flexibility in the area of customer "linking" or relationship categorization, helping management make better decisions about product positioning and cross-selling for various types of customers.

Institutions adopting a "relationship" perspective are faced with the challenge of breaking down the "Chinese Wall" built over time between some divisions of the bank, most commonly the retail and trust areas. The ability to make full use of relationship profitability information depends largely on bank culture. Where internal communication barriers or nondisclosure rules exist, the value of relationship information will diminish. Not only will the data needed to populate the system be more difficult to collect, but a lack of collaboration between business units will inhibit efficient use of the information once it becomes available.

Examining the full relationship with the customer brings additional data requirements into play. Typically, these requirements contain elements not readily available in the institution's information systems. Including these elements often requires significant changes to basic data application systems. Thus, this phase, like Phase 5, can involve a sizable investment of resources.

Also important in this phase is the determination by management of an acceptable profitability range for each type of customer. Besides looking at historical levels of customer profitability, management must develop profitability goals that may vary according to demographics, credit risk characteristics, or the type of service customers use. Decisions can then be made about retaining relationships that do not meet these goals.

Phase 8—Product Modeling

Here, management progresses beyond reviewing only historical profitability information. Attention turns to strategic planning and to modeling products, customers, and the right mix of the two. The interaction of organizational, product, and relationship profitability—historically and on a projected basis—is the central concern.

Product modeling expands the uses of performance information. For example, Phases 4 and 5 facilitate tactical decisions about products, for instance, involving pricing, cost reduction opportunities, and deployment of marketing dollars. In contrast, Phase 8 gives managers the capability to make better strategic decisions, such as whether to introduce a new product or how best to position existing products. Each decision's potential impact on profits can be anticipated, thus guiding future actions.

Because historical information alone no longer suffices, and because management must rely more on planning, on-line access to relevant information becomes an important part of this phase.

Phase 9—Integrated MIS

Ideally, a performance measurement system would be structured as an integrated database storing financial and nonfinancial data on products, customers, segments, delivery channels, and the like. Advantages of an integrated and centralized performance measurement system include:

- Consistency in reporting data on each component of total profits

- Increased efficiency in processing data through elimination of duplicate steps

- Audit-trail reports on allocations that tie back across products, customers, centers, etc.

- More effective control over the information gathered

Integration provides a multidimensional picture of the contribution of products, customers, organizations, and segments toward an institution's total profits. This analysis could conceivably extend further by drilling down to the real drivers of value.

An integrated performance measurement system can facilitate this process by allowing successive layers of performance data (at any reporting level) to be removed.

For example, product expenses may be viewed as the sum of the institution's costs to perform the activities necessary to sell and maintain the product. By drilling down to the activity level, managers can determine which activities add value or may be altered to improve the efficiency with which the product is brought to market or maintained once it has been sold.

Phase 10—Value-Based MIS

The shift toward a stakeholder-value orientation in many financial institutions has led executives to demand information measuring the performance of centers, products/product lines, and customers in terms of return on equity hurdle rates and market comparable ROEs.

When business lines or products are viewed as stand-alone entities and ROE data for each (adjusted for business-specific risk) is measured against a cost of capital "hurdle rate," actionable information is generated. This can then be used to guide strategic or tactical steps toward maximizing stakeholder value. As a limited and inexpensive source of funding, capital should be diverted from unprofitable businesses and products and toward areas that enhance the value of capital contributions.

Obviously, selection of a capital-allocation methodology is a critical aspect of a value-based information system. Many institutions with advanced performance measurement systems already in place use a risk-adjusted allocation of capital to product lines as the foundation for their ROE performance benchmarks. Risk-adjusted allocations recognize that capital exists primarily to cover unexpected losses arising from the risk inherent in the banking business. Equity allocations based on regulatory requirements or market comparables are considered viable alternatives to the risk-based method, but do not take into account the institution's specific credit and interest rate exposure characteristics.

Phase 11—Strategic Performance Measurement Systems/Balanced Scorecard

Strategic Performance Measurement (SPM) and the Balanced Scorecard approach may incorporate the performance measurement information derived from any of the previous phases, yet it advances beyond these phases by recognizing profitability as only one measure of success. In other words, financial measures share the spotlight with nonfinancial measures in determining where the institution has gone and where it should go in the future.

For example, internal measures of performance may include quality considerations, and customer measures may be devised to take into account loan approval response times and queue "wait" times. This should not replace the performance measurement systems already in place, but instead should supplement these capabilities with other variables which may facilitate forward-thinking managerial decision making.

SPM and Balanced Scorecards identify where value is being created, where improvement opportunities exist, and how well the institution is advancing toward its strategic objectives. In the banking area, they may provide an integrated approach to highlighting the activity, product, and process variables which are most critical to the institution. This serves to direct the focus of managers toward the proper performance measures. These measures must be tied back to the institution's strategy to determine which measures are most important, and ensure that those selected produce management responses that are in line with corporate objectives. Finally, care must be taken to see that the chosen measures are actionable and do not conflict with other measures.

Advancement along the Continuum

Institutions constantly seek to improve performance measurement by moving to the next phase of the continuum, or to another phase if a nonsequential progression is being followed. Such movement is not always by careful design. Some is achieved indirectly by taking steps to address specific problems, for instance, developing account analysis systems (Phase 6).

The typical evolutionary movement along the continuum depends on a wide variety of factors. Each phase represents different degrees of performance measurement knowledge, staff capabilities, and technology. An institution's commitment to acquiring or developing the human and technological resources needed to advance its position on the continuum will determine how quickly it reaches the next phase.

This commitment may sometimes be determined by an institution's size: the larger it is, the greater its need to understand how well its wide range of products and large number of organizational units are performing. Since each phase also represents different management information needs, position also can be a function of an institution's environment. For example, institutions with lower-than-average performance in a very competitive market typically need product and customer performance information to determine their profit improvement strategies. As a result, they may be further along the continuum than their size alone would suggest.

The key to successful management accounting is being aware of an institution's position on the continuum, and planning so that progression along the continuum will match the progression of management information needs. Achieving this goal, however, requires progression along a parallel continuum—the information systems continuum Figure 4-2 shows the two continua as parallel vectors, with the relative sophistication of each increasing from left to right.

Information systems range from no automated systems at all (manual processing) to highly integrated database architecture systems. Because each phase of the performance measurement continuum requires different basic data, each implies a certain position along the information systems continuum.

The clearest example is the development of relationship profitability (Phase 7). While there are many ways to develop a relationship performance system, it is impossible to do so unless the underlying information systems are integrated at least to the extent that all systems can identify and supply information about each customer.

Most institutions suffer a serious lag between their information systems capability and their performance measurement information objectives. An obvious solution is for the institution to progress efficiently in its information systems effort before

---

Figure 4-2—Performance Measurement and Information Systems

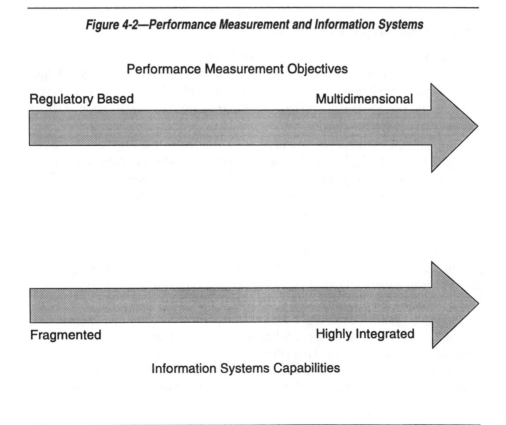

Performance Measurement Objectives

Regulatory Based   Multidimensional

Fragmented   Highly Integrated

Information Systems Capabilities

attempting to move along the performance measurement continuum. Such a solution, however, is a double-edged sword. The system needs are determined by the needs of the performance measurement phase, but by the time the systems catch up to that phase, management information needs probably will have progressed even further. This in turn leads to further systems revision, and the cycle continues.

Another solution to the problem of lagging information systems development is to "make do" with the current systems. This solution is so prevalent, in fact, that it has led to the establishment of a performance measurement phase: ad hoc product profitability (Phase 4). The problem with this approach is that the underlying systems never progress adequately, thereby limiting the development of performance measurement information.

What is needed is a process that addresses both continua simultaneously, as shown in Figure 4-3. The desired management information needs are identified first to determine the extent of performance measurement information development required. Then, through a data review and an analysis of the current systems, the current position along the information systems continuum is determined. Once these steps are completed, two critical pieces of information are available: where the institution wants to go and what it is currently capable of supporting.

Given that information, the institution can take a dual approach to solving its management information problem. It can build a bridge that uses current systems to support its desired position on the performance measurement continuum to the extent possible. This bridge is usually just an interim solution, such as loading data manually into microcomputers to develop product profitability or attempt product modeling.

Concurrently, the institution can develop an information systems plan that moves its systems toward the level required to support its desired performance measurement position. It might be said that in the later phases of the performance measurement continuum, an institution moves from the "processing age" to the "information age." In this transition, planning for the future is critical.

This dual approach has several advantages. It provides useful management information without forcing the institution to wait for major system enhancements. It also produces a useful, long-term information systems plan based not on technology but on management's information needs. As a result, the institution can meet its ultimate goals in a rational, ordered approach for both performance measurement and the supporting information systems.

Linking Information to Strategy

Executives who are involved in defining strategy and setting strategic objectives should be involved in the definition of management information needs. Performance

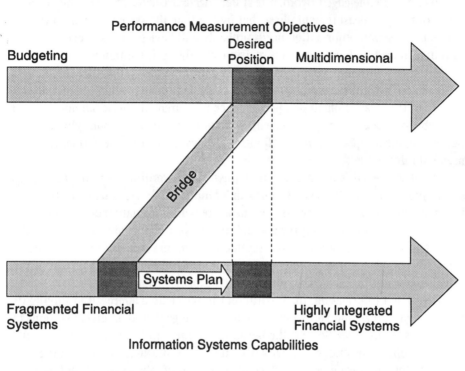

Figure 4-3—Developing Performance Information

measurement reports are inherently most useful in determining progress toward the institution's strategic earnings goals. These define where the institution wants to be in the future with respect to product, product line, or organizational performance.

Such objectives most often begin as incremental, achievable, short-term performance goals for portfolios of bank products using ROE or ROA (bearing in mind risk-return trade-offs). Frequent performance measurement reporting provides a vivid picture of how successful the institution has been in approaching its goals.

However, nonfinancial information may also support strategic decision making, and thus should be found in internal accounting reports. For example, performance measurement information could help indicate the validity of pursuing a particular strategy, such as the decision to target the affluent retail customer segment. Yet reporting only profitability results ignores the impact of such segment-specific variables as the size of the market, the institution's existing market share, and share growth trends.

Because the information needed to support strategic planning can be extensive and difficult to obtain, the institution's MIS strategy must be ambitious enough to meet these demands. Therefore, executives must outline an MIS strategy based, at least in part, on the information they need to measure progress toward strategic goals.

Stakeholder-value maximization, the stated goal of most financial institutions, also drives the close link between management information and corporate strategy. Increasing numbers of consolidations, business line restructurings, and asset securitizations attest to the greater emphasis being placed on this strategic objective.

Before the widespread adoption of a stakeholder-value measurement framework, profitability information along organization lines was sufficient for management use. However, without ROE data on individual business lines and products, supported by systems designed to provide value-based information, existing measures of an institution's success in maximizing shareholder value are suspect.

SYNOPSIS

Management accounting has evolved as the financial services industry has changed. Providing management accounting information has become increasingly important—particularly the information that can be generated by performance measurement.

Performance measurement in financial institutions can be viewed as an 11-phase continuum, and every institution can be positioned in at least one of the phases. Parallel to this performance measurement continuum there exists an information systems continuum. Institutions often find that their progress along the latter does not keep pace with their progress along the former.

What is needed, then, is a two stage approach to meeting performance information requirements. The first stage is an interim solution, a bridging process that uses current systems to support the desired performance measurement needs. The second stage, which should take place concurrently with the first, is the development and implementation of a plan for advancing information systems capability to the position required to support the institution's evolving performance measurement needs.

PART II

Income Statement Components of Performance Measurement

CHAPTER 5

Defining the End Product

OVERVIEW

The success of performance measurement systems often lies in the timely and accurate reporting of the defined measures. The final product must reflect the agreed-to measures and report them accurately, fairly, and clearly. Whether the end product is a report package or a sophisticated Executive Information System (EIS), it must be well defined, carefully implemented, and easy to understand.

This chapter highlights the many issues related to developing and designing the final reports. Although the end results may be presented electronically instead of on hardcopy, the format issue is the same. The chapter will discuss the various issues involved in presenting and classifying the income statement components.

There is a need to present management information across multiple views of the financial institution, including organizational, line of business, geographical, product, and customer views. Sample report formats are presented for all dimensions of the institution. A discussion of the various approaches for presenting/classifying information on these reports is provided, along with how the different presentations aid in the analysis and the conclusions which can be drawn from the reports. Performance measurement information in general can be highly motivational and lead the organization in a direction consistent with financial and strategic objectives. However, caution should be exercised during the initial stages of report production to insure that the desired behavior is achieved and the focus is placed on overall reporting objectives and desired behavioral changes throughout the institution.

INCOME STATEMENT PRESENTATION AND CLASSIFICATION

The most complicated report to be defined is the income statement. The income statement is the most focused on of all the financial institution's reports; all other reports and measures ultimately affect the income statement. The topics discussed below largely focus on expense classifications and presentation within the income statement. Revenue components are presented in Chapter 6.

Report Format Design

An essential component of any management information system is the presentation of profitability and performance information. In the financial services industry, there exist myriad reporting conventions and reporting options, including a variety of line item classifications and levels of reporting detail. During the initial design phases for the development of profitability and performance reporting systems, it is important not only to determine what information will be provided, but how the information will be used and reported. It is also important to decide who the intended audience is, as well as what decisions they will make or actions they will take based on the information reported. Samples of report formats for organizational, product, and customer profitability and performance reporting are presented below. Accompanying each sample report is a brief discussion of the format, intended purpose, and intended/target users, as well as frequency suggestions.

Report Data

A typical summary-level profit and loss statement for a profitability measurement system is shown in Figure 5-1. Because of the extensive detail required for noninterest expenses, a variety of detail report formats usually are included to support the noninterest expense component of profitability. This detail usually is addressed in subsequent detailed report formats.

These reports provide additional detail for direct noninterest expenses, based on the summary level categories found in the general ledger, for instance, salaries and benefits, occupancy, computer operations and systems, and "other." The reports also show the indirect expenses developed from the cost allocations. Figure 5-2 illustrates a typical profitability statement using these detailed categories. The terms "direct" and "indirect," as used in Figure 5-2 and in the following paragraphs, are discussed below.

Figure 5-1—Typical Summary-Level Profit and Loss Statement

Interest Income
Interest Expense
Credit/Charge for Funds

Net Interest Income

Provision for Loan Loss

Net Interest Income after
  Provision for Loan Loss

Other Income

Noninterest Expense

Income before Taxes

The particular format shown in Figure 5-2 is well suited to organizational profitability. The line items for direct expenses usually are general ledger summaries, which makes the organizational profitability system easy to implement and allows an easy transition for users. Just as important, the line items shown on the organizational profitability statement usually match those on plan or budget reports. As a result, developing this type of statement using this format does not require users to reclassify or translate direct expenses.

The format in Figure 5-2, however, does not provide detail for indirect expenses and represents a summary-level report of these expenses. The detail of indirect expenses may sometimes appear on a separate report as shown in Figure 5-3.

Figure 5-3 offers an example of a detailed indirect expense report. In this example, the report shows how much expense has been allocated or assigned from computer operations, loan processing, and other units. The amounts allocated to a particular organizational unit would be determined using one of the cost allocation techniques to be explained in Chapter 7.

A similar reporting concept can be used in reporting from any dimension, including product, branch, organizational, or customer profitability. For example, the expenses shown on the product profitability report would reflect the allocation of product-related expenses.

Figure 5-4 is an example of a product profitability report. This format is particularly useful in a functional organizational structure because it identifies specific

Figure 5-2—Typical Organizational Profitability Statement

Interest Income
Interest Expense
Credit/Charge for Funds
_____

Net Interest Income
Provision for Loan Loss
_____

Net Interest Income after
   Provision for Loan Loss
Other Income
_____

Net Revenue
Direct Expense
    Salaries and Benefits
    Furniture and Equipment
    Occupancy
        Telephone
    Professional Fees
    Travel and Entertainment
    Other Direct Expenses
_____

Total Direct Expense
Indirect Expense
_____

Total Noninterest Expense
_____

Income before Taxes

managers, through the units they manage, as the source of the reported expenses. The report therefore can reflect the institution's structure and responsibility assignment approach. An organizational alignment report is easier to implement in a *full-absorption* cost system that generally allocates each unit's total expenses. The data for the organizational alignment report are simply the result of those allocations.

Unfortunately, the product profitability report format shown in Figure 5-4 does not easily provide information about specific processes and activities which relate to

Figure 5-3—Indirect Expense Statement

Human Resources
Loan Processing
Deposit Processing
Computer Operations
Item Processing
Security
Building
Office Services
Other

Total Indirect Expense

Figure 5-4—Sample Product Profitability Statement

Interest Income
Interest Expense
Credit/Charge for Funds

Net Interest Income
Provision for Loan Loss

Net Interest Income after
    Provision for Loan Loss
Other Income

Net Revenue
Direct Expense
Indirect Expense
    Data Processing
    Loan Processing
    Item Processing
    Branch System
    Marketing
    Other

Total Noninterest Expense

Income before Taxes

Figure 5-5—Product Profitability Statement—Activity or Process View

Interest Income
Interest Expense
Credit/Charge for Funds

Net Interest Income
Provision for Loan Loss

Net Interest Income after
    Provision for Loan Loss
Other Income

Net Revenue
Direct Expense
Indirect Expense
        Account Origination
        Deposits
        Cashed Checks
        Cleared Checks
        Statements
        Account Closings
        Other

Total Noninterest Expense

Income before Taxes

---

the products being measured. For example, it does not furnish data about the costs associated with opening and maintaining a demand deposit account. This drawback can be overcome by using a report format that aligns expenses by product activity or transactions processed, as shown in Figure 5-5. This format is particularly well suited to a cost approach based on Activity Based Costing methodology. (See Chapter 8 for a discussion of Activity-Based Costing methodology.) Data for each line on the report are determined by multiplying the activity unit cost of the transaction by the appropriate activity count or transaction volume.

Expense information also can be presented using the approach shown in the organizational profitability report (Figure 5-2), using such categories as salaries, occupancy, and equipment. This format usually is required if information on categories of expense is desired; it could explain, for example, how much labor expense is associated with a particular product. But implementation is difficult, because line item expense data are seldom captured and recorded by product and because the resulting information is infrequently used. As a result, the format is seldom used.

Customer profitability statements can be designed in a fashion similar to product reports, with a few exceptions. Customer reports generally reflect all the identified relationships associated with a customer and sum the individual account profitability to determine overall customer profitability. (See Chapter 17 for a further discussion of customer-related issues.) Figure 5-6 below illustrates a sample customer profitability statement. Very similar views of expense details can be viewed at the customer level, but most institutions tend to favor a format which reflects activity and transaction unit cost detail as shown in Figure 5-6.

Figure 5-6—Sample Customer Profitability

	Total	Lines and Commitments	Loans	Fee Services	Deposits
Interest Income	$50		$50		
Interest Expense	(10)				$(10)
Credit/(Charge) for Funds	(10)		(40)		30
Net Interest Income	30		10		20
Provision for Loan Losses	(1)		(1)		
Net Interest Income after Provisions for Loan Losses	29		9		20
Waived Fees	(29)			$(29)	
Other Income	42	$10	2	30	
Noninterest Expense	(39)	(2)	(1)	(35)	(1)
Contribution	3	$ 8	$10	$(34)	$19
Overhead Expense	(4)				
Income before Taxes	$(1)				

PROFIT AND LOSS VERSUS CONTRIBUTION REPORTING

A reporting issue even more fundamental than the presentation of detailed expense information is whether reports should include all or only some expenses. Three basic methods of reporting profitability address this issue: the fully absorbed accounting approach, the contribution approach, and the "above the line/below the line approach." In addition to some basic report differences, the two reporting conventions differently impact the issues of responsibility for expense assignment and control.

Fully Absorbed Accounting Approach

Under this approach, the sum of the profits/losses of all reported units equals the profits/losses of the entire institution, regardless of whether the reported units are organizational units, products, customers, or any other aspect of an institution's business. All income statement items are assigned or allocated and are "fully absorbed" in the individual income statements. For example, if reported units are products, then the sum of the reported profits of the products would equal the institution's overall profits.

The fully absorbed approach requires that all expenses ultimately be distributed among the reported units of the institution and that no expenses be left undistributed at any level.

The advantages of this approach are:

- All expenses are included when profitability is reported and analyzed. This reduces the possibility that certain expense items will be ignored and remain unmanaged or not factored into such decision-making issues as establishing product prices.

- Managers become aware of all expenses in an institution, which facilitates expense management.

- Having fully accounted for all income statement items, individual business line, branch, product, or customer "hurdle rates" can be established that are congruent with the overall organization's goals. Every measure is in line with the corporate goal as it all contributes to the total.

The disadvantages are:

- Some expense distributions which are less exact or not based on ideal cost drivers are required to ensure that all expenses are included in the reported profitability. Managers of the reported units may feel accountable for expenses that they might consider beyond their control. This can result in challenges to the credibility of the information and sometimes increased frustration on the part of managers.

- The profitability information could distort the value of the institution's individual units. A product or center may generate revenues that more than cover processing and operating costs, but fall short of what is necessary to exceed reported overhead costs, resulting in a reported loss, not a profit.

Contribution Approach

Unlike the fully absorbed approach, the contribution approach does not require all expenses to be distributed among the reported units of the institution. Instead, it identifies expenses associated with different organizational levels, and includes those expenses in the reporting for those levels only. Expenses associated with the head of retail banking, for example, would be reported only at the retail banking administration level, not distributed to each branch.

This approach allows undistributed expenses to remain at different levels of reporting. As a result, the sum of the profits from reported units will not equal the profits of the total institution without factoring in the higher-level units which house certain expenses.

Figures 5-7 and 5-8 illustrate the contribution approach. Figure 5-7 shows a simplified organization chart containing different levels of management and the expenses of each respective level. Using examples from the chart, Figure 5-8 shows the reports that would be used under the contribution approach.

Contribution levels can be illustrated even more clearly when a matrix reporting format is used. The matrix format (shown in Figure 5-9) lends itself to a "layered reporting" which makes it easier to match level of detail to the level of management using the report.

The advantages of the contribution approach are:

- Allocations can be based strictly on activity/cost drivers, which enhances the credibility of cost allocations and reporting at all levels of management.

- Managers are held accountable only for expenses they control, and expenses are included only in reporting at the level at which they become controllable.

- The resultant information sometimes is viewed as better for product management and marginal pricing decisions, because only those costs directly related to the product are used in the analysis.

The disadvantages are:

- Because some expenses are undistributed, it is possible for all the institution's profit centers to appear profitable while the institution as a whole may operate at a loss.

- Products or centers may appear to be profitable at one level of reporting but unprofitable at the succeeding level. For example, a checking account product

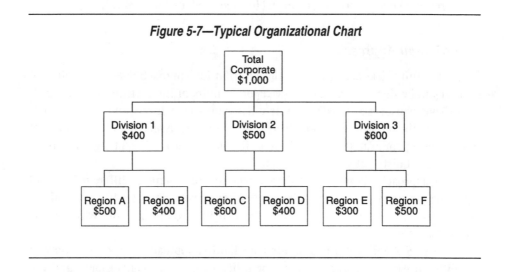

Figure 5-7—Typical Organizational Chart

Figure 5-8—Contribution Approach Profitability Statement

	Division 1	Region A	Region B
Net Interest Income after Provision for Loan Loss	$1,400	$ 600	$ 800
Other Noninterest Income	600	400	200
Net Income	2,000	1,000	1,000
Region Expense	(900)	(500)	(400)
Contribution from Regions	1,100	$ 500	$ 600
Division Expense	400		
Contribution from Division	$ 700		

Figure 5-9—Matrix Reporting Format

	Total Corporate	Division 1	Division 2	Division 3
Net Interest Income after Provision for Loan Loss	$4,000	$1,400	$1,200	$1,400
Other Noninterest Income	2,300	600	900	800
Net Income	6,300	2,000	2,100	2,200
Region Expense	(2,700)	(900)	(1,000)	(800)
Contribution from Regions	3,600	1,100	1,100	1,400
Division Expense	(1,500)	(400)	(500)	(600)
Contribution from Divisions	$2,100	$ 700	$ 600	$ 800
Corporate Expense	(1,000)			
Profit/(Loss) before Taxes	$1,100			

Division 1	Total	Region B	Region B
Net Interest Income after Provision for Loan Losses	$1,400	$ 600	$ 800
Other Noninterest Income	600	400	200
Net Income	2,000	1,000	1,000
Region Expense	(900)	(500)	(400)
Contribution from Regions	$1,100	$ 500	$ 600

may be profitable at the profit center or branch level, with regional and divisional expenses unallocated. The same product may be unprofitable at the next level when regional expenses, such as those for marketing, are added.

- There is a possibility of making incorrect pricing decisions given that all expenses may not be accounted for.

- Performance measures would need to be set higher than overall company measures to account for the unallocated line items. This can create confusion as to the varying levels of performance measures.

Above the Line and Below the Line Approach

Some institutions have begun using a combination of the above approaches. That is, they fully allocate all expenses but segment the reporting of those expenses into two categories—above the line and below the line. Those expenses above the line are considered more controllable and those below the line less controllable. Figure 5-9 illustrates the concept. This compromise approach allows managers of branches, products, or customers to account for the full profit impact without being held accountable for uncontrollable expenses. For example, incentives may be placed for margins above the line, but below-the-line information is provided for the development of pricing decisions. This method provides the advantages of both methods explained above. Its disadvantages are the same as those of the fully absorbed approach listed above.

EXPENSE COMPONENT CLASSIFICATIONS

Expense classifications offer the greatest complexity, as various ways exist to present and classify expenses. Many institutions have their own individual methods of reporting and subsequently controlling expenses. While each approach performs a useful function, each treats expenses slightly differently and may even use different terms, such as "allocated," "noncontrollable," or "below the line."

Also, each expense allocation is unique. A major prerequisite for implementing effective management information is developing a conceptual framework for expense transfer within the institution. This includes selecting expense transfer theories and methodologies that are both practical (within the limits of available data and technology) and consistent with the institution's stated strategic and operational goals.

Listed below are a number of ways to classify and report expenses within a financial institution, as well as the varied and often controversial theories and methodologies used to assign expenses and develop cost information. An overriding principle will be the acquisition and development of data that provides a useful level of information and allows consist results across multiple views of the organization.

Assigning Expense Responsibility

A profitability measurement system helps management meet expense management objectives by making it easier to assign responsibility for all expenses, establish control and authority for each expense, and report and monitor the results of the expense management effort.

Several factors make the assignment and reporting of operating expenses in financial institutions particularly problematic. First, many fixed expenses are not directly proportional to the volume of transactions processed. An institution's computer operations expense is a good example. Second, a high percentage of joint expenses is incurred when the same activity is performed for many independent users. Again, computer operations is a good example. Third, financial institutions must contend with the peaks and valleys of transaction volumes, which impede management's ability to completely control expense levels. Finally, to ensure adequate customer service during peak periods, allowances must be made for unused capacity. Production efforts are dictated by demand, and it is virtually impossible to maintain a constant level of effort over an extended period of time.

The initial step in managing expenses in this environment is to differentiate them by "type of expense." Expense types are similar to the line items on financial and budget reports and typically include:

- Salary expense (for full-time and part-time employees, temporary and contract employees, and so forth).

- Benefit expense (medical and insurance plans, pension plans, and so forth).

- Occupancy expense (including rent, utilities, maintenance and repairs, building depreciation, and so forth).

- Furniture and equipment expense (personal computers, microcomputers, office furniture, and so forth).

- Other operating expense line items (telecommunications, postage, stationery, and so forth).

The definitions are vital because they allow reporting to differentiate among expense categories. Treating the categories separately provides a clearer evaluation of expenses and the factors driving them. Furthermore, grouping certain expenses together allows assignment of responsibility to the individual(s) most qualified to control the category or type of expense (e.g., centrally managed benefit expense). One problem is that certain expense types are too broad for effective reporting. It becomes difficult to associate expenses with their benefits, and it is unrealistic to hold a single individual accountable for an entire expense type (such as salary) when control of the expenses is the responsibility of many individuals throughout the institution.

In response to these needs, the next logical step is to regroup the expense types so that they allow effective reporting and reflect a realistic span of control. These new expense groups normally are assembled by function/process/activity/task, location, product, or customer segment. Examples of each might be as follows:

- *Function/Process/Activity/Task*—all expenses incurred in performing the proof and encoding function are grouped and reported together.

- *Location*—all expenses associated with running a branch are grouped and reported together.

- *Product*—all expenses related to providing the lockbox product/service to customers are grouped and reported together.

- *Customer Segment*—all expenses incurred in support of providing products/services to the affluent/high net worth customer.

Every profitability measurement system contains expense groupings based on these and other similarities. Normally, each such expense group represents or corresponds to an organizational unit and overall management reporting structure. A manager or supervisor can be assigned responsibility for the expenses in each organizational unit, achieving a reasonable span of control. The unit then is referred to as a responsibility center (or simply "center").

Responsibility and control must coexist if a financial institution is to implement effective expense management. Responsibility without control can frustrate line management, and control without responsibility can render senior management unable to guide the actions of others toward achieving the institution's goals.

A related problem is that some expenses incurred by a responsibility center are not completely controllable by the center's manager. Very often the volume of work a center performs is determined solely by the activities of other centers. This is especially true of back-office activities where transactions either originate elsewhere in the organization, such as in the branch, or are associated with accounts acquired by those areas. Proof and encoding, for example, has no control over its workload, yet it does have control over and responsibility for expenses incurred in the timely processing of its work in support of the branch network and other centers.

In such cases, the center realizing the associated benefits (e.g., the branch) has partial control, generally through the volume of transactions processed, over the expense incurred in the center that processes the transactions. These expenses should be reported in both centers in response to the different needs of control and resource allocation. A related issue is that the cost of many items, and hence the level of expense incurred for those items, is determined centrally, based on institution-wide policies. Employee benefit expense developed from institution-wide policies, and occupancy expense, where a center's location often is determined by others, are primary examples.

Both issues suggest a common solution: When the control of expense is shared by two centers, responsibility for the expense must be borne by both. This dual responsibility is most effectively implemented through the concepts of direct and indirect expense reporting. The expense would be reported as a direct expense of one center and an indirect expense of the other center.

Direct and Indirect Expenses

A responsibility center incurs direct expenses by carrying out its activities and tasks. Generally, these expenses are highly controllable. They include the expenses budgeted by a center and listed on its general ledger responsibility report. Salaries are a good example of this type of expense.

Direct expenses also include expenses that a center requires to operate, but that, for control purposes, may be budgeted and monitored elsewhere. Another center reports these expenses because it may have the expertise needed to manage the expense, or because it can achieve better economies of scale. Examples of expense items often handled this way are benefits, occupancy, and telecommunication expenses.

Indirect expenses are expenses that support the activities of a responsibility center but are incurred elsewhere in the institution and allocated to the users of such activities or services. Every indirect expense is a direct expense of some other center. Indirect expenses can support activities that assist a center in performing its tasks. One example is the recruiting expense incurred by a personnel center to provide other centers with staff to perform their functions. Another is the purchasing expense grouped in one center for economies of scale but incurred to service other centers. The support expense also can be for activities that complement a center's efforts in providing products and services to customers. An example is the expense that proof and encoding incurs to service the checking account customers of the branch network. This activity could be handled in each branch, but is centralized for control and economy of scale.

Indirect expenses are somewhat controllable by the receiving center, generally to the extent of the volume of services provided. General and administrative expenses, however, are not controllable by the center but are reported as indirect expenses for other reasons. These expenses are discussed later in this chapter.

An example helps to illustrate the concept of direct and indirect expenses. Suppose all telephone expense incurred by a network of 10 branches is grouped in another center (e.g., the telecommunications center) to ensure proper control. The telephone center also includes the expense associated with a system that tracks telephone use and expense by branch and ultimately pays the telephone bills. In this case, the following would be true:

- The telephone expense is a direct expense of each branch because it is incurred to conduct business at the branch.

- The tracking system expense is a direct expense of the telephone center because it is incurred to enable that center to carry out its function. The tracking system expense also is an indirect expense of each branch because it is incurred to support the branches by paying their bills and controlling the overall level of telephone expense.

- If the tracking system expense is small relative to total telephone center expenses for convenience, it can be factored in and included with the telephone expense as a direct branch expense. If the tracking system expense is large, it may require a separate allocation.

Figure 5-10 further illustrates the matrix of direct, indirect, controllable, and noncontrollable expenses.

Additional Responsibility Assignment Issues

As mentioned earlier, expense component terminology complicates the discussion of expense management. Certainly this problem applies to assigning responsibility for expenses. For example, does management assign the responsibility according to whether the expense is direct or indirect, or according to whether it is controllable or noncontrollable? Does it assign responsibility by center type or by expense category type? The complications caused by these differing concepts not only encumber the development of a profitability system but also severely hinder any expense management effort. Benefit expense provides a good example.

Benefits are an expense whose management and control require specific expertise. As an expense type, benefits can be assigned to the person responsible for managing that expense, making profitability measurement on an organizational level quite straightforward. But from a product or customer profitability standpoint, the solution is not so simple. Clearly, it would be to the institution's detriment to ignore the benefit expense in developing the profitability statement for a product or cus-

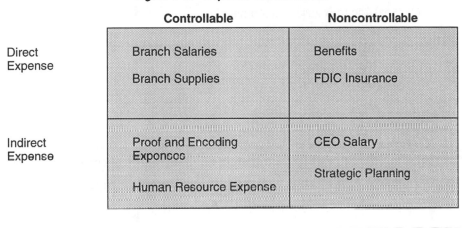

Figure 5-10—Expense Classifications

	Controllable	Noncontrollable
Direct Expense	Branch Salaries Branch Supplies	Benefits FDIC Insurance
Indirect Expense	Proof and Encoding Expences Human Resource Expense	CEO Salary Strategic Planning

tomer or for a line profit center. Yet to include the expense in the statement requires several decisions to be made. For example, is the benefit expense controllable or noncontrollable? Is it direct or indirect? Should the product manager, the line manager, or the customer relationship manager be held accountable and responsible for it as it relates to each one's personnel?

Perhaps the simplest way to solve the problem is to decide whether the benefit expense is direct or indirect. To reiterate an earlier point, when benefit expense is booked as an expense on the general ledger of the personnel department, it is a direct expense of that department and usually is treated as an allocated direct expense of the centers for which it is incurred.

Developing Information for Decision Making

Although costs and expenses are related, there is a clear difference between them. Expenses represent the way in which resources are obtained and paid for by an institution. For example, labor is a resource obtained and paid for by a "salary" expense. Activity-related costs, on the other hand, are the collection of resources (measured in financial terms) used to provide a specific product or service. For instance, the cost of cashing a check includes such expenses as salaries for tellers, equipment depreciation for proof and encoding machines, and lease expense for telephones. Techniques used to develop activity based costs are described in detail in Chapter 8. Certain basic concepts of developing activity costs are reviewed here.

Costs often must be broken down into component parts to provide the appropriate information analysis and decision making. Depending on the desired information, one of the following two breakdowns can be used:

- Fixed and variable components

- Marginal and fully absorbed components

Detailed explanation of these components is included in Chapter 19.

Marginal and Fully Absorbed Components

Marginal costs consist of expense items incurred as a result of adding one incremental item. Fully absorbed costs are based on the average cost of the entire volume. Marginal cost development can play an integral role in product management and pricing decisions. In addition, management can use marginal cost components to develop internal marginal cost analyses and "what if" volume/cost pricing analyses. (See Chapter 17 for a further discussion of pricing methodologies.)

Responsibility Center Classifications

Just as expenses are grouped by type, so are responsibility centers. This procedure facilitates control and allocation of the centers by capitalizing on the many features that are consistent within each class but vary dramatically across classifications. Such features include managers' technical skills, performance measurement criteria, and behavior-influencing decisions. Grouping responsibility centers according to these features increases flexibility and control in management and staffing, and achieves economies of scale.

One of the initial efforts needed to establish the framework for the conceptual design of the cost assignment process is to group all centers within the organization into major cost accounting center classifications. A center's classification is important in determining its reporting requirements, overhead distribution, and revenue and expense treatment. Additionally, within the cost transfer module of a system it may be necessary to identify, group, and classify centers by type in order to establish an appropriate cost assignment and close out sequence.

Centers can be grouped into one of the following center classification types:

- Profit Centers

- Processing Centers

- Staff Support Centers

- Administrative Centers

- Corporate Overhead—General

- Corporate Overhead—Specific

- Miscellaneous Centers

Following are definitions of the various center classifications and the general performance measurements that can be used for each type of center.

Profit Centers

Profit centers sell products and services to customers. These centers focus on individual customers and may offer one or many products. Their managers contribute to overhead and profits and are responsible for direct customer contact as well as for generating revenues to cover costs.

Branches, commercial lending units, and personal, corporate, and employee benefit trust units are generally profit centers, because they are organized to enhance profitability. Profit center activities include sales and business development, pricing, marketing, and customer service. They also may service customers by processing transactions. Performance measurement criteria for profit centers should include sales, growth, market share, and profitability.

Staff Support Centers

A staff support center performs services that cannot be directly aligned to products and services. Staff support services are not assigned revenue generation responsibility. They primarily provide support functions such as information flow, technical support, and resources to other centers throughout the institution. They also ensure that processing centers are able to provide the services sold by profit centers. Human resources, security, and the mail room are examples of staff support centers. Their objective is to provide centralized services to other areas throughout the institution in an efficient manner and at a specified level of cost.

Staff support center activities tend to be procedural and technical, and may include transactional activities of a nonbanking nature (e.g., mail processing and training). Such services are provided to each unit individually. Staff support centers should be evaluated by measuring how well they operate at prescribed expense levels and how well they assist other centers in achieving their respective objectives, including providing the appropriate level and quality of customer service.

Processing Centers

Processing centers also can be called product processing or customer processing/servicing centers. A processing center performs operational tasks in support of the bank products and services sold by profit centers. Processing centers typically handle customer transactions but are not assigned revenue generation responsibility. Their objective is to provide a desired level of service at the lowest possible cost. These centers focus on individual products or groups of similar products, and on groups of customers. They may be responsible for indirect customer contact, which does affect customer satisfaction, and for controlling expenses. Examples of processing centers include proof and encoding centers, deposit accounting, loan operations centers, trust operations, and processing centers.

Activities at these centers generally involve high volumes of transactions and the processing required to deliver services to customers. Performance measures should reflect the centers' ability to meet desired service level agreements and service quality levels, and to maintain or reduce the cost of processing transactions.

Administrative Centers

Administrative centers can include Line of Business Overhead, Processing Center Overhead, Affiliate Overhead, and other administrative overhead centers. Administrative centers supervise and coordinate the activities of units under their control. Their objective is to ensure that each unit they manage achieves its individual objectives. Thus, they set each unit's goals, provide guidance in achieving those goals, and monitor that achievement. Administrative centers typically administer the activities of processing and profit centers and have no revenue generation responsibility. Usually these centers focus on groups of units in the institution, but if they are within profit centers they may focus on groups of customers. Examples of administrative centers include regional branch administration and wholesale lending administration. Administrative centers should be evaluated on the same basis as the units they manage, as well as on the aggregate success of those units in meeting their objectives.

Corporate Overhead—General

This category includes general and administrative centers that manage the institution's overall operation and guide it in achieving its objectives. General overhead centers include planning (both strategic and tactical), corporate communications, and finance centers including tax and performance measurement and management areas. Again, these centers focus on and provide services to the institution as a whole and not to individual groups of units within the institution. This distinguishes them from line of business, local, and affiliate overhead centers.

General corporate overhead centers perform administrative, technical, and planning-oriented activities. Their performance should be measured by the institution's success in achieving its objectives and by the appropriateness of those objectives.

Corporate Overhead—Specific

Within the general category of overhead, certain centers have been identified and grouped as a particular type of overhead, in order to more specifically assign their costs to other units within the institution. The definition of these centers is the same as that for general corporate overhead centers. However, allocations for these centers can be developed using more specific cost drivers than can be used for assigning general overhead centers. Specific corporate centers include credit policy, risk management, and legal.

Miscellaneous Centers

Miscellaneous centers are special-purpose cost centers that have been set up to facilitate the pooling of expenses for development of costs. Examples of these centers can be process/activity cost pooling centers, consolidation or elimination centers, or dummy/temporary centers.

Units with a Dual Nature

Responsibility centers often are classified in several ways because their responsibilities and features overlap the defined classification. Consider a typical commercial bank branch. The branch officers originate and maintain customer account relationships, consistent with the branch's operation as a profit center. The branch tellers process transactions for the customers of the branch, which also is in keeping with the profit center role. However, the tellers also process transactions for customers of other branches and units, which is an activity consistent with the processing center classification.

The confusion can be resolved in two ways. One is to split the center into two or more units and classify each unit appropriately. This action requires additional effort because the new units need to be reported, analyzed, and so forth. However, the additional level of detail aids in pinpointing problem areas and enables managers to focus on specific areas of the organization while maintaining overall control. Splitting the center into distinct units also facilitates the development of appropriate performance measurement criteria for each unit. Those criteria will differ according to the various units' characteristics.

The other approach to the problem is to maintain the center as a single entity and, for profitability measurement purposes, to treat each function of the center separately. This method also requires additional effort as well as a significant level of automated system complexity. Centers were classified based on the type of work performed or the responsibilities of a particular center. Classification based on center titles alone is often misleading. Centers also were identified that fit into multiple classifications. Therefore, it is necessary to desegregate a center's expenses and treat a portion of the expenses differently for cost assignment purposes. Other situations may dictate the actual division of a center into two or more centers to facilitate proper treatment within the cost transfer module of the measurement system.

Figure 5-11 shows a listing of centers by classification which are included and used in the cost transfer module.

Figure 5-11—Sample Listing of Centers by Classification

Center Classification	Examples
Profit Center	Middle Market Lending Branches Personal Trust
Processing Center	Item Processing Trust Operations Loan Accounting
Staff Support Center	Purchasing Human Resources Mail Services
Administrative Centers	Wholesale Administration Branch Administration Trust Administration Affiliate Administration
Corporate Overhead—General	Executive Management Finance
Corporate Overhead—Specific	Credit Policy/Risk Management Legal
Miscellaneous Centers	Cost Pools Dummy Centers

SYNOPSIS

The assignment of responsibility for expenses is an important profitability measurement issue and one fraught with complications. Compared to the assignment of responsibility for balance sheet and revenue components, expense concerns are broader in scope and more controversial to resolve.

One group of issues involves reporting. Institutions must make fundamental decisions about which report format to use and whether to select the contribution or the profit and loss approach to expense reporting. Knowing the relative merits of each option is crucial to making the right decision.

This chapter discusses the various classification options and issues related to centers and account types and discusses the merits of each.

Further controversy arises from the various ways in which expenses can be characterized. Institutions can assign responsibility according to whether an expense is direct or indirect, or controllable or noncontrollable. They also can assign responsibility by responsibility type or expense type. Familiarity with these concepts and their advantages and disadvantages is therefore essential.

These challenges notwithstanding, a primary benefit of assigning responsibility for expenses is the ability to convert expenses into costs for analysis. Through a clear understanding of what expense must be borne by whom, managers can make informed decisions and increase profitability.

CHAPTER 6

Income Statement Components

OVERVIEW

Operating expense allocations represent only one of the challenges in performance measurement allocation. Comprehensive profitability analysis requires that all income statement items be assigned at the appropriate measurement level (i.e., product, organizational, or customer). Funds transfer pricing, described in Chapter 10, distributes the institution's net interest margin among the sources and users of funds. Remaining on the income statement are noninterest revenues from fees, taxes, loan loss, branch delivery expenses, transaction charges, and commissions, the allocation of which is the subject of this chapter.

Performance measurement results influence many aspects of management decision making and employee actions, including:

- Behavior

- Product strategy

- Pricing

- Service quality

- Cross subsidization

Without a reliable gauge of whether revenues are sufficient to cover the costs of offering bank products or services, the decisions about how to address or resolve any of these issues become "best guesses." The importance of accurate revenue allocations and of matching expenses to revenues in performance measurement systems becomes particularly clear when viewed in this light.

Evolution of Revenue Generation in Financial Institutions

Products and services provide banks with a variety of revenue streams, the principal ones being interest, fees, transaction charges, and commission and gains from investments. Deregulation, and its impact on competition in the banking industry, have diminished institutions' ability to generate historical levels of income from net interest margins. At the same time, the need to meet the constantly changing requirements and demands of customers and stakeholders have created new opportunities for revenue generation and product/service differentiation. In response to these developments, financial institutions have become increasingly adept at raising revenues from fees and commissions, such as those charged for bankcard products and trust services.

For this reason, the simple assignment of interest income is no longer sufficient to address the broader issue of revenue allocation in performance measurement systems. This chapter will discuss several emerging issues which need to be addressed as a result of this evolution in revenue generation within financial institutions.

REVENUE COMPONENTS

Revenue Assignment for Interrelated Products/Services

As the number of revenue-raising alternatives has increased for banks, performance measurement at any level has grown more complex. Management accounting departments have struggled to keep allocation methods and assignment rules for bank revenues in pace with the evolution of revenue generation. To illustrate this point, we will examine two significant developments in the area of bank product/service offerings.

First, expansion in the array of traditional bank businesses, particularly through involvement in such areas as discount brokerage, mortgage banking, and insurance, has created the problem of interrelated revenues. Because the services offered by these businesses are related to traditional bank services, arguments frequently arise regarding which revenues should be associated with the newer businesses. These interrelationships complicate the task of performance measurement.

For example, consider the sale by a bank of credit life insurance on an installment loan. Allocation of revenues to the branch and the insurance subsidiary in this case is relatively straightforward. The insurance premium (typically included in the monthly loan payment to the branch) is allocated to the insurance subsidiary; in turn, the subsidiary pays the bank a commission for the sale and a fee for servicing.

For the purpose of measuring product performance, the situation is much more controversial. One line of reasoning holds that the insurance product would not exist without the installment loan, so the loan should receive all revenues (and an appropriate share of the subsidiary's operating expenses). On the other hand, without revenue (and cost) allocations to the insurance product, it becomes difficult to determine whether such an option should be provided to borrowers.

A second development in bank offerings which has complicated revenue allocations is product "bundling" or "packaging." Bundling attaches "free" or "discounted" products or services to, for instance, a demand deposit account, and markets the resulting compilation as a single product. Credit cards, debit cards, and seniors' accounts are common examples of such attachments.

Determining how revenues should be attributed to stand-alone products is usually fairly simple, as most application systems have been designed along product lines and allow balances and revenues to be easily associated with individual products. Most difficulties related to assigning revenues to unbundled products/services have to do with determining average balances and accruals for interest and fees not yet charged. Also, legacy systems (those which have evolved with the business and do not offer all the features of modern banking applications) may not provide detailed revenue data on a product-specific basis.

However, product bundling raises an entirely different array of revenue allocation questions. Foremost among them is how to properly credit the underlying "free" products and services for their contribution to the bundled product's performance for measurement purposes. Equally important is the need to ensure that the costs of providing the underlying products are matched with the appropriate revenues.

By way of example, consider a bundled demand deposit account—which we will call *Premier*—which has an annual fee of $240 and combines:

- A demand deposit account ($500 minimum balance)

- Free cashier's checks or money orders

- A no annual fee credit card

- An EFT/ATM card (debit card)

- Direct debit facilities

- Home banking

- Discounts on personal loans of 25 basis points

Each product could be sold separately, with fees levied individually at a standard price. However, for marketing and competitive reasons the bank has combined the products into a single product. Figure 6-1 shows the difference in pricing between the individual products and the *Premier* account.

Figure 6-1—Pricing: Individual versus Bundled Products

	Average Customer Usage	Annual Revenue—Individual Pricing	Annual Joint Revenue Single-Fee Account
Premier Account		N/A	$240.00
Demand Deposit Account	1	60.00	—
Cashier's Checks	4	16.00	—
Credit Card	1	18.00	—
Traveler's Checks	$500	15.00	—
EFT/ATM Cards/Usage	12	60.00	—
Home Banking	1	60.00	—
Personal Loans			
Auto	$20,000	$50.00*	—
Home Improvement	$10,000	$25.00*	—
Total		$304.00	$240.00

* Loss of interest to the bank from the customer using the discounts applicable for personal loans. In pricing the bundled product the marketing function assumes certain behavioral characteristics and sets the price using those assumptions. In this case, if the customer's behavior perfectly matched the design assumptions, the bank would have provided a discount of $64.00 per year.

There are several ways to recognize the $240 for the purpose of measuring product performance. The method used should be simple to implement, transparent to information users, and a positive enabler for the behavior desired by the bank.

One way is to recognize *Premier* as an product in its own right and assess its performance by comparing all revenues to costs. In this case, the revenues would include interest receivable on the two loans after applying the 25 basis point discount to each loan, and the commission of $240.

A second way is to allocate the $240 to the individual products in proportion to the individual fee schedules of the unbundled products. Figure 6-2 shows such an allocation.

A problem with this approach is that customer use of the products or services that have been bundled is rarely consistent with the product-design assumptions. Variance between expected and actual usage may make the theoretical prices inappropriate for allocation purposes. Although this approach allocates the fees to the individual products on a consistent basis, it may not provide truly accurate information on product performance.

Figure 6-2—Assigning Bundled Revenues to Products

	Theoretical Revenues Under Ind. Pricing	% of Total Ind. Pricing Revenues	Allocation of $240 Yearly Fee
DDA Account	60.00	23.0	55.20
Cashier's Checks	8.00	3.1	7.44
Credit Card	18.00	6.8	16.32
Traveler's Checks	5.00	1.9	4.56
EFT / ATM Cards	60.00	23.0	55.20
Home Banking	60.00	23.0	55.20
Loans			
Auto	25.00	9.6	23.04*
Home Improvement	25.00	9.6	23.04*
Total	$261.00	100.0%	$240.00

---

* This element of the fee should be recognized as interest. The overall fee was calculated assuming a discount of 25 basis points on loans of $10,000.

An alternative approach would be to allocate the $240 in proportion to actual usage of the individual products by the purchasers of the bundled account. This approach treats the *Premier* account as merely the sum of the individual products rather than a product in its own right. Because this method fails to recognize *Premier* as a single product, it may not properly credit *Premier* for its role in securing a broad relationship with the customer.

Implicit Revenues

Issues related to revenue allocation for interrelated products and services involve revenues actually received from customers. Another set of allocation questions arises for income not directly paid to the bank in the form of fees. The most common example of such implicit revenues is where compensating balances replace regular fees to pay for cash management services.

A relationship manager may decide to waive certain cash management fees to secure customer balances. Therefore, the earnings potential associated with the balances compensates the bank for the income passed up when the fees were waived. Funds transfer pricing would credit the deposit product or branch holding the deposit for an appropriate share of the interest income (net interest margin) derived from the product, thus rewarding the deposit product/holder for the balances. However, under this scenario, no benefit accrues to cash management for its services, although it incurred some cost to provide them. As a result, it will be difficult to assess the overall performance of cash management services.

Because these compensating balances are maintained at the bank to pay for cash management services, a mechanism should be devised to ensure that the cash management process covers its costs and receives credit for its role in securing and maintaining customer relationships. One such method would be to charge the compensating balance product for the amount of the waived fees and treat this as cash management income. (It also can reasonably be argued that cash management should receive some share, if not all, of potential revenues on the balances.)

Because this approach creates revenues that may or may not be collected, the performance measurement system will not balance to the institution's accounting systems. One solution to this problem is to treat the revenue assigned to cash management as an expense to the officer who has the compensating balances, therefore ensuring that debits equal credits for the transfer.

The treatment of the charge to the compensating balance product/holder warrants further discussion. The traditional approach would be to deduct the expense after calculating the margin (using funds transfer pricing). This method would have no impact on the product's interest margin. However, the fees were waived in the first place to secure the deposit. Therefore, possibly a more equitable approach is to recognize the charge as a reduction of interest on the deposit product before the margin is determined, as shown in Figure 6-3. Although this results in the same net income, the alternative method reports revenues more appropriately at all stages of the transaction.

Shadow Accounting

The preceding cash management example brings to light an issue that is becoming increasingly important for performance measurement in financial institutions: how to handle situations in which more than one individual is responsible for delivering or maintaining a particular service or product.

For example, traveler's checks normally are assigned to an institution's branch system because that is where the service is performed. But if a customer of the institution's corporate division issues the checks, the corporate division would be responsible for some revenues as the relationship manager. Further, a product manager could hold responsibility for all branch fee services. In all, three different managers might have a hand in delivering the service, thus having a claim to a portion of its revenues.

In essence, the problem is that each of these managers should receive some credit for the traveler's checks revenues, yet there is only one set of revenues to assign. Some

---

Figure 6-3—Cash Management Revenue Allocation—Alternative Approach

Assumptions:

Balance	$10,000
Interest Applied	7.0%
Cost of Funds	6.0%
Fees Waived	$100

	Traditional Approach	Alternative Approach
Funds Transfer Credit	$750.00	$750.00
Interest	600.00	600.00
Associated Interest Cost		100.00
Margin	150.00	50.00
Direct Cost	100.00	
Net Income/Contribution	50.00	50.00

---

banks resolve this situation through the use of shadow accounting. Under this mechanism, revenues are double or triple counted, once each for several managers. Despite its benefits, this method obviously poses problems in reconciling performance measurement statements to financial reports. As a result, shadow revenues normally are handled in special memo accounts, and clearly identified as shadow revenues on management accounting reports. Special care should be exercised when using such a methodology so as not to distort overall total profitability and at the same time not to disenchant the line.

Credit for Cross-Selling

A more complex problem arises when one individual sells a service on behalf of the institution even though responsibility for providing that service clearly lies with another individual. Cross-selling is an effective means of leveraging existing customer relationships to sell a wider range of services. For that reason, both performance measurements and reward systems should acknowledge the cross-selling efforts of managers.

An example is the sale by corporate division relationship officers of services to top corporate executives. These individuals are also likely to be targeted by the institution's high net worth customer program. The manager responsible for the program is normally in an area completely different from that of the corporate division officer, such as the retail or trust division. Clearly it benefits the institution overall if the relationship officer cross-sells such services as trusts, investments, and loans. However, if these services are for the executive's personal use, the corporate division officer has no reason from a performance measurement standpoint to sell them. All profit from such services will be assigned to the high net worth program manager. Furthermore, time spent cross-selling means less time spent selling the corporate division's services.

Shadow accounting could be used to solve this problem, namely by crediting the corporate division officer with revenues from cross-sold products. However, reconciliation problems again arise between performance measurement and financial reports. A more common alternative is to create a one time "referral fee" for the officer, negotiated between the corporate division and the high net worth program.

Determining the process to use for paying referral fees may be difficult. For instance, should the corporate division officer receive the fee as soon as he or she makes the referral, or only after a sale is made by the high net worth program manager? Also, should fee rebates be put in place for cases in which loans to executives become nonperforming? These and similar questions should be addressed by management accounting and the respective departments prior to implementing a referral fee method to credit managers for cross-selling.

Process Performance

The preceding sections of this chapter have examined some of the challenging issues in the allocation of revenues to products and organizational units. This section takes the analysis a step further by introducing the concept of revenue allocations to processes (i.e., the activities which combine to build the product or service).

Since the 1980s, cost allocation methods have become increasingly sophisticated. By using such techniques as Activity Based Costing (ABC), management has been able to evaluate process costs and develop business process redesign or improvement programs that have significantly reduced operating costs and changed the way organizations view and manage themselves.

While major advances have been made in cost measurement, allocations, and management information systems, the revenue recognition techniques have become largely outdated. Banks have traditionally assessed performance of strategic business units by attributing most revenue to profit centers (usually a branch). Although the value-adding activities supporting products are performed by a number of departments, operating units, or even separate companies, banks typically allocate revenues exclusively to the account/relationship manager.

Revenue allocations based on these methods hinge on who owns the customer relationship rather than on the realities of production cost or economic benefit. The account holder, branch, or base product is rewarded to the detriment of support centers performing the activities which actually bring the product or services to market. Such differences in the advancement of cost and revenue allocation techniques cause a disequilibrium in the way banks measure performance on the expense and revenue sides.

In reality, interest and fees are the economic reward for a series of processes that are combined to make a product. Therefore, just as operating cost may be assigned to process activities, revenues may be allocated to processes. Such a system provides a clearer understanding of how economic value is created in the bank by products, business units, and customer relationships. Not only is this information useful in determining the cost/benefit relationship of specific activities, but it also helps align the risk and reward components of pricing decisions.

A typical high-level process diagram for a consumer loan product is shown in Figure 6-4.

It is misleading to treat all revenue as sales revenue, which would result in a 100% allocation to the branches originating the loans. A method for allocating both interest and fee income should properly reflect the contribution of each of these departments/activities toward total product profitability. Doing so matches activity expense allocations derived from Activity Based Costing with the revenues derived from these allocated costs. From this analysis, information users develop a clearer picture of which product- or service-related activities add the greatest or least value. Figure 6-5 illustrates how a revenue-expense matching exercise, characterized as a "process value statement," might look.

Revenue Recognition

Performance measurement traditionally has been accounted for over statutory reporting periods (economic cycles that are defined by statute, such as annual or quarterly periods) rather than over product or relationship life cycles. In assigning revenues to products or processes, the timing of revenue recognition should be considered, taking into account the underlying economic realities of the entity which generates that revenue.

Figure 6-4—Loan Product Process Diagram

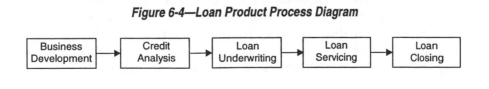

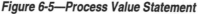

Figure 6-5—Process Value Statement

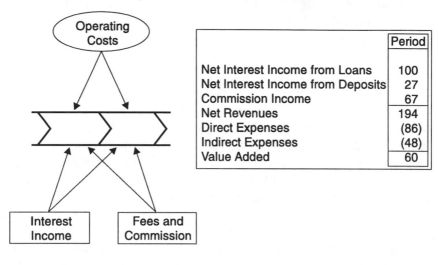

	Period
Net Interest Income from Loans	100
Net Interest Income from Deposits	27
Commission Income	67
Net Revenues	194
Direct Expenses	(86)
Indirect Expenses	(48)
Value Added	60

Examples from the financial services industry may prove useful in illustrating this point. For banks, commissions on a loan product in the form of an arrangement fee should not be fully recognized upon receipt if a portion of the fee is intended to compensate for prepayment risk. Instead, because not all of the commission relates to origination, it should be amortized over a longer term, possibly over the entire life of the loan.

In the case of the life insurance industry, methods have been implemented to improve revenue recognition techniques by analyzing expected profits over the life of a product or relationship. Banks could borrow from these techniques by using discounted cash flow analysis and adjusting for probabilities of default and early redemption in order to assess the real value of each relationship. The difficulty in applying this approach lies in the uncertainty arising from risk factors inherent in the banking business, such as credit risk, economic risk, and prepayment risk. Periodic reviews of the assumptions used for the analysis are necessary to minimize the impact of changes in these risk factors.

Figure 6-6 illustrates the concept of applying revenues to appropriate stages of the product or relationship life cycle for performance measurement purposes. The table identifies the underlying reasons for several fee types typically charged by banks. It indicates the difficulty of accurately determining the source of each fee. As is apparent, not all fee or commission allocations are equally complex.

Figure 6-6—Fee Allocation over Life Cycle Stages

	Product Development	Relationship Management	Sales and Marketing	Account Maintenance
Arrangement	•	•	•	•
ATM Usage				•
Overdrafts				•
Insurance	•		•	•
Home Banking	•	•	•	•
Safe Custody		•	•	•

OTHER INCOME STATEMENT ITEMS

Taxes

The issue involves the wide variety of tax structures and rates with which financial institutions operate. Because tax rates vary by country, state, and city, calculation of a tax effect should reflect the differences. The difficulty in implementing a differential tax rate system, however, has led many institutions to use a single, average tax rate when taxes are included in profitability reports.

New Products and Start-Up Operations

New products and start-up operations pose special problems. Because their initial volume tends to be relatively small, and because many new financial products are fixed asset-intensive or system-intensive, their expenses can be large. As a result, most such operations and products appear to be extremely unprofitable. Great care must be exercised in using profitability measurement approaches that would not prevent a product or service's implementation or bring about premature discontinuance.

Some institutions resolve this problem by adopting an approach used by many industrial concerns: They cover the new expenses with the profits of current products. Start-up costs, research and development costs, and other related items are not charged or allocated directly to the new product or start-up operation; instead they are considered an overhead expense. This approach is ideally suited to the contribution reporting methodology, because the new product expense can be treated as just another item for the contribution to cover.

Another way to handle these items is to expense them against the respective product, organization, or customer at the time the expense is incurred. This approach makes it easy to reconcile profitability measurement to financial statements. However, because the expenses do not affect reported profitability after the year in which they are incurred, a manager has no incentive to ensure that all of the expenses will be recovered in subsequent years. This is particularly true if the expenses are considered amortized for pricing and expense recovery purposes.

To address this problem, some institutions develop reporting systems with trend reports that span several years. A large expense incurred in year one to develop a new system, for example, would be expensed that same year. For a $1 million expenditure in year one to develop a system with an expected life of five years and an expected capacity of five million items per year, the additional cost to recover would be $1 million over 25 million items, or four cents per item. The report would show the $1 million expensed in year one, but the four cents per item would be used only for pricing and similar activities. The multiyear report would indicate whether the profit of succeeding years recovered the initial $1 million. Figure 6-7 illustrates these computations.

Ideally, a new business or start-up operation would develop a plan, such as a five-year plan indicating that the break-even point would be reached in year two. A reporting system with a multiyear trend then could be used to monitor performance against each of the target years. Even with the major expense in year one, for example, the final actual results still could be compared against the five-year plan; at the end of year one it could be determined whether the operation was on, below, or above target. The same could be done for each of the ensuing years.

Research and Development

Research and development expenses or systems and programming expenses frequently present challenges for developing profitability information. Some of the difficulty arises from the difficulty of determining who has responsibility and accountability for these expenses.

Figure 6-7—Unit Costs for Multiyear System

Expenditure	Expected Life	Cost per Item
$1 Million	÷25 Million Item-Years = (5 Million Items per Year for 5 Years)	$0.04

A relatively straightforward way of solving this problem requires an understanding of the types of research and development expenses. There are three general classifications. The first, system maintenance expenses, consists of expenses incurred to keep a system operational or to meet regulatory requirements. The second, system modification expenses, relates to the expense of changes requested by users (but not required to keep the system operational). It also includes minor enhancements for new product introduction or product modification. A good example of this type of expense is the modification of deposit accounting systems that took place when debit cards were introduced. The third type of expense consists of true system development expenses, where extensive systems work is performed and entirely new systems are developed. An example is the development of a new cash management system.

With these differentiations in mind, it is relatively easy to determine who is responsible and who should be held accountable for each expense category. System maintenance expense typically is an operational consideration; it is charged to and is the responsibility of the area that operates the system. In a loan accounting system, for example, system maintenance would be charged or allocated to the loan accounting area as an indirect expense. The expense then would be included in the costs developed for the loan accounting area. From there it would flow naturally to all of the related organization, product, and customer profitability reports.

System modification expenses typically are assigned directly to the person or organizational area requesting the change. In the debit card example above, the expense would have been charged and allocated as an indirect expense to the product manager for debit cards (assuming there was such a product manager), or to the retail area responsible for those accounts.

System development expenses typically are one-time expenses and can be treated in much the same way as the start-up operations discussed earlier in this chapter.

Advertising

The main problem associated with advertising expenses is that their benefits usually extend well beyond the time period in which the advertising occurs. Further, the benefits are difficult to quantify in the normal cost allocation sense. Consequently, there are alternative ways to allocate advertising expense. Financial institutions handle advertising expense in three different ways for profitability measurement. The first method treats advertising as an overhead expense of the appropriate management level. General "image" advertising, for example, could be treated as corporate overhead, while advertising for certificates of deposit could be treated as overhead for the retail division. This approach is relatively easy to implement, but it is restricted to organizational profitability; it does not report expenses to product or customer levels.

This disadvantage can be mitigated using the second of the three approaches, which treats the advertising expense as a product overhead expense allocated in the current period. Certificate of deposit advertising, for example, could be allocated as a current period expense to the reported profitability of the certificate of deposit product. The drawback is that this method does little to allocate the expense to customer or organizational profitability reports.

The third way to handle advertising expense is to use a simple allocation basis (such as the number of certificates of deposit) and to develop an average advertising expense per product unit. In essence, this method treats the expense as an overhead to a customer account. Because the account is automatically associated with a customer, a product, and an organization, this technique allows more effective allocation of the expense than do the other two methods. Like the second method, it also could allocate the average amount per account in the period during which the advertising expense occurs, but this action usually produces expense fluctuations in profitability statements. A more widely accepted practice is to amortize the advertising expense as follows:

$$\frac{\text{Advertising expense}}{\text{per account per month}} = \frac{\text{Annual budgeted advertising}}{\text{Number of accounts} \times 12 \text{ months}}$$

Other Large and Infrequent Expenses

Several financial institution expense categories share two characteristics: they are large, compared to regular monthly expenses, and they may not occur every period. Depending on an institution's accrual and accounting policies, many expenses can fall into this category. Examples include postage for Form 1099 mailings in January, quarterly equipment maintenance contracts, annual real estate taxes, and of course advertising.

The problem posed by these expenses can be solved by changing the accounting approach and establishing monthly accruals. Fluctuations are eliminated, and normal cost accounting techniques can be used. However, creating monthly accruals for all such expenses may not be practical. In such cases, the three methods described for advertising expense are acceptable alternatives.

Loan Loss Provision

An important component of a financial institution's profit and loss statement, at least for lending institutions, is the loan loss provision. Several methods can be used to handle the provision. The simplest is to not allocate it, an approach often used in smaller institutions. However, this is misleading because the loan loss provision is a major component of product and customer profitability.

Another way to deal with the loan loss provision is to allocate net charge-offs (gross charge-offs less recoveries) to the appropriate center, product, or customer as an element of the profit and loss statement. This technique is relatively simple to implement because the gross charge-offs and recoveries are known and can easily be charged to the appropriate organizational centers, products, and customers. However, it does have a few shortcomings:

- Charge-offs can occur long after the credit decision. If the manager of the product, customer, or organization has changed between the initial booking of the loan (the credit decision) and the charge-off, the current manager's profitability is influenced by someone else's decision.

- Similarly, recoveries can occur long after the charge off. The risk is the same as with a charge-off, except that recoveries favorably affect the new manager's profit and loss statement.

- The variability of charge-offs can destroy the incentive to achieve plan results. A single large loan, charged off against profits, can make it impossible for a manager to meet a year's goals. For example, if a center with a planned profit of $500,000 has an unanticipated $1 million charge-off in January, it has virtually no hope of meeting—and therefore no incentive to try to meet—its other goals for the year.

- Because net charge-offs generally do not equal the provision, this technique increases the difficulty of reconciling the management accounting information to the institution's financial statements.

These methods for handling the loan loss provision do not account for changes in credit risk in the reported profitability. That presents a problem, because if there is an increase in credit risk, there should be an increased loan loss reserve with a corresponding provision to account for that increased risk. One allocation method that deals with this change in risk involves the computation of a calculated loan loss reserve. The loan loss reserve and loan migration analysis method approach is discussed in detail in Chapter 11.

Approaches to Branch Costing and Profitability Reporting

The branch network system often represents the largest share of a financial institution's non-interest expense. Branches serve as the link between the customer and the bank by directly offering many products and services. In addition, branches refer customers to other areas of the bank, including Trust, Bankcard, and Investments. As a result, it is important to fully understand what activities branches are performing and which products or users benefit from those activities. Once this is determined, costs can be matched with appropriate revenue to derive profitability. This section outlines various methods of allocating branch-related costs for both product and organizational profitability purposes. In addition, it will review and discuss several related issues such as alternative approaches for account ownership and depreciated versus leased facilities.

For organizational profitability purposes, branch expenses must be understood to determine whether any costs are incurred to support other profit centers. If so, these costs should be allocated to the centers benefited. For product profitability purposes, all branch expenses must be allocated to the products and activities they support. A product is a service provided by the bank to the customer and is sold separately in the marketplace. Activities are subsets of products and are defined as transactions or tasks that support products. These include items deposited, loan payments processed, stop payments, loan origination, and account maintenance. Every product and activity must be defined before product allocations begin. Chapter 8 discusses activity based costing in more detail.

Sampling Approach

To determine branch cost allocation methodologies, all activities, activity volumes, and time associated with performing the activity must be known. Developing this information requires collecting data from the branch network. It would be very time-consuming and labor-intensive to visit every branch. Fortunately, branches generally offer similar products and perform similar activities across the entire branch network. And the amount of time required to perform an activity varies little between branches. One approach that has worked for many banks is to interview a representative sample of branches and use the results to determine cost allocation methodologies for their entire branch system. The sample may include, but is not limited to, the following type of branches:

- Large deposit base (established branches)
- Small deposit base (de novo branches)
- High commercial loan volume
- Mall locations (transient relationships, commercial deposit relationships)
- College towns (turnover in account base)
- Downtown locations

After the criteria have been chosen, select a representative sample that will most likely reflect all branches in the system. This sample of branches will be interviewed in order to develop appropriate allocation methodologies for the activities and/or services. The interview questions will be focused primarily on the amount of time required, on average, to perform the activity or service. The next section will discuss the use of surveys to collect the required data.

SURVEYS

Once the branches have been selected for interviewing purposes, surveys need to be developed to determine the time required to perform each activity. For product profitability purposes, the surveys should include all retail and commercial depository transactions, retail loan transactions, and all possible types of transactions (including referrals) that branches perform. In addition, the surveys should include all internal product-related tasks such as originating and servicing accounts. For organizational profitability purposes, the surveys should include all activities that support other profit centers, including trust referrals, investment services, bankcard applications, etc. Unlike product surveys, organizational surveys will not be an all-inclusive list of activities performed by the branches. This is because most branch expenses should remain with the branches; only expenses related to referrals should be allocated to other profit centers.

The surveys can be mailed to the selected branches or used in conjunction with on-site interviews. Interviewing generally provides more accurate information and tends to have less bias than mailed surveys because of the extra feedback provided from interviewees. However, interviewing is a more time-consuming and costly alternative than mailing.

After the activities have been identified, a table must be established that describes the activity, the time required to complete it, and its respective volume. The table in Figure 6-8 illustrates a sample survey for product profitability.

The initial product survey should include all activities performed and have blank columns for noting the time and volume associated with them. The purpose of the survey is to interview branch personnel to determine the time spent to perform each activity, rather than how much time is spent on the activity during a given period. Once an average time has been developed, that time will be multiplied by the respective activity volume to determine a weighted average time spent on that activity, relative to other activities performed by the branch.

Multiple surveys may be developed, including surveys for:

- Sales-related activities

- Service-related activities

- Functional responsibilities such as tellers, mortgage officers, etc.

Next, the survey results are consolidated. If multiple surveys are used, then each type of survey is consolidated separately to derive an average time by activity for each survey. These surveys are then weighted according to the resources devoted to each type of survey. For example, if tellers represent 35 percent of a branch's salaried resources, then 35 percent of branch expenses are allocated based on teller allocation methodologies.

For product profitability reporting, the total branch network volumes are required for each activity. However, if multiple surveys are used, then volumes may be required for each type of survey. For organizational profitability reporting, volumes are required by branch for total debits and credits and any other service-related volumes.

Figure 6-9 illustrates a product profitability survey after the results have been compiled. In this example, multiple surveys are not used.

Assuming this was an all-inclusive representation of a branch's activities, 30 percent of the branch's resources would be devoted to "receiving deposits." As volumes change on a period-to-period basis, the resulting percentage of time spent on each task will change to reflect the new volumes.

The same approach applies for organizational profitability with the exception of the activities listed. As mentioned earlier, the activities would include only those supporting other profit centers, and only a portion of expenses would be allocated out.

Figure 6-8—Sample Survey for Product Profitability

Activity	Time	Volume
Receive Deposits		
Accept Loan Payments		
Process Night Deposits		
Originate Car Loan		
Originate Home Equity Line		
Open IRA		

Figure 6-9—Completed Product Profitability Survey

Activity	Time	Volume	Weighted Volume	Percent
Receive Deposits	1.5	400	600	30.0%
Accept Loan Payments	3.0	50	150	7.5%
Process Night Deposits	20.0	20	400	20.0%
Originate Car Loan	45.0	10	450	22.5%
Originate Home Equity Line	60.0	5	300	15.0%
Open IRA	20.0	5	100	5.0%
Total			2,000	100.0%

OTHER BRANCH ISSUES

Account Ownership Issues

Account ownership issues exist when a customer opens an account at one branch and conducts business at a different location. As a result, the customer's balance remains at the originating branch while all service-related costs are incurred at the service branches. This violates the matching principle, which states that revenues from a relationship be matched with expenses incurred from the same relationship.

Below are five alternative methods to resolve account ownership issues:

- Extensive systems can be purchased or developed that enable institutions to track each transaction and cross-charge branches based on their volume of transactional activity relative to their customers' transactional activity conducted at other branches. Each branch will have its own unique cost structure, used to determine incoming and outgoing charges. This is an accurate but complex methodology that is expensive to implement.

- Another complex approach is to credit servicing branches with the account relationship. This can be accomplished by reviewing the prior month's transactions and assigning relationships to the branch with the most account activity for the period. Thus, the account ownership may occasionally shift between periods to branches where customers conduct the most business.

- The pooling approach takes all costs associated with transactional activities throughout the branch system and divides by the total transactions to derive an average transaction unit cost. This unit cost is then applied to each branch based on the number of transactions incurred by their respective customers. This approach applies the matching principle but ignores the efficiency levels between branches.

- The net approach takes the difference between a branch's total transactions and the total transactions incurred by its customer base. This difference is then multiplied by a unit cost per transaction (described above) to derive a net charge or credit. For example, if branch A had 1,000 transactions and its customer base had 1,200 transactions that were incurred throughout the network system, then branch A would be charged for 200 transactions multiplied by a standard unit cost. This approach is more accurate than the pooling approach because the branch's efficiency is considered for part of the equation (1,000 transactions). However, the pooling approach is still used for the unit cost calculation (the remaining 200 transactions).

- Finally, account ownership issues may be ignored with the hope that the interbranch transactions net out. This approach does not match account revenues with expenses but requires no real implementation efforts.

Depreciated versus Leased Facilities

Branch profitability can be greatly influenced by whether the branch was purchased or leased. Depreciation and leasing expenses are important to know and understand. However, branch managers should not be held responsible for these costs. To resolve this issue, several alternatives exist:

- For profitability reporting purposes, depreciation and leased costs can be treated as a separate line item after the contribution margin.

- All branch facility expenses can be pooled and charged out to branches based on square footage.

- All facility expenses can be isolated from the profitability reports and a facilities manager held responsible for maintaining costs.

- Facilities charges can be reported only to senior executives involved in strategic branch decisions, without managers being held responsible.

- Depreciation and leased costs can be included within total branch operating expenses.

SYNOPSIS

The development of performance measurement systems requires the keen analysis of all aspects of the income statement and balance sheet. Included in this analysis is the proper matching of revenue items with the associated expenses. The nature of the banking environment presents several challenges in the process to assign or allocate revenue and expense items.

First, revenues may be generated in a bundled relationship. For example, a seniors' checking account may be packaged with several products and priced with one monthly fee. The chapter reviewed the related bundling issues and presented several alternatives to deal with the allocation of revenues to achieve the matching principle of revenue with expense.

Additional complications relate to the referral of business between units. For example, a retail branch may refer a high-deposit customer to the Trust Department. Again, the chapter presented several alternatives, reviewing cross-selling issues, shadow accounting, and referral credits.

On the expense side, several expense items require special consideration, including taxes, loan loss provision, advertising expenses, and branch expenses. This chapter reviewed these items and presented several alternatives for a rational allocation.

CHAPTER 7

Cost Accounting Approaches and Methodologies

OVERVIEW

Development of cost information is one of the most labor-intensive exercises of a financial institution's performance measurement project. Management relates more closely to cost allocations than any other performance measurement issue. Great debates often accompany the development and reporting of unit-cost or cost assignment information. Ironically, the information is not the most material part of overall profitability. However, with the current trends in cost management and process reengineering, management places great emphasis on measuring and knowing costs.

With the industry focus on cost management, great care should be given to the identification and selection of costing methodology, approach, and key assumptions. Because each institution has its own agenda, scope, and objectives, no one costing methodology or approach will satisfy all. This chapter highlights the various methodologies and approaches to developing cost information, and the strengths and weaknesses of each.

Cost Methodologies

The first step in developing an appropriate costing methodology is deciding what and how much of the organization's expenses will be assigned—especially overhead and administrative expenses. There are three main approaches and several nuances in dealing with this issue.

Full-absorption costing is a method under which, by definition, all costs are fully accounted for. Expected costing is where costs are developed based on expected expenses and/or volumes. With expected or standard costing, expenses assigned may be greater than or less than the actual expenses.

FULL-ABSORPTION COSTING (AVERAGE ACTUAL COSTING)

Full-absorption costing, as its name implies, allocates all costs in the development of unit costs. The unit cost is developed by dividing actual expenses by actual transaction volume, and represents the institution's average cost of processing a transaction (unit) over a given time period. It does not reflect what the transaction "should" cost, or what it was expected to cost when a department or institution's budget was created.

Under the full-absorption approach, fixed costs are included in the unit cost, as well as any indirect or overhead costs related to the particular organizational unit. However, unit costs could be developed to represent direct unit costs and indirect unit costs. Under full-absorption costing, these unit costs are assignd to users based on transactions processed, multiplied by unit cost. Full-absorption costing therefore results in the allocation of a base expense that equals the unit's total expense.

Under full-absorption costing, all variances due to fluctuations in expenses and volume are ultimately borne and paid by service users. These variances are referred to as spending, or rate variances and volume variances. Total expenses are allocated regardless of how much excess or available capacity exists. When transaction volumes and/or expenses fluctuate, costs are spread over actual volume levels and users are charged varying unit costs so that the total base expense is allocated.

Volume variances occur when budgeted or expected volume differs from actual volumes. Figure 7-1 illustrates the treatment of volume variances in full-absorption costing. At the budgeted volume level, there is an associated level of budgeted expense. The further the activity volume is from budget, the greater the associated variance.

Advantages

The provider's expenses are fully allocated, with no residual left in the provider center. If volumes rise or operating efficiency increases, service users reap the benefits of reduced unit costs. No expense residuals are left in the support units once the allocations have been completed.

Full absorption's main advantages are simplicity and understandability. Allocations are based on actual expenses and actual volumes.

In addition to avoiding confusion as to what expenses are or are not included, full absorption circumvents debates between service providers and users as to what

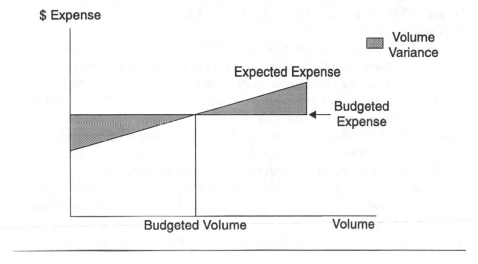

Figure 7-1—Volume Variances under Fully Absorbed Costing

should be considered relevant. This fact assumes added importance when allocations are used for several purposes.

For example, expenses considered relevant when measuring product, organizational, and customer profitability often are not considered relevant when analyzing pricing issues. Mandating that all expenses be used establishes understandable ground rules. Further, by treating all expenses as relevant, full-absorption costing recognizes that, in the long run, prices established for products and customers must cover all the institution's costs. Unit costs reflect actual institution costs, not expectations, marginal costs, or costs under ideal operating conditions.

Full-absorption costing creates the additional advantage of assuring that the entire institution's profitability equals the sum of the profitability of its components. No residual expenses need to be factored in to derive total institution profitability. This consideration becomes especially important when all components of the institution are analyzed. The sum of the parts equals the sum of the whole.

Disadvantages

Unit costs derived using the full-absorption method can vary significantly from period to period due to fluctuations in transaction volume. Such variances can be confusing when using the data for pricing decisions; in fact, they can render the information less meaningful. Consider proof and encoding unit costs. demand deposit and savings account products are serviced by the proof and encoding unit and receive allocated expense. If transaction volumes fall, unit costs increase. If transaction volume of one product—say savings—falls, unit cost rises for both the savings and demand deposit products. This may, in turn, affect the profitability of the demand deposit product and the price selected for processing checks, even though there has been no change in the demand deposit volume or product characteristics.

This brings up another shortcoming of full-absorption costing, namely that volume changes of any one service user can affect the allocations received by all other users. It contradicts the expense-management concept of matching responsibility for expenses with control of those expenses. If a unit performance can be affected by volume growth or decline of other users of the same services, management might decide to continue unprofitable lines of business to mitigate the impact of cost increases in other lines.

Full-absorption costing also is prone to fluctuations in unit cost due to one-time or periodic "big hit" expenses. Because unit costs are based on actual expenses, significantly greater expenditures will take place in some time periods. One example is the seasonality of some expenses, such as postage for mailing tax forms (1099s) in January. In the same way, advertising campaigns might have a large periodic impact on unit-cost calculations.

Another disadvantage of full-absorption costing is its inability to measure the productivity or efficiency of operating areas. When allocations are based on expectations and standards, rate variances and associated unallocated residuals typically reflect varying levels of operating efficiency. With fully absorbed costs, all expenses are allocated and the service/activity user bears all variances.

Excess capacity also is left unrecognized. The resulting volume variances are borne by the service users, creating little incentive for service providers to reduce operating costs. These managers have considerable control over expenses, but no responsibility for them because all expenses are allocated to the service users.

EXPECTED COSTING

As its name implies, expected costing develops unit-costs that are expected, based on planned volumes and budgeted expenses. Expense allocations are determined by extending actual transaction volumes by the expected unit cost. The expense base allocated generally does not equal the actual expenses incurred during each time period; residual expenses can therefore be left unallocated at the end of each period.

Under this method, fixed, indirect, and overhead expenses are included in the base expense and are incorporated in the unit cost, based on expected transaction volumes. If fewer actual transactions occur than expected, a portion of the center's expense will remain unallocated. Expected costing differs significantly from full absorption in its treatment of variances. Here the service provider bears all rate variances when actual expenses vary from plan or budget. This is not to say that the budgeted expenses are optimal or represent peak efficiency. If operating efficiency is not expected to be optimal, that cost will be passed on to the service user. But the service provider can allocate only those expenses based on expected unit costs; any additional expense will remain in that unit as a residual.

Because expense allocations are based on actual transaction volumes, one would expect volume variances to be borne by the service users. However, these variances actually are borne both by users and providers. (See Figure 7-2.)

Expected-costing allocations are based on a unit-cost charge derived from the expected activity volume and its associated expense level. The total allocation for all volume levels is a multiple of this charge and is represented in Figure 7-2 by the expected cost allocation line.

Advantages

Like full-absorption costing, expected costing is relatively easy to implement because the calculations are, for the most part, straightforward. It also is comparatively easy to understand, and the data it requires often are readily available through the institution's budgeting process.

Another advantage this method shares with full absorption is the treatment of all budgeted expenses as relevant for allocation purposes. Debates are avoided as to which expenses should be incorporated into the unit cost. Like full-absorption costing, the expected method recognizes that, in the long run, pricing must cover all costs.

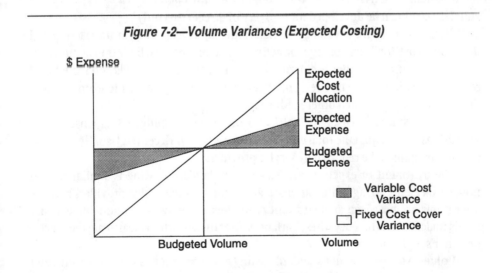

Figure 7-2—Volume Variances (Expected Costing)

However, unit costs developed under expected costing can be held stable over time—typically three or six months. This stability facilitates the use of unit costs in the pricing process.

Disadvantages

The main drawback is that expected costs may not acurately reflect actual costs due to poor budgeting techniques or unexpected occurrences. In addition, changes in strategic direction and external factors require that unit costs be periodically updated and adjusted.

The expected-costing method also is more complex and more resource intensive than the full-absorption approach. Unallocated expense residuals must be addressed, and unit cost-factors need to be examined and recalculated on a regular basis.

STANDARD COSTING

Under standard costing, unit costs represent the most efficient operating environment that can be achieved. The calculated unit costs are used as one criterion to measure actual performance, and unit-cost rates are extended by actual transaction volumes to generate expense assignment. Standard costs are predetermined according to defined operating standards, time and motion studies, or workflow analysis, and are derived assuming a certain level of operating efficiency. Fixed costs are incorporated assuming activity/transaction volumes at full operating capacity, although standard costs can be developed for recovery of direct costs only.

Standard costs are developed by examining all aspects of each transaction and deriving a cost for each component activity. The extent to which transactions are broken down into activities is determined by the institution's needs and the level of resources available. For this reason, standard-costing approaches tend to be more detailed and complex than other methods.

Because standard costs are not based on actual or budgeted expense levels, allocations rarely equal the total expense for any given work center. Usually, residual expense remains to be reported by service providers.

The treatment of expense variances under standard costing is similar to that under expected costing. Rate variances are borne by the service provider, because allocations are based on standard unit costs. Measured against attainable expense levels under peak efficiency, these variances offer insight when measuring the service provider's performance.

Volume variances under standard costing affect the user as well as the provider of services, as does expected costing. The variable cost component of the variance is borne by the service user. The fixed-cost component, however, is allocated to user and provider in offsetting manners. When actual volumes fall below expected levels, a smaller portion of costs is allocated to users. Because a portion of the cost is left unallocated, the provider shows the residual as an unfavorable variance. When activity volumes exceed expectations, the amounts of the variances are reversed.

COMPONENTS OF STANDARD COSTS

Standard costs can be broken down into two basic components: rate and volume. The rate component is developed from the following variables:

- The employee time required to complete an activity or transaction. Tasks that take longer to complete—by the same person—should have a proportionally longer unit time. This is especially important in costing such labor-intensive tasks and procedures as deposit processing, where commercial deposits usually require more teller time than retail deposits.

- The equipment time required. If it takes less time for a computer to process a transaction, the unit cost should reflect that fact. The differentiation becomes especially important in costing automated tasks and procedures.

- The additional resources, such as telephones, postage, and supplies, required to complete the task. Most activities performed in a financial institution can be associated with specific expenses. For example, statement rendering for commercial checking accounts often requires a significant and varying amount of postage due to the volume of enclosed checks. Rendering loan statements, however, requires minimal postage because there are generally no enclosures (unless by design). Standard unit costs will reflect these differences.

- The cost of these three variables—manual time, equipment, and additional resources. Salary rates generally vary by job classification and duties. Equipment costs include depreciation, maintenance, and supplies, while the costs of additional resources comprise utilities, floor space, telephone, supplies, and other expenses.

The second standard cost component, volume, is developed under the assumption that all operations are conducted at full usable capacity. Full capacity, however, does not assume continuous operation, because equipment downtime and required reserve capacity must be taken into consideration. On the labor side, factors for breaks and fatigue must be figured into the developed standards. Standard costs should reflect the maximum operating efficiency that can be achieved and sustained over a given period of time.

To develop capacity measures, two issues must be addressed: machine standards and standard-cost allowances. The first relates to machine capacity and the second to labor capacity.

- *Equipment Standards.* Equipment standards introduce several unique considerations into the unit-costing process. Examples of equipment stardards that are developed in financial services might include developing standards for reader/sorter and proof and encoding equipment or standards for CPU equipment within a computer operations department. The most important of these are operating characteristics, operator skill, equipment costs, work availability, and matching activity with capacity.

- *Operating Characteristics.* The operating characteristics that should be considered in the unit-costing process include equipment speed, durability, and employability. Equipment speed determines how many items can be processed, and this maximum capacity can be used as the basis for unit costing (discussed in the information technology costing chapter.)

Equipment durability indicates the frequency of necessary repairs and/or replacement. The concept of employability is a reflection of the equipment's capability to operate on a continuous basis or its need to remain idle, or "rest." Equipment breakdowns and maintenance time can be looked at as a combination of planned and unplanned events. Planned maintenance is detailed in the equipment specifications; normally, it will be X hours per month or per Y transactions. It should be accounted for during the development of unit cost data. Unplanned maintenance, however, must be determined based on historical operating statistics or manufacturer experience. This can be quantified but will only be an estimate.

- *Operator Skill.* The operator is the focal point of the equipment's operation. He or she is responsible for "getting the job done" correctly, and the operator's capability drives the equipment's output. If the operator is not completely familiar with the equipment, it might be appropriate to reduce the expected output until he or she is "up to speed." An operator who is thoroughly knowledgeable, however, can meet the equipment's output potential. The analyst must therefore evaluate the situation and calculate operator limitations when determining equipment rates. An example is the different processing speeds, skill, and error rates of experienced versus inexperienced check encoding equipment operators.

- *Equipment Costs.* Equipment costs that should be considered include deprecia-tion, lease payments, and maintenance agreements, the largest expense cate-gories associated with equipment. Periodic equipment expenses—whether monthly, quarterly, or annual—that vary substantially from one period to the next can create management confusion regarding the delivery cost of products and services. A "smoothing" of these periodic expenses by the analyst will provide a better representation of the actual delivery cost of a product or service.

- *Work Availability.* The actual availability of work also should be considered. Simply put, the ability to continuously process work depends on the receipt of that work. For example, envelope-opening equipment in the lockbox depart-ment cannot be used until the envelopes are received from the lockbox drop and are ready to be fed into the equipment.

- *Matching Activity with Capacity.* When developing unit-cost data, the analyst encounters situations in which there is limited use of particular equipment. A decision must be made regarding the equipment's capacity to be used in devel-oping unit-cost data. Three types of capacity are usually considered: theoretical (the maximum attainable capacity in an ideal environment), practical (the maximum capacity in the current environment), and usable (the expected capacity in the current environment).

Theoretical capacity assumes the most efficient operation in an ideal environ-ment; the use of theoretical equipment capacity is a standard-costing approach that focuses on maximum attainable output. In order to develop practical and normal capacity and subsequent unit costs, theoretical capacity must be adjusted to account for the impact of environmental factors.

The expected equipment downtime due to breakdowns, maintenance ,and repair, as well as operator fatigue, reduces theoretical capacity to practical capacity. Practical capacity is the maximum attainable output within the existing operating environ-ment, and can be reduced further to reflect the expected equipment use. In this instance, a number of questions must be considered:

1. Will the equipment be used by one, two, or three shifts?

2. Will it be used five, six, or seven days a week?

3. Is the equipment's usage controlled by external factors, such as an envelope opening equipment that is used only after mail delivery?

The answers need to be figured into the capacity calculations. Usable capacity is the result—the expected equipment usage—given all environmental factors that affect it.

- *Standard-Cost Allowance.* Standard-cost allowances are another important capacity issue. They typically are developed to account for nonproductive activities, which can be separated into three general categories: personal (time spent for lunch, breaks, and so forth), fatigue (time spent for rest breaks, slowdowns in productivity, and so forth), and incidental operations (time spent in project set-up, reconcilement activities such as teller balancing, and so forth).

Unit-cost data should account for these factors as part of the normal course of business, and the analyst should establish reasonable allowances for each activity. Incidental operations can affect more than one product or function. Allocation of the expense among the affected products/functions can be accomplished through detailed analysis or general allocation. The best approach should be determined by a cost/benefit analysis and the materiality of the time and expense in question.

Personal and fatigue time normally is not associated with a specific product or function; consequently, an allowance is required to factor the normal course of human operations into the unit costs. This adjustment can be made by removing personal and fatigue time from the development of the hourly rate, or by adding a cost-allowance factor to the appropriate unit costs.

Advantages

One of standard costing's principal advantages is that standard costs remain stable over a period of time, which facilitates their use in the pricing process. Prices based on these costs are the most competitive the institution can offer while covering developed unit costs. Because standard costs assume optimum use of resource capacities, they allow prices to be set with longer-term objectives and viewpoints.

Under standard costing, unit costs are predetermined using engineering or operating data, timings, and analyses. These unit costs therefore provide an objective basis for use in measuring the productivity and efficiency of operating areas. Because the allocation process does not transfer inefficiencies to the service user, the service provider's performance can be monitored.

Standard costs are developed assuming transaction/activity volumes at optimum or standard levels, and all volume variances are reported by service users as well as service providers. In order to minimize volume variances, service providers must minimize unused or excess capacity.

Because of this, standard costs can be used as a motivational tool. If reasonable and attainable standards are established, service providers will work to decrease variances and increase productivity. In addition, providers will be motivated to maintain available capacity at levels close to those of the actual requirements.

The amount of residual expense reported by operating units reflects either a higher-than-optimum level of unit costs (rate variance) or a lower-than-optimal volume (volume variance). Operating expenses can be controlled, in part, by monitoring attainment of the standard costs developed. Service providers can become "income producers" for the institution by surpassing standard levels of efficiency and capacity use, resulting in favorable variances. Assuming accurate standard-unit costs, favorable variances represent "contributions" to the institution's profitability.

Disadvantages

Chief among the disadvantages of standard costing is its significant resource requirement for development and maintenance of costs. Standard costs are derived by detailed examinations of activities and transactions, and developing the necessary database is time consuming. The level and complexity of calculations usually mandate use of automated processing. Furthermore, the level of detail inherent in standard costing may make obtaining the necessary transaction/activity volume data difficult.

Many financial institution transactions/activities are not readily available or captured in an automated manner, and developing standard costs for them is extremely difficult and not particularly useful. Customer service, for example, is imprecise when it comes to time spent and resources required. Development of a standard cost for this activity would require use of averages that do not correspond to most actual occurrences. Also, in a rapidly changing environment, significant changes in volume can present standard cost allocations that are very different from actual. This can adversely affect the pricing process by factoring in costs that may not reflect the current state.

An additional disadvantage is the double-edged impact of developed standards on employee behavior. When perceived as reasonable and attainable, standard costs can be an excellent motivational tool, but if perceived as unattainable the standards may undermine management integrity and become demotivating.

TECHNIQUES FOR UNIT COST DEVELOPMENT

Financisl institutions can use any of several techniques for developing unit costs. A discussion follows on some of the more common approaches.

Predetermined Time Standards

Under this approach, management identifies the tasks within a given activity and assigns to each a time value based on engineered time standards. The various time values are then summarized into a total unit-time value, which is converted into a unit cost through the extension of unit time by hourly rate. The hourly rate calculation (described in detail below) is computed from the expense associated with the center's support of the activity, based on the selected cost-accounting methodology.

Information developed under the predetermined time standard technique can help ensure a high degree of accuracy in the computation of unit cost, and also can feed productivity measurement, efficiency measurement, business process, and methods analysis. This technique offers further value in the measurement of routine, short-cycle repetitive tasks, because it eliminates the bias and inefficiencies that would result from less accurate techniques.

Predetermined time standards are not useful in measuring qualitative and non-routine tasks. Further, because unit times and expense rates are developed separately, the analyst must be well trained and experienced to become proficient at this technique. Resource commitments for the development and maintenance are significant as well, in comparison to other techniques, especially regarding database development and maintenance.

The predetermined time standard approach often is used for such highly repetitive volume-intensive activities as lockbox services. Such services consist of many small, definable components, any of which may or may not be desired by specific bank customers. For example, a customer may request tapes of payments with multiple sorts of the transactions (e.g., by dollar amount; from smallest to largest payment; by account number; or by alphabetic customer listing). These lockbox services are short-cycle, highly repetitive tasks requiring little or no decision making or judgment. They can therefore be measured individually using predetermined time standards, and customer unit costs can be "built" using the appropriate service/activity components.

Self-Log/Time Ladder

This technique captures employee time by task within an activity; employees are required to document the time spent on each task over a set time period. The information gathered during the collection phase is used to establish standards for each task, which will correlate to a specific level of transactions/activities processed during the same logging period. Unit-cost calculations are then determined by extending the unit time by the computed hourly rate.

Principal among this technique's advantages is that both analyst and user find it easy to use and understand. It also allows for the sampling/measurement of a relatively large number of employees while providing management with information that also can be used to measure productivity.

Unfortunately, this information is only as accurate as the data capture effort behind it. Inaccuracy can result if tasks are performed infrequently or if employees misrepresent their time. In addition, if an employee fails to monitor his or her time at regular intervals, his or her dependence on memory may lead to further inaccuracy. The technique therefore requires good documentation for all tasks—a chore that can distract employees from their "real" work. Further, because the logs are typically kept during a survey period, the results may not reflect a complete set of actual ongoing activities. The branch platform operation particularly lends itself to measurement under the self-log/time ladder technique because of the nonstandardized nature of human interaction. The tasks performed are varied; no two types of transactions require the same amount of processing time.

Stop Watch

This technique uses a stop watch to carefully measure the tasks or elements of each activity performed by a sampling of employees. Tasks that cannot be separated are measured at the lowest discernible level. The unit cost is calculated by extending the measured-unit time by the computed hourly rate.

The stop-watch technique can exhibit a high degree of accuracy, and it can serve as a useful tool to verify unit times calculated in other ways. Because it can be applied to different levels of activities and tasks, the stop-watch technique can lead to meaningful productivity, business process, and methods analysis. Its key advantage, however, is its efficient measurement of unit times; all nonproductive time is eliminated from consideration during the stop-watch measurement.

This technique has several disadvantages, however. Foremost among them is its resource demands for both implementation and maintenance. Another concern is the impact of the actual timing process; employees can become self-conscious knowing they are under scrutiny, and their perception of a "hidden agenda" can have an adverse effect, skewing the results.

A third disadvantage involves the actual measurement. If the transaction level is low, the analyst will either have to spend large blocks of time trying to capture infrequent transactions, or use a small sample. Neither is desirable.

The stop-watch technique often is used to measure such structured environments as ATM transactions. The ATM is a highly structured delivery system that processes a series of different transactions. Each transaction is easily captured for measurement and cost allocation. Such ATM tasks as cash disbursement and deposit acceptance, for example, are invariably performed in the same sequence and in the same amount of time, regardless of transaction size or operator skill. The focal point of measurement is equipment processing time, because that is where the expense lies.

Percent of Time/Managerial Estimate/Historical Records

This interview technique evaluates allocation drivers based on conversations with employees who perform the duties. A list of activities or tasks performed is compiled and estimates are made of the time spent performing each task, based on historical records. This systematic approach of relating historical and current input to historical and current output leads to the development of the unit cost.

This technique is easy to use, because measures are based on past experience and/or current knowledge of the work environment, including employee skill level and transaction volumes. Analysts and users can comprehend it, and it can be successfully applied to qualitative or quantitative tasks.

For the analyst, the main advantage is the reduced effort required for developing unit times and costs. The analyst focuses on expenses while the users or managers develop the task-usage data. Overall, this approach is cost effective and can produce reliable results if approached at the right level of detail and with discipline.

Basing unit cost on this technique, however, can incorporate inefficiencies of the past and present. Unlike other techniques, it does not identify changes in procedures and workflow, and the attitude of "this is the way we have always done it" can persist. Further, costs developed this way may not tie in with productivity measures and efficiency measures, which focus on current rather than ideal processes.

The loan-decision process often uses the interview technique because of its broad requirements for information while executing the task/process. Each loan is considered separately; some loans may require additional information while others may be processed quickly. A $200,000 home mortgage, for example, requires more detail and analysis than a $10,000 car loan. A manager can therefore target an estimated average for the "typical" loan process by type of loan, and this average can be translated into the relevant unit cost.

Relative Ratio

Under the relative-ratio technique, each task for each employee is assigned a rank, according to estimated time to complete. The rankings of all employees are consolidated. A unit time is then established for the base task, and all other tasks are related to the base task. The rating factor is used to develop each unit cost, by multiplying the base task time by the rating factor and then extending the unit time by the hourly rate.

The relative-value technique is easy to use, because it focuses on developing a single common measure; there is no need for a high level of task information or detail. This ease of use translates into a reduction of analyst time, leaving more time for attention to more pressing matters.

Using this technique on a single common measure has its drawbacks, however. The lack of task detail/measurement prevents productivity measurement, efficiency measurement, business process, and methods analysis. The analyst thus is unable to draw meaningful conclusions about a task without refining the measurement techniques. Use of a common measure creates inefficiencies in the unit times, because the weights given to any individual task could be inappropriate. The common measure also requires the development of separate unit times and expense rates.

An example of this technique can be easily seen by looking at the teller function, which is composed of many different tasks. Some, such as deposit acceptance and cash balancing, are normally associated with the function, while others, such as check encoding, are not so common. The total time commitment for any particular function is directly related to the volume of the activity: the greater the total volume, the longer it takes to complete the task. The analyst thus has to decide whether to invest in the development of a sophisticated time-accounting system for the teller function, and a meaningful cost/benefit relationship that will support the expense.

Normally, such an expense cannot be justified. The analyst must therefore determine a more appropriate way to measure this function. The relative-value concept lets the analyst capture all the possible teller duties and provide a means for computing unit cost data. Each task or activity is weighed in relation to the entire function, and teller time is then translated into unit costs based on the weight of each function and the total teller expense.

CHOOSING AN APPROPRIATE TECHNIQUE

In deciding which unit-cost development technique to use, management should consider two main factors: the cost-accounting method employed and the key attributes of the function to be costed.

The first factor affects management's decision because certain costing methods are particularly well suited to certain cost development techniques. Figure 7-3 shows appropriate pairings of costing methods and unit-cost techniques.

The second issue is the key attributes of the function to be costed. Following is a list of some of these attributes and some points to consider when evaluating them:

- *Volume of Work Processed*—Greater accuracy is required for a higher volume.

- *Aggregate Processing Time*—Greater accuracy is required for large blocks of processing time.

- *Nature of Work*—Management must gauge the capability of the measurement technique to measure routine versus creative tasks.

- *Cycle/Volume Relationship*—Greater accuracy is required for short cycle/high volume processing.

Figure 7-3—Cost Methodologies and Unit Costing Techniques

Unit Cost of Techniques

Costing Methods	Predetermined Time Standards	Self-Log/ Time Ladder	Stop Watch	Percent of Time	Relative Value
Standard	•		•		•
Expected		•	•	•	•
Full-Absorption		•	•	•	•

- *Magnitude of Work Force Covered*—Management must weigh the percentage of the work force hours covered against the analyst time required to develop the unit costs.

Assessed against these key attributes, the unit-cost measurement techniques should be chosen as follows:

- *Predetermined Time Standard*—Short cycle/high-volume operations, with limited decision-making or judgment involved; situations requiring a high degree of accuracy.

- *Self-Log/Time Ladder*—Operations characterized by high volume or by large amounts of processing time, for all types of work.

- *Stop Watch*—Machine-controlled activities; externally controlled tasks requiring a high degree of accuracy; may be used to verify a unit time established by another technique.

- *Percent of Time/Managerial Estimate/Historical Records*—Long-cycle operations requiring considerable decision-making and judgment; creative activities; activities with low aggregate processing time not requiring a high degree of accuracy.

- *Reactive Value*—Short-cycle routine activities requiring a relatively high degree of accuracy; used in conjunction with other measurement techniques.

HOURLY-RATE CALCULATIONS

Once the unit-cost development technique has been chosen, it is often helpful to express the unit in terms of a unit of time. The first step in developing the hourly rate is to establish available hours. Available hours equal theoretical hours (100 percent utilization) less allowances for lunch, personal time, breaks, downtime, and so forth. The next step is to determine the level of operating expenses to be related to the available hours. This process can be undertaken using various approaches.

For example, consider an institution that develops expected unit costs, requiring the determination of expected operating expenses.

First, the institution calculates the salary grade midpoint plus related expense. The "salary plus" figure generally represents the function. It is not the objective of cost analysis to selectively charge for a particular individual or piece of equipment, because that may only aggravate a situation of great demand for the best or the cheapest service provider. Second, the institution determines the additional direct and indirect expense burden, based on historical norms. It then combines these two computed figures to form the expense base for the function. When the base has been determined, the institution can take the final step in the hourly rate calculation and divide the expense base by the number of available hours.

RELATED ISSUES

In choosing and implementing a methodology, financial institutions encounter a number of different yet related issues. Some of the most important are discussed below.

Line Management's Role in Selecting a Methodology

Line management concerns must be considered when selecting a cost accounting methodology. It is imperative that these managers understand, accept, and ultimately support the cost approach and methodology. One of the main purposes of developing cost and profitability information is to provide meaningful data that line managers can use. They need to be fully comfortable with the information and how it is derived, especially when that information is used to evaluate performance. A process that is not supported can result in more time spent discussing the validity of the information than using it. For many institutions, this argues for a simple but comprehensible methodology.

Choosing among Several Appropriate Methodologies

There are several "right" answers to each issue regarding cost allocations and accounting. The allocation methodology, allocation parameters, and costing method all can be addressed in several ways. The solutions lie in the characteristics of the financial institution and the areas being studied, and in how the institution intends to use the cost, profitability, and performance measurement information.

This often necessitates compromises when implementing a performance measurement system to ensure its acceptance and smooth operation. It is important to remember that management accounting information can be worthwhile even if it is less than 100 percent accurate.

Keep in mind the four M principles outlined in Chapter 3. Following them can present a rational approach to matching expenses with revenues, and benefits with their associated costs.

AUTOMATION

The frequency of reporting has a significant impact on the effort required and the techniques used for data acquisition and maintenance. Data acquisition for monthly profitability analysis requires efforts different from those for periodic ad hoc analysis of profitability. Frequent data acquisition, however, can be very time consuming unless it is based on current data available through automated means. Automated data capture that has been well defined and validated can enhance the timeliness, responsiveness, credibility, and usage of the profitability-measurement system.

A thorough knowledge of the dynamics of each center's activities is required to select the most appropriate measure, and to efficiently capture the information. One way to achieve both goals is to give the centers responsibility for collecting the data, with the cost-accounting staff monitoring the process for accuracy and impartiality. Assigning the responsibility for data collection to each allocating center can lead to improvements in interactive budgeting and transaction volume planning.

Resultant budgets will more closely follow transaction volumes, and expenses will be easier to control. If data acquisition responsibility is to be spread among the centers, then specific guidelines are required to ensure that all information is usable, relevant, collected on a consistent and appropriate basis, and received on a timely basis.

Given the complexity of today's financial institutions, automation is almost a requirement for accurate cost calculation. Fortunately, today's technology offers the flexibility and capability to do the job at a reasonable cost. Hardware and software are constantly improving, providing analysts with the tools to develop a sophisticated activity-based profitability and performance measurement system. Further discussions of these and related topics appear in Chapters 15 and 16.

LEVEL OF ACCURACY

The cost-accounting approach that offers the most precise, accurate information is not always the best choice. The question is whether the additional benefit outweighs the incremental costs of delivering the benefit.

For example, the financial timing may not be right for a state-of-the-art system that requires a significant investment. An interim solution might be more appropriate.

Management also must ascertain whether the supporting cast of operational and financial controls is sufficient to use a sophisticated system properly and reap the potential benefits. In this vein, care must be taken to avoid "misleading accuracy." A "guessed at" three divided by an "estimated" five and a half will be a "highly authoritative" .545455 when carried to six decimal places, creating perceived accuracy that is not supported by the underlying methodologies. Automation tends to lend credibility and assurance of accuracy and can sometimes be carried to ridiculous extremes.

COST TRANSFER APPROACHES

The selection of an overall cost transfer approach is important because it helps to determine the initial recipient of each distributed expense, affects interim cost build-up, and the development of final costs. Any of three such transfer approaches, direct allocation, sequential allocation, and simultaneous allocation can be used but the "right" one depends on the complexity of the institution, its available resources, and the intended use of the information.

To clarify the differences among the three transfer approaches, each will be discussed using the following example. Financial Institution A has four centers: a lending office, a branch, a human resources department, and a computer operaions center. Pertinent information is as follows:

Center	Employees	CPU Usage (Sec.)	Direct Expenses
Lending office	20	250 million	$400,000
Branch	10	500 million	$100,000
Human Resources	N/A	250 million	$150,000
Computer Operations	20	N/A	$900,000

The lending office is a sizable operation that maintains customer lending relationships. These require few ongoing transactions once the loan is on the books, so systems usage is relatively low. The branch is a typical high-transaction operation, located in a shopping center, with heavy systems usage resulting from the transactional nature of its customer account relationships. Human resources supports the other three centers by providing recruiting and salary administration services. The most appropriate basis for distributing human resources expense is staff size/headcount. Computer operations also supports all the other centers by maintaining all automated systems, including the payroll system for human resources. The computer operations expense, comprised of hardware and software expense, is best distributed based on systems usage, as measured in CPU seconds (see Chapter 9—Information Technology Costing for a discussion of this measure).

The lending office and the branch are profit centers and, as final beneficiaries of all expenditures, they ultimately receive all allocated expenses. The example assumes—for simplicity's sake—that the lending office and the branch do not support each other, although this arrangement could certainly be incorporated into the costing approach.

DIRECT ALLOCATION APPROACH

The direct allocation approach consists of concurrent, independent allocations and distributes all expenses directly to the final beneficiaries. In other words, the expenses of each center are allocated to profit centers, products, or customers directly; no expenses are allocated initially to intermediate users. Processing, staff support, administrative, and overhead centers receive no expense allocations under this approach.

In the example, human resources, a staff support center, provides services to computer operations and to two profit centers: a branch and a lending office. Computer operations supports human resources, the branch, and the lending office and has a dual nature (processing and staff support). Under the direct allocation approach, all human resources and computer operations expenses would be allocated directly to the branch and the lending office. Those two centers are the ultimate beneficiaries of all expenditures since they maintain responsibility for all customer relationships. Computer operations would not receive an allocation of human resources expense even though the former is supported by the latter. The reverse is also true. Human resources would not receive an allocation of computer operations expense despite its support of that center. The general cost transfer flow in this case is illustrated in Figure 7-4.

Continuing with the example, the costs related to computer operations and human resources would be allocated directly to the final beneficiaries: the lending office and the branch. Since the lending office has twice as many employees as the

---

Figure 7-4—Cost Transfer Flow—Direct Allocation Approach

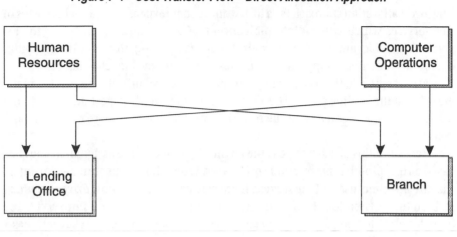

---

branch, it receives two thirds of human resources' $150,000 expense while the branch receives one-third. However, since the branch uses twice as many CPU seconds as the lending office, it receives two-thirds of the $900,000 operations expense while the lending office receives the remaining one-third. With direct allocation, then, the allocation of indirect expenses would be as follows:

	From Computer Operations	From Human Resources	Total
Lending office	$300,000	$100,000	$400,000
Branch	$600,000	$ 50,000	$650,000

Advantages

The direct allocation approach has several advantages over other approaches. First, it is uncomplicated and easy to understand. The flow of information and cost is clear, and line managers can easily trace their allocated costs back to the center of origin. In addition, the distribution of expense to other units, as an indirect expense, is easy to follow. Each allocation originates as the direct expense of a specific support center.

As an outgrowth of this simplicity, the system and overall effort required for the direct allocation approach is much less extensive than for other approaches. Each unit's expenses are distributed only once, keeping the number of allocations to a minimum.

Disadvantages

The direct allocation approach fails to distribute some expenses to the actual users of the service, which contradicts the concept of assigning responsibility for expenses/costs in conjunction with control. For example, suppose that the computer operations center only supported human resources, not the branch. Under the direct allocation approach, the computer operations expense would still be allocated to the branch and the lending office. This decision probably would appear arbitrary to the managers of those centers, and the resulting information could lose credibility as a result.

Related to this disadvantage is the possibility that expense assignment could be based on inappropriate measures or cost drivers. When allocations are made to centers that are not direct users of the service, there may be no relevant cost driver on which to base the distribution. If, for instance, computer operations did not service the branch and the lending office but its expenses were allocated to them, what valid basis could be used? For human resources expense distribution, a relevant cost driver might be number of fulltime equivalent employees. Should this measure then be applied to computer operations as well, since operations supports human resources? The problem becomes even more unwieldy and significant in an institution with a more complex structure, since there are more units supporting other units.

Direct allocations also fail to afford the opportunity to measure the productivity of centers other than the final beneficiaries. While expense variance analysis can be performed for all centers, meaningful productivity comparisons cannot be made of intermediate centers.

Another disadvantage inherent in direct allocations is the difficulty of relating expense allocations to transaction volumes or other activity counts. This problem results from basing allocations to profit centers on a single or direct transaction. Ignored are transaction volumes that reflect services provided to support centers from other centers. This built-in inconsistency ultimately reduces the credibility of the allocations. In our example, the human resources system uses 250 million CPU seconds, as does the lending office. The branch, however, uses 500 million CPU seconds to process its work. Under the direct allocations method, one-third of the computer processing expense is distributed to the lending office and two-thirds is distributed to the branch. Human resources uses as much processing time as the lending office but receives no allocation. The branch uses only half the processing time but is charged for two-thirds.

SEQUENTIAL ALLOCATION APPROACH

The sequential allocation approach is an iterative process consisting of a series of allocations in a specified order or sequence. Unlike the direct allocation approach, the sequential approach distributes a center's expenses to any center utilizing the particular service, including processing, support, and overhead centers.

The expenses of a staff support center can be distributed among other staff support centers that are intermediate users of the particular service. During a subsequent step in the process, the expenses of these intermediate users are distributed to the ultimate beneficiaries/users of the services.

Under the sequential allocations methodology, once a center's expenses have been distributed, that center is "closed" in the sense that it can no longer receive any incoming allocations. One by one (or in groups, if sufficiently independent) the centers are closed, their expenses distributed, and the number of centers eligible to receive expense allocations is reduced. After a number of iterations, the only centers left open and still eligible are the final beneficiaries of the activities/services provided.

If this allocation method is applied to the example, the allocation sequence could be as follows:

1. Human Resources
2. Computer Operations
3. Lending office
4. Branch

Human resources would be distributed among computer operations, the lending office, and the branch, because all use human resources' services. Computer operations, a processing center, therefore receives an expense allocation from human resources. The human resources center would then be closed and become ineligible to receive further expense allocations, whereupon operations expense would be distributed only to the lending office and the branch. Although operations still supports human resources, it cannot allocate any portion of its expense to that closed center. Figure 7-5 illustrates the general flow of expenses for this example.

There is, however, another way to sequence the allocations. The order used above (Sequence A) can be replaced with an arrangement that switches the order of computer operations and human resources (Sequence B). The final allocations under each of these methods are as follows:

	Sequence A	Sequence B
Lending office	$380,000	$475,000
Branch	$670,000	$575,000

Figure 7-5—Cost Transfer Flow—Sequential Allocation Approach

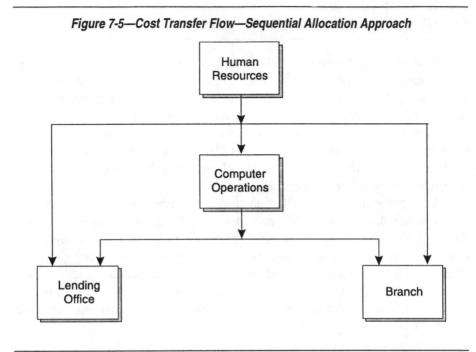

As shown by these figures, the key to the sequential allocation approach is the order in which centers are closed and their associated expenses distributed. The sequence of center closings determines the eligible recipients for future expense allocations and affects the resulting cost calculations.

SEQUENCE DETERMINATION

Deciding on an appropriate sequence for closing out centers and allocating the associated expenses follows several rationales. The order can be based on the institution's organization chart, on center classification, or on the amount of service provided or received.

The simplest method of developing the close-out sequence is to follow an institution's organization chart. The expenses of the highest level of the structure, generally the executive management function, are distributed among all other centers, and then the center is closed. The expenses of the next center on the chart, for example, strategic planning, then are distributed to all centers except the closed Executive management center. Centers at the same level are closed out in a predetermined order.

The process continues until only the final beneficiaries remain. At that time, all expenses are distributed among those centers.

The sequence also could be based on center classifications. A typical sequence under this approach would be as follows:

1. Administrative centers

2. Staff support centers

3. Processing centers

4. Profit centers

All administrative centers are closed out first, and all associated expenses allocated. Next all staff support centers are closed out and their expenses distributed. The process continues until only the profit centers remain. The centers within each classification can be closed out concurrently (if there is enough independence of operations) or in a predetermined sequence. If the latter method is chosen, another order of close-out and distribution must be established.

A third approach to sequencial allocation involves the extent of services received by a center. The center that receives services from the least number of centers is closed out and allocated first. The rationale is that the center that uses the least amount of services would be receiving the fewest allocations. Thus it could be closed out early in the process with little negative effect on the accuracy of subsequent allocations. The remaining centers would be closed out and allocated in ascending order of services and allocations received. The last centers to be closed out would be those that receive the most service support; generally, the final beneficiaries of services.

This approach also could be employed by performing the allocations in descending order of services provided. In other words, the expense of the center providing the most services would be distributed to its users first, before other centers are closed and ineligible to receive allocations.

Advantages

The primary advantage of the sequential allocation approach, compared to the direct allocation approach, is its potential for greater accuracy. The increased accuracy stems from the capacity to perform allocations between support units. More actual users can directly receive allocations in conjunction with actual services received. The process does require additional effort and resources when compared to direct allocations, but the benefits often outweigh the additional effort. Further distinguishing the sequential approach from the direct approach is its capacity to allocate expenses from one unit to another.

The sequential allocation approach also allows for an increased use of transaction/activity based measures as the basis for expense assignment. This feature improves the accuracy and credibility of the cost transfers, and provides additional performance measures and information to be used in decision making.

Yet another advantage of the sequential allocation approach is its distribution of expense directly to actual users of a given service, whether they are intermediate or final users. This practice is in accordance with the concept of assigning responsibility (through allocations) where there is control. The use of an arbitrary basis for expense distribution is therefore less likely because transaction/activity based cost drivers are readily available.

Disadvantages

Under the sequential approach, once a center allocates its expense it is closed and is ineligible to receive subsequent allocations. Consequently, two centers that provide services to each other cannot allocate expenses to each other under this method. In our example, the human resources center could not receive an allocation from computer operations because it was the first center closed. Likewise, if human resources had been left open to receive an allocation from computer operations, then computer operations would have been closed before it could receive an allocation from human resources.

Another disadvantage of sequential allocation approach is its complexity relative to the direct allocation approach. Since the total number of allocations is higher, sequential allocations are more time-consuming and require more analysis and data handling. The sequential allocation process also is more difficult to understand intuitively. The manager of the branch in the example provided, probably can accept the allocation he or she receives from computer operations because that center provides services to his or her center. But he or she may question why that allocation contains expenses stemming from human resources' allocation to computer operations.

A third problem involves tracking expenses. Compared to the direct allocation approach, the sequential allocation process makes it difficult to track the flow of expenses through the organization and to keep an audit trail.

The essence of the sequential allocation approach creates another disadvantage, namely, that the final costs developed are highly dependent on the sequence selected. As shown in the example, different allocation sequences will result in different calculated costs, even though the allocating centers and their expense levels remain unchanged.

SIMULTANEOUS ALLOCATION APPROACH

The simultaneous allocation approach allows each center to distribute its expenses to all other centers that use its services and concurrently receive allocations from the same centers. The expenses of each center are distributed among its actual users, which may be support centers (also known as intermediate users) or final beneficiaries. The distribution can occur without requiring any center to close. Simultaneous allocation is a very sophisticated process, involving extensive mathematical equations. Hence, this method is rarely, if ever, implemented without some type of automated processing.

Two mathematical techniques are commonly utilized to perform simultaneous allocations. One is a process of continuous iterations in which each center's expense is distributed to all centers that receive services. When a support center receives an allocation, that expense is distributed to the center's service users during the next iteration. With each succeeding iteration, the incoming expense allocations decrease because each is a fraction of a fraction of the preceding level. The iterative process continues until all the support centers are left with negligible expenses, signifying that virtually all expenses have been distributed to the final beneficiaries.

Another mathematical technique used to perform simultaneous allocations involves a massive set of simultaneous equations. These equations can be solved using either matrix algebra or linear programming. (Further discussion of either of these techniques is beyond the scope of this book.)

If we apply the simultaneous allocation approach to our example, human resources and computer operations each would be able to allocate a portion of their expense to each other, as well as to the lending office and the branch. The lending office and the branch could allocate expenses to each other as well. These allocations could reflect services provided for the other center's products and customers. They also could compensate branches in high transaction level locations, such as shopping centers, that tend to require a high level of direct expenses. Figure 7-6 illustrates the general flow of expenses in this example.

Advantages

The simultaneous allocation approach has the flexibility to distribute the expense of any center to all other centers it provides service to and then leave the center open to receive additional incoming allocations in subsequent iterations. If utilized properly, this method will produce the greatest accuracy as well as provide the flexibility to

Figure 7-6—Cost Transfer Flow—Simultaneous Allocation Approach

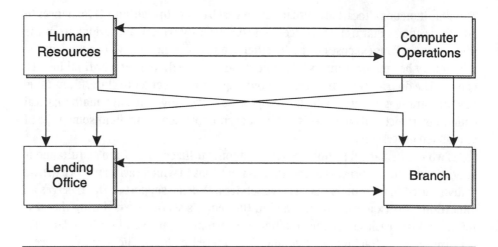

ensure that expenses are allocated to the actual users of services throughout the institution. Responsibility is therefore aligned with control to the maximum extent possible, minimizing the chance of arbitrary allocations.

The accuracy advantage that the simultaneous allocations approach has over the sequential allocation approach, however, is limited to centers that provide services to one another. Another major distinction between the two approaches is that with simultaneous allocation the result of cost allocations are always the same, whereas the sequence of allocations affects the results of cost allocations under the sequential allocation approach.

Disadvantages

Perhaps the most apparent disadvantage of simultaneous allocation is the inability of line managers to follow, understand, and accept the allocation results because of the mathematical equations used. Generally, there is no way to verify expense allocations by analyzing center expenses and transaction volume/activity cost drivers. Simultaneous allocations result in the "black box effect," where numbers go in and answers come out, and no one can easily explain, beyond mathematics, what transpires in between. In addition to being confusing to line managers, the simultaneous allocation approach is more difficult than the direct and sequential approaches with respect to tracking cost transfer flows with audit trails.

Another disadvantage of simultaneous allocations are their dependence on computing resources. The difficulty of the required calculations precludes manual applications. If attempted manually, the process would be cumbersome and time-consuming, with a greater chance of error.

The additional benefits derived from using simultaneous allocations have to be weighed against the additional resources required. As previously stated, the flexibility to allow cross-allocations between centers is seldom needed.

CHOOSING THE RIGHT COST TRANSFER

Each allocation approach can provide reasonably accurate and relevant information in the appropriate environment. When deciding which of the three cost transfer approaches is best for a given financial institution, one must remember to consider the intended use of the information, the complexity of the organization structure, and the extent of available resources. In a relatively simple organization, the problems of interdependent support centers and cross allocations are minimized, so the direct allocation approach might be favored. The additional benefits and accuracy provided by more sophisticated approaches may have a limited impact on the final allocation results. In a relatively complex organization, however, the resultant information may not be as meaningful unless the flexibility of a simultaneous allocation process is utilized. Given the extent of center dependency and the materiality of the enhanced accuracy, a sequential allocation process might then be the preferred approach.

While it is difficult to pinpoint which method is best for a given financial institution, it is important to emphasize that each method can result in different allocated cost results. As shown by the examples, this difference stems from the combination of expense recipients and the order of allocations under the various approaches.

IMPACT OF UNIT COSTING

This discussion of cost transfer approaches is based on the assumption that the total expenses of each center are distributed to other centers. Consistent with this philosophy, this approach distributes the institution's expenses so that they can be aligned with revenues and reported in a meaningful manner. Profitability measurement often includes the technique of unit costing, which alleviates many of the disadvantages mentioned earlier. For example, when predetermined unit costs are developed and extended to distribute expenses, the tracking and verification of allocations cease to be a problem.

The development of unit costs requires that expense allocations be based on transaction volumes or well-defined activity cost drivers. This requirement cannot always be met, especially in staff support, administrative and overhead centers. Furthermore, not all methods of unit cost development are equally effective in dealing with the problems discussed. Thus the utilization of unit costing does not, in and of itself, resolve the issue of which approach to use. The selection of a cost transfer approach is, however, affected by the unit costing technique chosen. Each aspect of the cost allocation process is affected by the decisions inherent in the other aspects, and all parts should be viewed as mutually dependent.

The issues related to the utilization and selection of unit costing techniques are discussed in more detail at the beginning of this chapter.

MULTIPLE CENTERS

Two situations involving multiple centers have an impact on the various cost transfer approaches and therefore merit discussion here. The first is the performance of similar functions by more than one center, for example, a series of proof and encoding centers located in different geographic areas. The two most common solutions to this problem when performing allocations are described as follows and illustrated in Figure 7-7.

Figure 7-7—Functions Performed by Multiple Centers

Site	A	B	
IT Processing Costs	$400,000	$600,000	

Branch	1	2	3
Number of Transactions	2,000,000	2,000,000	2,000,000

Approaches:

Distribution to Actual Users

Branch 1—20¢ per transaction ($400,000 ÷ 2,000,000)

Branch 2 & 3—15¢ per transaction ($600,000 ÷ {2,000,000 + 2,000,000})

Distribution to all Users at Average Cost

Branch 1 & 2 & 3—16.67¢ per transaction ({$400,000 + $600,000} ÷ {2,000,000 + 2,000,000 + 2,000,000})

- Distribute each location's expenses among its actual users. By allocating actual expenses to actual users, the costs developed in each location differ for identical transactions, products, and services. Resulting cost data are considered the "cost of doing business" at each location—one reason why this approach often is preferred over the other.

- Combine the expenses and transaction/activity volumes for all centers and develop average transactional costs. These average costs then are used to distribute portions of the total processing expense on the basis of transaction volume. This approach is frequently employed to normalize costs when the institution rents some locations and owns others (especially if **fully** depreciated). It does not penalize users of locations with higher than average costs, such as out of the way locations with travel cost or downtown locations in high-rent areas. It does penalize users of efficient locations for the inefficiencies and excess capacities of other units, in the form of higher allocations.

The second problem involving multiple centers arises when they perform identical services for one another. It usually affects branch networks where each branch services customers of other branches. ATM networks present similar challenges. Following are three approaches to handling this situation:

- Develop internal transfer charges for each unit's transactions. The transfer charges for each location reflect its cost base, and each location "charges" the service users for every transaction. This approach, however, is cumbersome and requires extensive calculations and computer system time. It also penalizes the user location for any inefficiencies and excess capacity at the supporting location.

- Develop a single transfer to charge each location for services provided. This approach rewards more efficient locations and penalizes less efficient ones. Utilizing average unit costs, for example, rewards locations that provide efficient service by allocating to users more expense than the location incurs in providing the service. Conversely, locations that provide inefficient service are penalized by allocating to users less expense than the location incurs in providing the service.

- Create a pool (or multiple pools) to collect the total expenses associated with a transaction (or transactions), then allocate to each location its proportionate share of the pool (or pools). This approach avoids numerous interallocations while maintaining the benefit of matching expenses.

CHOOSING AN EXPENSE DISTRIBUTION MECHANISM

Once a financial institution has determined which centers will receive allocations and which cost transfer approach will be used, its next concern is choosing the proper methodology under which the centers' expenses are allocated.

The allocation basis should be structured to distribute the centers' expenses in the most appropriate manner. Some centers, such as those in the computer operations area, might use identical allocation parameters, but those measures probably would not apply to staff support services such as mail, duplicating, or statement rendition. In determining the best allocation basis for each center, management should consider the following general criteria.

Fairness

The basis must distribute the expense of the center in an impartial manner, and the expense allocated must reflect the extent of services provided. Allocation bases that favor certain users can distort the cost results, adversely affect credibility, and mislead managers when making decisions.

The concepts of cost allocation and profitability require assignment of responsibility for expenses and the matching of expenses with the derived benefits. The perceived fairness of cost allocations is vital to the success of any performance measurement system. When the fairness of the cost allocation is questioned, the system loses its credibility with the business and product line managers. It then may not be used to its full potential because key managers will not rely on the cost and profitability/performance information and may not provide the needed support for the process. In addition, more time and effort will be spent defending the calculated costs than deriving them.

User Comprehension

If line managers are to be held accountable for indirect expenses, they must clearly understand the nature of those expenses, why they are responsible for having incurred the expenses, and how the expenses are allocated to them.

Managers frequently point to their inability to understand the allocation basis when allocations, expenses, and profitability are not at desired levels. More effort is then expended in analyzing and discussing the appropriateness of the allocation basis than in developing the cost assignment.

Given this consideration, it generally is preferable to avoid an overly complicated cost assignment basis. Use of cost drivers that can be understood only by the service providers prevents business and product line managers from understanding and managing the resultant costs.

Expense assignment is much more effective when stated in understandable terms, and could result in additional benefits such as cost reductions. Consider, for example, computer printout expense. If this expense were distributed on the basis of number of pages, as opposed to a highly technical information technology measure, it probably would increase the chances of reducing duplicate copies or discontinuing redundant reports.

Cost Effectiveness

Sometimes the most appropriate distribution mechanism is a measure of transaction/activity volume that requires significant resources to isolate and then capture. Often, however, other easier to use measures could be substituted and still provide a reasonable level of accuracy. Thus it is important to ascertain whether the additional benefits to be derived from a more sophisticated measurement approach outweigh the incremental resource requirement.

Consider, for instance, a revolving credit product offered by a network of branches. It would be difficult in this case to track bad debt collection activity by branch and would require significant effort and resources. However, collection activity generally is proportional to delinquencies, and tracking delinquencies by branch normally can be accomplished easily by an automated loan system. Delinquency rates therefore can be an excellent indicator of collection activity, assuming that collection efforts are similar for all delinquent accounts associated with a given product. Of course, other parameters (such as loan size) would be important in establishing loan delinquency and collection relationships. The expense and effort required to track actual collection efforts would probably outweigh the additional accuracy that could be derived.

While each case should be evaluated on its own merits, a systems evaluation is also in order. If many of the cost assignments require significant, additional efforts for data capture and maintenance, the system could "die of its own weight."

Consistency

Ideally, a consistent cost assignment basis can be applied, at least conceptually, to all similar centers. This is not to say, however, that the identical assignment basis should be utilized across the board; no one basis will be appropriate for all centers. But cost assignments for similar centers should be performed utilizing the same conceptual approach.

All processing center expenses, for example, should be distributed on the basis of true cost drivers to activities and cost objects. Activities in these centers generally are transactional in nature, and because the activities are often repetitive, with each requiring identical effort, transaction/activity volumes are the most effective measures.

However, there are exceptions. For instance, processing centers with nonrepetitive functions require different treatment. Still, the establishment of a general concept lends direction to the process, and presents a point of reference to help in isolating exceptions and determining an appropriate cost assignment basis.

Selecting the appropriate basis often entails compromises in data availability and cost versus benefit derived, and these compromises may result in interim solutions. But regardless of whether the approach is interim or long term, its selection can be aided by first developing a conceptual design to the assignment of expenses.

SPECIFIC SELECTION CRITERIA

In addition to the general criteria discussed, management must consider many specific factors when selecting the appropriate basis for a given center. Some of the more important questions to address are as follows:

- Are the expenses joint or independent? Of these two expense types, independent expenses are easier to isolate and assign to specific users, be they other organizational centers, products, or customers. Labor-intensive activities such as loan approvals provide a good example. Joint expenses such as computer hardware are much more difficult to assign directly and thus require transaction volume measures and other assumptions for allocation.

- Is the labor or equipment expense component predominant? It usually is appropriate to select a cost assignment mechanism related to the predominant component. For example, systems programming expense, which consists mostly of salaries, is generally distributed on the basis of programmer time measured in hours. Distributing this expense based on the number of accounts by application or product would be inappropriate.

  On the other hand, computer operations expense is predominantly equipment related and therefore more suited to distribution based on the extent of system use (generally measured in CPU seconds and other computer operations resource measures, as described in Chapter 9—Information Technology Costing).

- Are the tasks repetitive or specialized in nature? Repetitive tasks may appropriately utilize a transaction/activity based volume measure to assign expenses, because each transaction requires the same effort and can be weighted the same. Examples of such tasks include check capture, keypunch (the number of keystrokes may vary but each is the same), and duplicating.

Specialized processes, such as large commercial loan approvals, do not always require the same effort to process each transaction. Transaction volume counts, used in conjunction with weighting factors, can be appropriate bases. Sometimes, however, it is more effective simply to track the individual time spent.

- Are automated transaction/activity volume statistics available? The availability of automated statistics has a dramatic impact on the resources required to implement and maintain a cost accounting and profitability measurement system. For high-volume, repetitive transactions, automated statistics are necessary to ensure accurate distribution of expenses. Capturing data on an automated basis eliminates the need to burden the business and product line managers or the cost analyst staff with manual tracking.

If automated transaction statistics are not available, however, manual data must be gathered. This method of acquisition usually is not preferred, but it occasionally must be utilized because the most appropriate measure cannot be captured automatically.

Sometimes if the desired data are unavailable, a center will gather related or similar data that may be less accurate from a relevant cost driver perspective. Using this data as a compromise has a useful additional benefit. It eliminates the need to develop a specific capability to capture currently unavailable data. It is crucial, however, that the substitute data is appropriate and represents an appropriate and relevant cost driver.

- Does the center contain two or more functions? For organizational reasons two or more functions many times are contained within the same center. This arrangement presents a problem if there is no assignment basis appropriate for all functions. Two possible solutions exist. First is the use of multiple bases for assigning a center's expenses. This alternative requires the expenses to be segmented by function and treated independently. The second solution is to split the center into two or more centers, one for each function. This approach offers the advantage of helping management to control each function by providing more detailed and focused information than was previously available. Management control can be maintained by creating an additional summary level center on the management reporting system.

SOURCES OF VOLUME DATA FOR USE AS ALLOCATION BASES

Transactional volume measures generally make excellent cost drivers because they reflect the relative extent of effort required by users. Financial institutions use a number of sources for capturing these measures, including:

Application Systems

These systems exist for financial reporting and offer a wealth of account and transactional information. Utilizing application systems data as the basis for cost assignments requires little if any manual tracking, but some programming effort is needed. Application systems generally capture number of accounts, balance information, and some transactional data (examples of demand deposit transactions might include number of checks, number of deposits, and so forth).

Most application systems can capture specific transactions or the financial entries made in conjunction with the activity. For example, a demand deposit account application system may not track checks cashed and deposited but may capture the associated debit and credit entries.

Summary Level Data

This information can be modified within an application system through the use of established and historical transactional relationships. A good example of the use of summary level data is the relationship of loan payments as a percentage of total accounts for a given lending product. This relationship can be assumed to be the same at the responsibility center level (e.g., branch) as it is at the total organizational level.

On-Line Transaction Systems

If available, these systems present another opportunity to capture relevant data without additional manual effort. Transactional data are readily available on these systems, and the challenge of product identification can generally be met using account number identifiers. Example systems include on-line teller systems.

Automated Customer Information File (CIF) Systems

These systems can be used to match transactional data to products and customers. CIF systems typically are created for marketing analyses but also can provide account number/product relationships. They enable the user to assign account balances and transactions to specific products and customers.

SAMPLE SURVEYS

If automated data is not available, ongoing manual tracking can still be avoided through the use of sample surveys. Conducted periodically, these surveys can provide a snapshot of the center's activities. The surveys must capture a truly random sample of transactions and be conducted often enough to provide data that represents the changes in the dynamics of the business. To avoid distorted results, sample surveys should never be taken during periods of exception activity for certain products (e.g., quarter or year ends).

MANUAL LOGS

Time ladders (discussed earlier in this chapter) and other manual logs require significant effort because employees are responsible for tracking their own activities. This process can be disruptive and time-consuming but may be the only way to capture the necessary information. Highly specialized transactions, where effort varies significantly with each transaction, typically require this self-analysis.

The source of data for the cost assignment basis varies depending on the nature of the activity measured and the resources available to capture the data. The cost analyst staff must apply a flexible and creative approach and be willing to compromise when the benefit of additional accuracy may be outweighed by the extra effort required to obtain it.

SYNOPSIS

Management accounting can be reduced to two basic issues: what expense should be assigned and how should the expense be assigned.

As the analyst selects and employs the most appropriate approach for the financial institution, he or she must be aware of the relative strengths and weaknesses of the many possible methodologies and mechanisms. However, in addition to knowing how to capitalize on each method's advantages, the analyst also needs to consider some general guidelines. Business and product line management must be involved in the selection process and understand its relationship to the overall performance measurment objectives. The various methodologies and mechanisms should be evaluated in light of the institution's specific situation and characteristics. Advantage must be taken of technological advances in automation. The cost/benefit tradeoffs of each approach need to be weighed carefully. All of these considerations can be of immense help in untangling the complexities of cost accounting.

CHAPTER 8

Activity Based Costing

OVERVIEW

A number of market forces impact the profit margins of financial institutions and drive the need for better expense and performance measurement information. These market forces include the introduction of new low cost competitors and non-traditional products in the marketplace, the continuing technology explosion, and an emphasis on meeting ever-changing customer requirements for new product features, alternative product/service delivery channels, and improved product quality.

While institutions undertake many initiatives to maintain or gain competitive advantage, these also result in changing the institutions' cost structures and the financial services industry as a whole. And these cost structure changes are occurring at a time when financial institutions, like other industries, are placing an increased focus on cost management. In today's competitive arena, improved cost and performance management information are required not only to support tactical business decisions (e.g., competitive pricing and investment decisions), but are also necessary as input to the organization's long-term strategic decisions.

All of these factors necessitate the need for managers to better understand and manage costs. It is no longer enough to develop cost and profitability information. Managers must know why a cost exists, whether it is necessary, and how they can improve the bottom line. In today's business environment, managers must not only know which products, delivery channels, and customers are profitable or unprofitable. They also must know what drives their profits and losses, which activities and processes add to or subtract from overall profitability. They also must know what can be done to effect change in the current situation to meet customer demands, respond to competitive pressures, and ultimately improve profitability and shareholder value.

In addition to the need for better information that can be acted on to increase profitability, there is a heightened need to produce this information more frequently and to ensure that it can be developed on a consistent basis across multidimensional views of the organization (e.g., by organizational unit, market segment, product, customer, etc.). The need for consistent and credible decision-making information is critical to ensuring that management makes the proper decisions. In some institutions today, inconsistent methodologies and incomplete analysis make it possible for different groups to develop vastly different performance and profitability results for the same products and customers. Often the sum of the parts does not equal the whole, or profitability results constructed across multiple views, i.e., products, customers, and organizations, do not equal each other when summed at the top of the house. If the cost and profitability information is incomplete or incorrect, then the strategic and tactical decisions based on this information may be incorrect as well. One way to provide improved and consistent management information along multiple views of the corporation can be achieved through the implementation of Activity Based Costing techniques.

This chapter will focus on the application of Activity Based Costing (ABC) techniques in financial institutions. We begin by defining the concept of Activity Based Costing and its foundation in business process analysis. We discuss how Activity Based Costing supports the development of consistent cost data across multiple dimensions. Next, we provide a high-level overview of the Activity Based Costing process flow and present a bank-specific example. Finally we discuss how Activity Based Costing information has been used in service industries to not only develop improved cost information, but to analyze and act on the management information developed in order to enhance profitability and shareholder value.

To put Activity Based Costing in context with other methodologies discussed in this text, it is important to note that Ernst & Young's approach to measuring, reporting, and managing profitability is a set of methodologies collectively referred to as Total Cost Management (TCM). Activity Based Costing is but one component of a set of tools and methodologies that comprise TCM. The Activity Based Management Model shown in Figure 8-1 presents the methodologies that comprise TCM.

Two of the methodologies that comprise TCM will be covered in this chapter. The first is Business Process Analysis, which will be briefly discussed in regard to its use in Activity Based Costing. Business Process Analysis will be discussed further in Chapter 19, "Cost/Expense Management." The second methodology, Activity Based Costing, is of course the subject of this chapter. The third methodology is Continuous Improvement, which also will be discussed in Chapter 19. Finally, the development of performance measures also is considered integral to sustaining TCM in an organization. Not only is it important for an institution to measure and improve profitability and performance, but it is necessary to monitor business decisions by developing

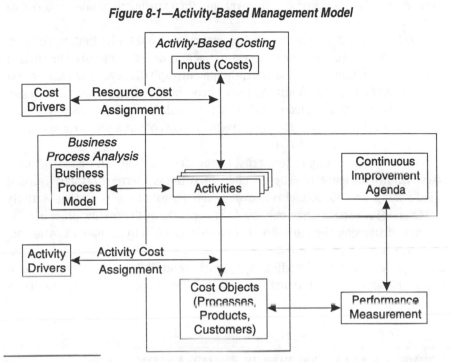

Figure 8-1—Activity-Based Management Model

Source: Adapted from the diagram in *The CAM-I Glossary of Activity-Based Management,* edited by Norm Raffish and Petter B.B. Turney, 1991.

performance measures, financial and nonfinancial, to track progress against goals and critical success factors. This concept was discussed in Chapter 3 and is mentioned here only to complete the full circle of the TCM approach.

ACTIVITY BASED COSTING DEFINED[1]

Activity Based Costing is a methodology which identifies and quantifies the cost of a financial institution's business processes and the associated activities that make up these processes, and accumulates these activity costs by meaningful cost object. One of the fundamental principles of Activity Based Costing is that all cost data should be

---

1   Terminology and definitions used in this chapter are drawn from and consistent with those presented in the *Glossary of Acitvity-Based Management,* edited by Norm Raffish and Peter B.B. Turney and *The Ernst and Young Guide to Total Cost Management,* by Michael Ostrenga with Terrence R. Ozan, Marcus D. Harwood, Robert D. McIlhattan (1992).

identified first at a process or activity level, and then attributed to one or more cost objects.

A cost object is any product, service, customer, market, distribution channel, project, etc., for which a unique cost measurement is desired. Initially, the costs of the institution's resources (e.g., salaries, equipment, capital) are assigned to business process/activity cost pools. A process/activity cost pool simply groups all processes and activities and their related costs into a cost pool. Next, these process/activity pooled costs are assigned to cost objects, based on a cost object's use or consumption of an activity, often volume drivers.

Activity Based Costing includes cost driver identification and cost assignment phases as shown in Figure 8-2. The first phase of costing is referred to as activity based process costing, and the second is known as activity based object costing. Activity Based Costing is the term commonly used to refer to the entire costing process.

Before discussing the more detailed mechanics of Activity Based Costing approach with a financial institution-specific example we will explain the concept of business process analysis. We will also explore how multidimensional views of cost information can be developed and supported within the context of Activity Based Costing.

ACTIVITY BASED COSTING'S FOUNDATION IN BUSINESS PROCESS ANALYSIS

A key approach used when conducting an Activity Based Costing study is to view the organization as a collection of business processes and activities, rather than a hierar-

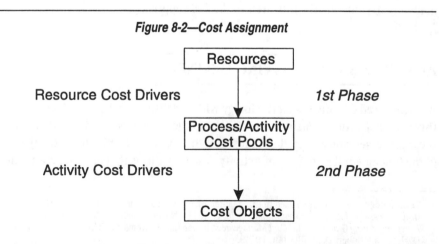

Figure 8-2—Cost Assignment

chy of accounts and organizational units within the general ledger. Many current costing approaches focus on cost allocation and cost assignment within a hierarchical framework. That is, all allocations occur on a hierarchical cost-center by cost-center basis, usually from organizational cost centers to the products those centers support. But using Activity Based Costing techniques, costs are first aggregated into business process/activity cost pools rather than general ledger cost centers and accounts, and then are allocated to one or more cost objects.

A business process is simply a series of activities linked together to accomplish a specific business objective. For example, the business process of loan origination includes such activities as completing the application, checking credit history, pricing the loan, and preparing and mailing the loan documentation. Likewise, the business process of processing a check involves a number of organizational units from the branch to the proof and encoding, and item processing areas.

Business processes rather than organizational/account hierarchies are important because they reflect the way customers view and interact with the institution. They more closely mirror the actual cost flow and cost dynamics of the business. The ability to model the flow of an institution's costs and identify the cause of these costs as they flow within and between organizational units provides the key to both capturing all relevant cost information and analyzing and improving an institution's cost structure.

It is important to note that the activities that make up a business process may cut across many departments. In the example of loan origination above, a number of departments within the institution were involved in the process, including the branch office or loan production office, credit, loan operations, marketing, and the mail room.

Figure 8-3 shows the difference between a department view and the Activity Based Costing process view.

Figure 8-3—Process versus Departments

Processes	Departments						
	Loan Office	Branch	Credit	IT	Marketing	Loan Operations	Mail
Process #1				•	•	•	
Process #2		•					
Loan Origination	•	•	•	•		•	➡
Process #4	•	•	•				
Process #5		•			•	•	

The business process and activity view is important because Activity Based Costing is based on the theory that it is not the organizational units, products, or customers within a financial institution that consume resources and incur cost. Instead, the business processes and activities which make them up consume varying amounts of resources and cause costs to be incurred. The fundamental concept is that a cost is caused, and that the cost being incurred can be identified and managed. Because it is important to understand the linkages between the cost incurred and the activity that required the cost, the initial steps in developing Activity Based Costing information include documenting:

1.   The entire set of activities that comprise a business process

2.   The costs for those activities

3.   The relationship between an activity and its cost

Understanding these linkages and cost flows within and between departments ensures that components of cost are not overlooked and that potential opportunities for reducing or eliminating duplicate and unnecessary costs are identified.

ACTIVITY BASED COSTING SUPPORTS CONSISTENT VIEWS OF PROFITABILITY MEASUREMENT

Currently, financial institutions desire to desegregate their organizations and measure profitability along multiple dimensions. They seek to understand the profitability of products and services (such as corporate trust or home equity loans), markets (such as geographic regions), customers, and distribution channels (such as branches). Moreover, they must ensure that the bases for profitability measurement along multiple dimensions are consistent. That is, revenue, funds transfer pricing, and cost assignment methodologies should be the same across various "cuts" of the institution. This requires more sophisticated and powerful costing tools than financial institutions have typically employed.

Properly implemented, Activity Based Costing can provide consistent views of cost along multiple "cuts" of the bank. Costs can be aggregated in any way the institution wishes, for example, by organization, product, customer or segment. Total costs will sum to the same number in each view. This is because Activity Based Costing takes costs to the lowest common denominator of activity that is relevant to measure. These activities and their associated costs can then be summed up across different views or cost object (product, customer, etc.). This contrasts with traditional methods that allocate costs down organizational or product hierarchies, or across

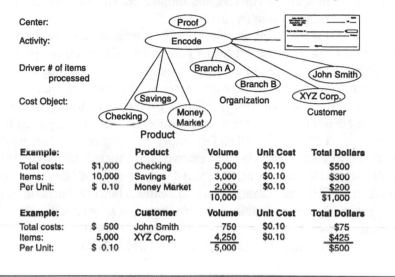

Figure 8-4—Sample of Activity Based Costing in Banking

Example:		Product	Volume	Unit Cost	Total Dollars
Total costs:	$1,000	Checking	5,000	$0.10	$500
Items:	10,000	Savings	3,000	$0.10	$300
Per Unit:	$ 0.10	Money Market	2,000	$0.10	$200
			10,000		$1,000

Example:		Customer	Volume	Unit Cost	Total Dollars
Total costs:	$ 500	John Smith	750	$0.10	$75
Items:	5,000	XYZ Corp.	4,250	$0.10	$425
Per Unit:	$ 0.10		5,000		$500

customers. When traditional cost allocation techniques are used, summing costs one way, for instance by product, usually leads to different results than if they are aggregated another way, such as by customer. As shown in Figure 8-4, the Activity Based Costing approach allows activity costs to be aggregated across multiple profitability views (e.g., product, customer, or organization).

HOW DOES ACTIVITY BASED COSTING WORK?[2]

The first phase of Activity Based Costing assigns general ledger resource costs (e.g., salaries, equipment, supplies, and capital) to business processes or major activities aligned to a process activity cost pool. In this first phase, resource cost drivers are used to assign cost to process or activity cost pools. A resource cost driver measures the quantity of resources consumed by a process or an activity. The second phase of cost assignment uses activity cost drivers to assign activity costs out of these process/activity cost pools to the end cost object (i.e., a product, customer, or delivery channel). An activity cost driver measures the quantity of activities used by the cost object.

One functional cost center may or may not equal one cost pool. Also, all expenses or cost elements within a cost center may be assigned to one or more activity cost pools

---

2   This section draws from: John Karr, "Activity Based Costing in the Financial Services Industry,"*Bank Accounting of Finance*, v.8, n.1, Fall 1994, pp. 30–36.

or specific cost elements. Line items of expense (e.g., salaries and benefits) may be assigned using one set of cost drivers, and another cost element such as equipment may be assigned using yet another cost driver.

A cost driver is any factor that measures the consumption of cost by a process, activity, or cost object. Cost drivers usually are measured in terms of a process or an activity/transaction volume. A cost driver is sometimes referred to as an economic cost driver, but for purposes of this book, the term cost driver will be used. Although the terms cost driver and root cause are often used interchangeably, again in this book the term cost driver will be used to indicate the measure used to assign cost to a cost pool or cost object. In Chapter 19 on Cost/Expense Management, where we discuss Process Value Analysis, we will use the term root cause to denote the underlying cause or event that results in costs being incurred. The term often takes on a negative connotation when the root cause indicates suboptimization of a process or increased cost for a cost object. For example, a cost driver used to assign reject-repair expense might be the number of reject items repaired. The root cause of that additional cost, however, may be preencoded items being accepted which do not meet machine-readable standards.

In summary, Activity Based Costing takes line item cost inputs and assigns them, based on resource drivers, first to process/activity cost pools. Process/activity cost pools are groups of related activities and their associated costs. The process/activity cost pools can be defined broadly (e.g., marketing, processing, or collections) or narrowly (e.g., dividend payment, redemption, or securities purchase). A resource driver is a measure of the quantity of resources consumed by an activity. In the next step process/activity-pooled costs are attributed to cost objects, such as products or customers using activity drivers, by using transaction counts. Overhead costs go through the same process of activity pooling and assignment based on drivers.

Of course, the actual mechanics of Activity Based Costing are a bit more complex than this summary suggests. Moreover, somewhat different technical approaches to Activity Based Costing exist. The following describes how costs are identified and assigned using one variant of an Activity Based Costing approach. Figure 8-5 provides a summary of the sequence of Activity Based Costing to be discussed below.

Step 1: Review General Ledger Centers and Accounts and Book Financial Transactions to Appropriate Accounts

In order to be useful and to support most allocation methods, expenses need to be properly accounted for. This means being booked into the institution's financial systems using the correct account codes. In many institutions, improper booking takes place more often than is generally suspected. A key step in Activity Based Costing analysis is to see that such problems are identified and rectified prior to cost assignment.

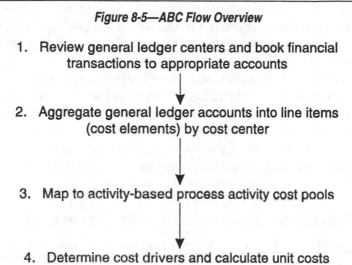

Figure 8-5—ABC Flow Overview

1. Review general ledger centers and book financial transactions to appropriate accounts

2. Aggregate general ledger accounts into line items (cost elements) by cost center

3. Map to activity-based process activity cost pools

4. Determine cost drivers and calculate unit costs

5. Drive pool costs to cost objects using drivers

Step 2: Aggregate General Ledger Accounts into Line Items (Cost Elements) by Cost Center

An institution's raw expense data, found in the general ledger or subledgers, are usually too voluminous for use in allocations. The individual account balances are therefore aggregated to higher line item level, for example, salaries and benefits, occupancy, or travel and entertainment. The line items, sometimes called "cost elements," are organized by cost center, another accounting classification. Cost centers are hierarchical in nature, with the highest level being the bank-wide consolidation and the lowest being the base responsibility center. Activity Based Costing typically uses a low cost center as starting point for allocation versus the detailed cost center. For example, the full Student Loan Marketing Department cost center may be used as a starting point, rather than a smaller center such as the Student Loan Department's advertising unit. This assumes that the two would be allocated using similar cost drivers.

For purposes of Activity Based Costing, cost centers are grouped into two categories. Category One includes centers that are internal support units and do not directly provide products or services to external customers. Instead, they provide support to other units of the bank. Examples include Human Resources and Planning and Finance units. Category Two includes cost centers that perform activities directly related to serving external customers, for example a Lending Group. This step is very much like that of determining the closeout sequence for cost allocations discussed in previous chapters.

Careful analysis is needed to separate Category One support centers from Category Two customer-oriented centers. Institutions often confuse their existing definition of "overhead" and operating units with true support and customer-related units. In fact, many units defined as "overhead" perform activities directly related to providing products or services for customers. For example, some banks term their Loan Review groups "overhead," when their activities can be directly related to serving customers.

Step 3: Map to Activity Based Process Activity Cost Pools

A critical element of Activity Based Costing is mapping cost center information to cost pools. Cost pools are process or activity based aggregations of costs. Possible examples of cost pools are loan marketing, loan servicing, and loan workout. Based on analyses of the cost center's activities, and which processes they support, costs are assigned to pools. By doing so, management can see how much cost is consumed by activities and processes, which can be a useful, nontraditional way of considering costs.

Step 4: Determine Cost Drivers and Calculate Unit Costs

Another feature of Activity Based Costing is the use of cost drivers to calculate unit costs. For each pool, a driver is identified, which relates pool costs to the ultimate cost object (defined previously). The driver can essentially be thought of as the causal force behind the cost pool. For example, loan marketing pool costs could be driven by the number of customer calls made or the number of loan proposals developed. Loan servicing pool costs could be driven by the number of active and inactive accounts. Drivers usually are transaction based. Using the relationship between the driver and objects, process pools costs are assigned. For example, if the driver for certain activity pool costs is the number of accounts, then the unit cost can be expressed on a per-account basis.

Step 5: Drive Pool Costs to Cost Objects

Cost objects are the components of the institution to which costs are ultimately allocated. Costs are driven to objects using two steps. First, internal support units' (Category One) costs are allocated to customer-oriented (Category Two) units. Then Category Two costs are driven to cost objects. Typical cost objects are products, customers, or accounts.

Driving the process costs to objects is straightforward. Consider the example of a cost expressed on a per-account basis. Per-account can be summed by product, using the account to product relationship; by customer, using the account to customer relationship; or by organizational unit, using the account to organization relationship. Other cost pools can be driven directly to product, customer, or organization by mapping drivers to the cost object. For example, if the driver is a transaction such as a returned check, cost per returned check can be directly attributed to product type (e.g., MMDA), customer, or organization (e.g., Retail Banking Group).

Complications can arise in the driving of cost to objects. For example, the link between driver and object may be difficult to determine. How can the cost per new sales call be attributed to specific products or customers? Solving this generally requires establishing additional objects such as "new customers" or "marketing products," or arbitrarily allocating such costs among existing objects.

Another complication can be that all transactions within a given class of driver do not consume an equal amount of costs. This is often encountered where one type of account entails more work than others, yet all accounts are treated as being equal by the institution's systems. To address such issues, cost weighting mechanisms can be developed. For example, high balance accounts could receive some multiple of the cost attributed to low balance accounts.

ILLUSTRATIVE EXAMPLE OF ACTIVITY BASED COSTING FLOW

The previous discussion outlined the basic process by which costs are assigned using Activity Based Costing. The following narrative and Figures 8-6 and 8-7 provide an illustrative example of Activity Based Costing, using hypothetical cost center expenses. The example includes descriptions of how costs are allocated within units. It also shows how costs can be driven from an internal support (Category One) unit to an external customer-oriented (Category Two) unit.

Starting with a Category One example, Figure 8-6 shows how a hypothetical support unit called Payroll is allocated using Activity Based Costing. The basic process follows the steps described in the previous section and as outlined in Figure 8-5.

The cost center's expenses are booked to the proper accounts and aggregated by line item. The Payroll unit's direct expenses (such as salaries/benefits and occupancy) total $72,000 for the period. The Payroll unit's expense from other support units also "upstreams" from it in the cost allocation flow. In the example, the Payroll unit receives usage-based charges from other support units totaling $9,000. Therefore, total expenses for the unit for the period total $81,000 ($72,000 plus $9,000).

Figure 8-6—Example: Payroll Units (Category One)

Step 1. Expenses Booked to Proper Account and Step 2. Aggregated by Cost Center and by Line Item	Step 3. Costs Mapped to Process Cost Pools	Step 4. Cost Driver Determined and Cost Assigned	Step 5. Costs Driven to Cost Object
Expenses for the Period MM/YY Cost Center 10XX: Payroll Direct Expenses Salaries $42,000 Travel & Entertainment 6,000 Occupancy 9,000 Telephone 3,000 Supplies 3,000 Printing 1,500 Postage 1,500 Depreciation 2,000 Miscellaneous 4,000 Total Direct Expenses $72,000 Charges from Category One Units Computer (usage × rate) $6,000 Cafeteria (usage × rate) 1,080 Etc. (usage × rate) 2,000 Total Support Charges $9,000 **Total Expenses $81,000**	**Process Pool A: Payroll Processing** Activities determined to consume 80% of center's costs: $81,000 × .80 = $64,800 **Process Pool B: Investigation** Activities determined to consume 20% of the center's costs: $81,000 × .20 = $16,200 **Total Expenses $81,000**	**Process Pool A Driver: Number of Payroll Checks** $64,800/10,000 checks = $6.48/check **Process Pool B Driver: Number of Inquiries** ($16,200/150 inquiries = $108/inquiry **Total Expenses $81,000**	Support unit costs are attributed to other responsibility centers on the basis of the number of checks and inquiries that they generate.

In the next step, the costs are mapped to process cost pools. In this example, the cost center performs two processes: A—Payroll Processing and B—Investigation. Analysis of the processes show that 80 percent of the unit's total costs ($64,800) are related to performing payroll processing, and 20 percent of the unit's total costs ($16,200) are related to investigations. Analysis of this sort typically involves examining the composition of the unit's day-to-day activities, and identifying associated costs with each significant process it performs.

The next step is to determine the cost driver for each process. The cost driver can be thought of as the operational or economic event that generates the process costs. In the Payroll unit example, the cost driver for payroll processing is determined to be the production of payroll checks.[3] The total volume is 10,000 checks, so that the cost per check in this example is $6.48 ($64,800 in process costs divided by 10,000 checks). Similarly, the driver for the investigation process is determined to be the number of inquiries that need to be investigated. The number of inquiries is 150, so that the cost per inquiry is $108 (or $16,200 in investigation process costs divided by 150).

Once the costs are assigned, they are driven to the cost object. For support unit costs, cost objects are other organizational units that use their services. For example, a Legal Department's costs can be driven to such other organizational units as Loan Workout or Human Resources. In the example shown in Figure 8-6, payroll costs would be driven to all other parts of the institution, based on the number of checks and inquiries they generate.

In order to prevent an endlessly circular stream of allocations to and from support units, a hierarchy or assignment sequence should be imposed so that costs are driven downstream but never upstream. That is, support units cannot pass costs to other support units above them in the hierarchy. Establishing the hierarchy and sequentially ordering the support units within it does not imply any judgment about the relative value of the services provided by the units. Instead, it is a simplifying mechanism designed to streamline the cost assignment process.

Support (Category One) unit costs are driven to external customer-oriented (Category Two) units. There, they are combined with the unit's direct expenses and further carried through to the ultimate cost objects. Figure 8-7 provides another example of how costs are handled, this time for a Category Two unit, a Home Equity Department.

The basic flow for external customer-oriented Category Two units such as a Home Equity Department is very similar. Direct expenses are booked to the proper account and aggregated by cost center and line item. Charges from Category One units, based on the Home Equity Department's usage, are added to the direct costs. In the example

---

3   If payroll processing involved two separate types of activity, hard copy check production and ACH transactions, then the basic process definitions might include "Payroll Processing—Check" and "Payroll Processing—ACH," each with its own process cost profile.

Figure 8-7—Example: Home Equity Department (Category Two)

Step 1. Expenses Booked to Proper Account and Step 2. Aggregated by Cost Center and by Line Item	Step 3. Costs Mapped to Process Cost Pools	Step 4. Cost Driver Determined and Cost Assigned	Step 5. Costs Driven to Cost Object
Expenses for the Period MM/YY Cost Center 20XX: Home Equity	**Process Pool A: Loan Marketing and Origination** Activities determined to consume 30% of the center's costs: $638,700 × .30 = $191,610	**Process A Driver: Number of New Loans** ($191,610/5,000 loans = $38.32/loan)	Costs are attributed to cost objects such as: • Customer/segments • Products • Organizations based on their relationship to the drivers.
Direct Expenses Salaries $550,000 Travel & Entertainment 10,000 Occupancy 12,000 Telephone 6,000 Suppliers 8,000 Printing 10,000 Postage 8,000 Depreciation 5,000 Miscellaneous 6,000 **Total Direct Expenses** $615,000	**Process Pool B: Active Account Servicing** Activities determined to consume 50% of the center's costs: $638,700 × .50 = $319,350	**Process B Driver: Number of Active Accounts** ($319,350/80,000 accounts = $3.99/account)	
Charges from Category One Units Payroll Processing (250 checks × $6.48) $1,620 Payroll investigation (10 inquiries × $108) 1,080 Computer (usage × rate) 10,000 Cafeteria (usage × rate) 3,000 Etc. (usage × rate) 8,000 **Total Support Charges** $23,700	**Process Pool C: Inactive Account Servicing** Activities determined to consume 5% of the center's costs: $638,700 × .05 = $31,935	**Process C Driver: Number of Inactive Accounts** ($31,935/20,000 accounts = $1.60/account)	
	Process Pool D: Delinquencies and Collection Activities determined to consume 15% of the center's costs: $638,700 × .15 =$95,805	**Process D Driver: Number of Past Due Accounts** ($95,805/3,000 accounts = $31.94/account)	
Total Expenses $638,700	**Total Expenses** $638,700	**Total Expenses** $638,700	

shown in Figure 8-7, direct costs are $615,000 and Category One charges are $23,700, yielding a total cost of $638,700 to be assigned.

In Figure 8-7, the Home Equity Department determined that it performed four basic processes: loan marketing and origination; active account servicing; inactive account servicing; and delinquencies and collection. Further analysis of the department's activities indicated that loan marketing and origination consumed 30 percent of the department's costs, or $191,610; active account servicing 50 percent, or $319,350; inactive account servicing 5 percent, or $31,935; and delinquencies and collection 15 percent, or $95,805.

Continuing with the basic Activity Based Costing flow, cost drivers are determined for each process cost pool, and costs are assigned on a per-unit basis using the driver. For example, the driver for the loan marketing and origination process costs was determined to be the number of new loans booked in the period.[4] Dividing the total process pool costs of $191,610 by 5,000 in new loans booked during the month leads to a cost per new loan of $38.32. Similar exercises are carried out for the other three process cost pools so that all of the Home Equity Department's costs are assigned.

Finally, the costs are driven to the ultimate objects, such as organizations, products, or customers, based on the object's relationship to the driver. For example, total customer or segment costs can be determined by summing the new loan and account-driven costs for the customers or segments.

The examples outlined above show one methodological approach to Activity Based Costing. Other, more sophisticated variants exist as well. For example, further analysis of process costs could identify which are fixed and which are variable. The fixed and variable components could then be carried through the rest of the Activity Based Costing flow. Another complexity might be to identify the costs associated with excess capacity, and to attribute them to the cost objects using Activity Based Costing principles. Activity Based Costing is a flexible enough technique to allow for numerous features in its design.

OVERALL APPROACH TO IMPLEMENTING ACTIVITY BASED COSTING

The following is a recap of the steps to be undertaken during an Activity Costing Project:

- Determine project scope and uses of cost information.

---

4   Clearly, other alternate drivers could be defined for this process. For example, the number of applications generated could be a driver.

- Review general ledger and other cost data; collect financial data.
- Identify business processes and their activities, cost objects.
- Design cost flow models (see Figure 8-8).
- Identify resource and activity cost drivers and sources of driver data.
- Collect cost driver data.
- Calculate process/activity costs.
- Calculate object costs.

This general sequence of events for performing an Activity Based Costing project is presented in Figure 8-9.

When designing and executing an Activity Based Costing program for the first time in an institution, it may be prudent to take a phased approach to the development of the cost information. A pilot area process can be selected so that the concepts and techniques of Activity Based Costing can be tried without attempting to undertake a massive costing project throughout the institution. What is learned from the first pilot project can then be refined, and the costing efforts expanded to other business processes and activities throughout the institution.

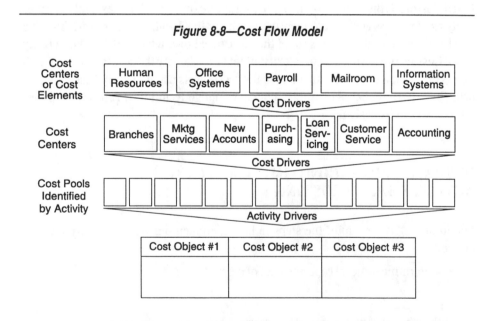

Figure 8-8—Cost Flow Model

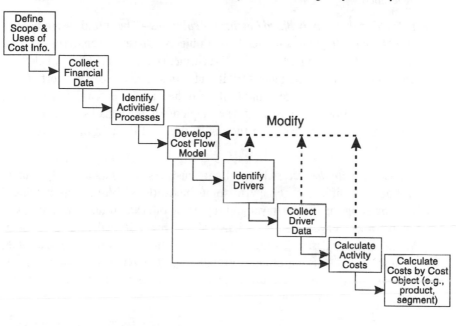

Figure 8-9—Develop Cost Model—Activity Based Costing Project Components

Commonly Encountered Issues and Pitfalls

Financial service firms that implement Activity Based Costing often encounter a similar set of issues and problems. The list below outlines some of the major ones.

- *Level of Detail*—Because Activity Based Costing is such a powerful tool, and often promises such a pronounced improvement over existing cost allocation methods, there is a tendency to design it at too low a level of detail. Process pools, drivers, and objects proliferate as successively finer "cuts" at costs and profitability are demanded. Besides raising the expense of the initial Activity Based Costing analysis, too much detail also makes system maintenance quite costly. Therefore, a balance should be struck in the Activity Based Costing system between the desire for detail and the benefits and costs of providing it.

- *Data Sources*—While much cost data is resident in institutions' financial systems, the data are not generally adequate for Activity Based Costing purposes. This is particularly true for cost driver data. Cost drivers are often operational in nature, and may not be captured by existing systems, or interfaced to the financial systems. Information about the "ideal" driver may be difficult to obtain and use in cost calculations. Typically, some type of work-around may be required until a more robust and efficient systems solution is developed.

- *Refreshing the Activity Based Costing Calculations*—The initial assignment of cost elements to pools, and then to cost objects, is based on analyses of point-in-time or historical performance. Over time, cost relationships can change. For example, a cost center may shift its activities to increase its support of loan setup. Therefore, the algorithms built into the Activity Based Costing system need to be periodically refreshed. The frequency of the updates will depend on the pace of internal change at the institution and the cost of renewing the analysis.

- *Discomfort with the Process View*—Using business processes as a way to identify and attribute cost is new to some institutions. While Activity Based Costing supports the portrayal and reporting of costs in terms of processes, many bank managers prefer to see costs shown in traditional, line item format. While Activity Based Costing can show line item costs for organizational, product, and customer profitability reporting, adding the process dimension is one of its most powerful features. Bankers should not ignore it, even if they are initially uncomfortable using it.

SOME IMPLICATIONS OF ACTIVITY BASED COSTING'S USE

The usefulness of the Activity Based Costing information includes not only the actual cost data being developed, but also the wealth of data available from the business process documentation, cost flow, and cost driver information that is developed as part of the process. This can yield insights that will be useful in improving the institutions' processes and cost structure. When analyzed and acted upon, it forms the basis for managers to make decisions regarding the products and services the institution offers, its product mix, and pricing, as well as who its customers should be and which markets it should be in. Even if the cost object is profitable, the information developed about the way a process or activity is performed may yield the opportunity to change the process or reduce the cost of an activity, therefore improving the overall profitability.

Activity Based Costing is increasingly being employed by a wide variety of financial institutions. Banks, securities firms, investment companies, and insurance companies are using Activity Based Costing tools and techniques. As indicated above, they have found that gaining a better understanding of costs has broader ramifications than initially expected. For instance, an insurance company used Activity Based Costing to better understand the profitability of its products. The Activity Based Costing exercises yielded an improved, and surprising, picture of which products were profitable and which were not. The company found that large quantities of "shared" operations expense, such as claims processing, had been inappropriately allocated among products. Activity Based Costing provided a more accurate picture of how new products consumed costs. The company repriced products and in some cases dropped the product lines if the price or volume increases, or cost reductions, were not feasible.

A provider of institutional trust services used Activity Based Costing to determine which activities were most responsible for its cost structure. As its customer account and assets under management numbers rose, its costs rose disproportionately, rather than benefiting from the economies of scale that management had anticipated. Activity Based Costing helped to identify excessive tailoring and customization of incremental business as a key cause of the rapidly rising costs. As a result, the company determined that certain of its business processes involved substantial amounts of such nonvalue added activities as reconciliations, rekeying data, and producing redundant reports. This analysis led to process redesign and other opportunities to reduce costs outright.

In another example, a large commercial bank used Activity Based Costing to improve its organizational profitability reporting. As a result of the process, a substantial volume of expense, previously thought of as pure overhead, was more accurately attributed to organizational units. The Activity Based Costing calculations were also easier for management to understand than the previous, arbitrary method of cost allocation. A clearer link between actions, cost, and profitability was established. Also, Activity Based Costing helped the bank to provide more consistent views of organizational, product, and customer profitability.

SYNOPSIS

This chapter has outlined some of the attributes of Activity Based Costing and the forces guiding its use in financial institutions. As discussed, Activity Based Costing can help to improve managers' understanding of their institutions' cost structures. Used in concert with a broader suite of performance measurement techniques and analytical tools such as Process Value Analysis, it also can help bankers more effectively manage their costs. Process Value Analysis will be discussed within the context of Business Process Analysis in Chapter 19 on Cost/Expense Management. The banking industry is likely to employ Activity Based Costing more and more frequently in its analytical tool kits and management reporting systems.

CHAPTER 9

Information Technology

OVERVIEW

In most financial institutions, the information technology (IT) function creates the largest functional expense and is a critical area of management concern. It affects virtually every product and management operation and therefore has a major effect on an institution's ultimate profitability. Accordingly, management needs specific information about this function, especially its costs.

Information technology, however, is a highly complex area and requires specific technical expertise to comprehend and manage. Because most managers do not have these skills, it is necessary to provide the nontechnical manager with a means of understanding and controlling his or her IT costs.

This chapter presents several methodologies for converting the technical aspects of IT into the more commonly understood elements of costs. First it describes the typical IT organization and its relationship to cost development. Then it addresses the specific issue of developing costs from a computer processing perspective, following with a discussion of the data collection required to support the costing methods. The chapter concludes by illustrating the conversion of the costs developed in the preceding paragraphs to product-oriented costs.

THE INFORMATION TECHNOLOGY ORGANIZATION

The IT organization generally includes three broad functions: Systems and Programming (S&P), Computer Operations, and Network Computing. (For purposes of this discussion, administration and management are included in each of the functions. Alternatively, administration and management could each be separate functions.) The first, systems and programming, consists of the programmers and analysts responsible for the development, maintenance, and enhancement of application systems. Sometimes known as application development, or by a variety of other names, this function employs the programmers who support the systems with which management is most familiar, such as demand deposits or commercial loan systems. Developing and reporting S&P costs are addressed later in this chapter.

Developing costs for computer operations is more complicated than for S&P because the process contains several independent but related functions. These functions can generally be described as follows:

- *Operations*—the function responsible for the day-to-day operations of the computer center, recovery of data streams, and implementation of the job scheduling plan. It typically includes expenses for hardware as well as for console operators, tape operators, and printer operators.

- *Planning*—the function responsible for computer capacity planning, system configurations, and equipment purchases and maintenance.

- *Systems Programming*—the function responsible for the selection, installation, tailoring, and maintenance of operating systems-oriented software such as the operating system, compilers, data base managers, transaction processing systems, and utilities.

- *Security*—the function responsible for developing and maintaining methods to help ensure security, integrity, and reliability of data and programs. It also can provide advisory, audit, or training assistance related to data security.

- *Production Control*—the function responsible for maintaining operational schedules, quality and integrity. It typically includes investigating, analyzing, and proposing solutions to recurrent operational problems.

- *Telecommunications*—the function responsible for designing, maintaining, and managing the institution's data communications capabilities. It also may be responsible for voice telecommunications networks.

Such general descriptions cannot, of course, describe all computer operations activities. More specific activities frequently are included in each area (e.g., performance measurement as part of systems programming). Larger areas such as user scheduling also may be considered elements of broad units such as production control. Nevertheless, the functions listed are used frequently as organizational units in computer operations, and as such, they contain the collection of expenses (salaries, benefits, depreciation, and so forth) that are essential to developing computer operations costs. The principles described here, however, can be applied to any organizational structure, regardless of whether it contains these units.[1]

The third and least well-defined IT area is that of network computing. This encompasses the rapidly emerging technologies of desktop computing and local area networks (LANs); and organizational units involved in these functions may be known as LAN support, office systems, information center, or PC support, among others. However, the functions can be described as follows:

- *Network Support*—the function responsible for the installation of physical network components including cabling systems, network hubs, bridges, routers, desktop and server computers. This unit is likely also to be responsible for network management, ensuring that network components are performing correctly. Expenses include hardware purchases, hardware maintenance, capital depreciation, usually telecommunications costs and personnel.

- *Network Administration*—the function responsible for supporting the network operating systems and communications software, as well as configuring the network, adding users to the network and managing the security of the network components. Software purchase and maintenance costs in addition to personnel costs are the major cost components.

- *Office Systems Support*—the function responsible for installing and assisting users with office productivity tools such as electronic mail, word processing and spreadsheets.

- *Help Desk*—the function that is dedicated to responding to user calls for assistance and coordinating the resources to resolve problems. Various software tools may be used to support this function.

Network computing has evolved from the use of personal computers, which initially was a departmental expense. With the implementation of more sophisticated technologies and the inter-connection of these "islands of automation," responsibility has migrated from departmental units to business units and central IT functions. However, financial systems typically do not move as fast as the technology and organizational changes and therefore, costs for network computing functions may be

---

1   Some institutions include item or check processing in computer operations. But because item processing is not a functional part of computer operations, it is not included in this discussion of IT costing. The cost accounting principles described in Chapter 7 can be used for developing item processing costs.

spread between end user and IT units. This fragmentation of network computing costs has resulted in a lack of management awareness of the total costs, often referred to as "hidden IT costs."

Assuming the functional areas that have been listed are organizational units as well, the resulting organization chart would be as shown in Figure 9-1. Unfortunately, such a chart does not help in the development of costs because the areas it comprises do not lend themselves to cost allocations. While loan processing, for example, can be allocated on the basis of loans, a unit such as production control cannot be dealt with so easily. For this and other computer operations areas, a different allocation method is required.

DEVELOPING COMPUTER OPERATIONS COSTS

Converting the expenses recorded in the organizational areas shown in Figure 9-1 requires multiple steps as detailed here. Conceptually, the process consists of creating a series of spreadsheets that distribute expenses to readily allocable pools, and then allocating the pools on a given cost driver basis. The use of sophisticated spreadsheet software has made it convenient for many institutions to use available microcomputer spreadsheet programs to do the cost development. Many of the figures accompanying this chapter resemble the output of such spreadsheets and can be used as general guides when using microcomputers to develop IT costs.

Step 1—Consolidation of Expenses

As noted, computer operations organizational units record the expenses of the functional areas. Not all expenses related to computer operations, however, are found in those units. Furthermore, the units may include expenses not related to computer operations. Voice communication line expenses, for example, frequently are found in the telecommunication unit. The first step in developing costs is to properly account for all expenses related to computer operations, whether they are in operations's organizational unit or not.

Expenses that may be recorded elsewhere (along with organizational units where they may be recorded) include:

- Depreciation for special equipment related to computer operations, such as chilled water systems or uninterruptible power supplies. These expenses might be recorded in facilities management or buildings improvement.

Figure 9-1—Typical Information Technology Organization Chart

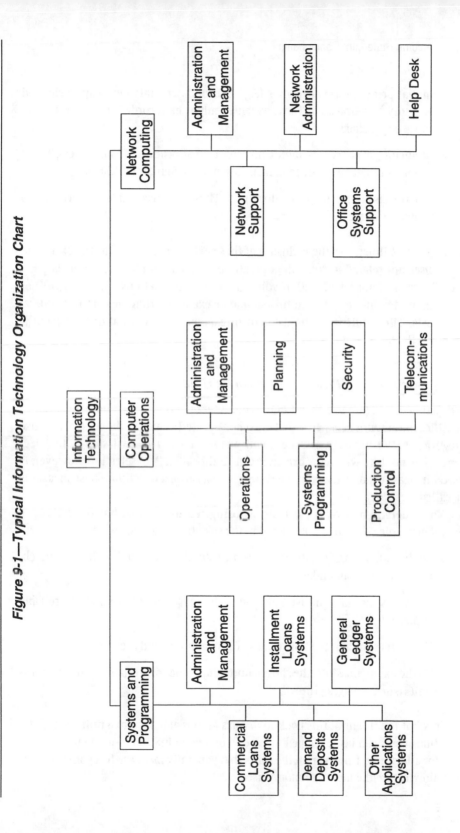

- Special printed forms expenses (e.g., consolidated statement paper) charged directory to a line area. These expenses might be recorded in supplies warehouse or purchasing.

- Occupancy expenses (assuming no prior cost allocation of floor space). These expenses might be recorded in facilities management or buildings.

- Benefits (assuming no prior allocation). These expenses might be recorded in human resources.

Figure 9-2 illustrates the inclusion of these extra costs as well as the exclusion of expenses not related to computer operations. The column labeled "Expenses Excluded" accounts for $400,000 of voice grade communications and $600,000 of data communications equipment that should be excluded from the computer operations costs. The result is the adjustment of expenses to the total of $6,130,000 (shown in the last column).

Step 2—Selection of Resource Units to Be Used

As illustrated in Figure 9-2, Step 1 of the computer operations cost allocation process identifies the amount of expense that must be allocated as well as the general expense categories (e.g., salaries, hardware, facility costs, etc.). The next step is to select appropriate pools to which the expenses can be allocated. Pool selection, however, is based on measures of activity in the computer operations function. These measures are called "resource units."

No predetermined rules exist for choosing resource units, but the following general principles should be considered in the selection process:

- To the extent possible, the resource unit should be defined so that a nontechnical manager can understand it.

- The units should be measurable and their measurement should be as reliable as possible.

- The units should reflect the trade-off between cost and accuracy.

- To the extent possible, the chosen units should be controllable by the business units (such as pages printed).

It is not the intent of this book to discuss all possible resource units; computer operations costs can be developed using one or a combination of many units as the basis for allocation. However, of the units that generally meet the foregoing criteria, the following are the most commonly used:

Figure 9-2—Computer Operations Expenses

	Operations	Planning	Systems Programming	Security	Production Control	Telecomm	Total Reported Costs	Expenses Excluded	Total Costs
Salaries and Benefits	$ 414,000	$312,000	$384,000	$102,000	$ 74,400	$ 111,600	$1,398,000	$	$1,398,000
Hardware									
Rent	1,750,000						1,750,000		1,750,000
Maintenance	400,000					100,000	500,000		500,000
Depreciation	550,000	250,000	40,000			15,000	855,000		855,000
Software									
Rent			300,000				300,000		300,000
Maintenance	150,000		100,000				250,000		250,000
Depreciation	25,000		25,000				50,000		50,000
Communications									
Voice (a)	7,000	4,000	5,000	2,000		404,000	422,000	(400,000)	22,000
Data (a)					2,000	600,000	602,000	(600,000)	2,000
Facility									
Occupancy	190,000	65,000	67,000	21,000		33,000	376,000		376,000
	5,000	2,000	2,000	4,000	27,000	7,000	47,000		47,000
Other									
Supplies									
General	15,000	5,000	10,000	7,000	8,000	19,000	64,000		64,000
Printer	265,000						265,000		265,000
Tape	65,000						65,000		65,000
Disk									
Outside services		10,000			80,000	15,000	105,000		105,000
Miscellaneous	25,000		18,000	15,000	17,000	6,000	81,000		81,000
Total	$3,861,000	$648,000	$951,000	$151,000	$208,400	$1,310,600	$7,130,000	$(1,000,000)	$6,130,000

Notes: (a) Expenses for voice and data are allocated directly to users.

- CPU seconds—for the costs of the central processing unit (CPU) and general operations. (There might be a special unit for on-line CPU seconds.)

- Disk megabytes per month—for the cost of on-line storage.

- Pages printed—for the cost of printing.

- Tape mounts and storage—for the cost of tape.

Many institutions favor the use of multiple resource units because they link costs with specific resource usage. For example, a manager might not understand what a CPU second is (or for that matter, how much work a CPU second can accomplish), but he can intuitively understand that daily interest accruals will require more CPU seconds than monthly accruals. Likewise, disk megabytes per month can be directly related to business-related items, such as length of retention or number of customers on file, that managers can understand easily.

Because the resource units listed are relatively common, they are used in examples throughout this chapter. It should be remembered, however, that they are not the only units that can be used.

Step 3—Allocation of Expenses to Resource Unit Pools

The next step in developing computer operations costs is to allocate the expenses to pools in selected resource units. Figure 9-3 is a spreadsheet that illustrates this procedure. (In addition to expense categories and resource units, Figure 9-3 includes a column labeled "General," which applies to expenses that cannot be directly allocated to a resource pool or that are not worth the time or expense to allocate directly among the resource unit columns. The "General" expense column is discussed later in this chapter.)

Expenses can be allocated to the resource units in a manner similar to that used for other cost accounting activities. For example, if salaries through out the institution generally are distributed on the basis of estimated personnel distributions, then the salaries for each operations organizational unit can be distributed the same way. (For general cost accounting techniques, refer to Chapter 7.) There are, however, three operations expenses that cannot be allocated quite so easily.

The first and largest single expense is equipment, and its allocation usually is intimidating because of its technical nature. The allocation of equipment expense generally requires an item-by-item review of the fixed asset listing of all IT equipment.

Most, but certainly not all, of this allocation is relatively straightforward, as shown in Figure 9-4. In other cases, however, the allocations can be more difficult. For example, switching units that allow reconfiguration of tapes, disks, and CPUs can

Figure 9-3—Allocation Skeleton—Expenses Allocated to Resource Units

	Total Expense	CPU	Disk	Print	Tape	General
Salaries and Benefits						
Hardware						
Rent						
Maintenance						
Depreciation						
Software						
Rent						
Maintenance						
Depreciation						
Communication						
Voice						
Data						
Facility						
Occupancy						
Furniture and Equipment						
Other						
Supplies						
General						
Printer						
Tape						
Disk						
Outside Services						
Miscellaneous						
Total						

be assigned to any or all of the resource unit pools that have been identified. In general, however, these units can be handled in the pool used for general operating units, which is usually the CPU resource unit pool.

An expense related to equipment is the cost of funds associated with purchased equipment. Although it is not included in the example used here, it should be incorporated in computer operations costs if it appears in the institution's other reports (e.g., expense budgets).

The second problematic expense area is supplies. In most organizational units within a financial institution, supplies represent a relatively small cost that can be allocated as a general expense of the unit (e.g., on the basis of salary allocations). For computer operations, however, supplies constitute a major expense category and it is important to allocate them directly to the appropriate resource unit pools. Examples

Figure 9-4—Operations Unit Allocation of Expenses to Resource Units

	Total Expense	CPU	Disk	Print	Tape	General
Salaries and Benefits	$1,398,000	$423,000	$	$ 76,000	$121,000	$ 778,000
Hardware						
Rent	1,750,000	722,000	600,000	58,000	370,000	
Maintenance	500,000	158,000	113,000	45,000	84,000	100,000
Depreciation	855,000	449,000	15,000	12,000	74,000	305,000
Software						
Rent	300,000	288,000		12,000		
Maintenance	250,000	209,000	15,000	8,000	18,000	
Depreciation	50,000	38,000	12,000			
Communications						
Voice	22,000					22,000
Data	2,000					2,000
Facility						
Occupancy	376,000	24,000	136,000	18,000	8,000	190,000
Furniture & Equipment	47,000					47,000
Other						
Supplies						
General	64,000					64,000
Printer	265,000			265,000		
Tape	65,000				65,000	
Disk						
Outside Services	105,000					105,000
Miscellaneous	81,000					81,000
Total	$6,130,000	$2,311,000	$891,000	$494,000	$740,000	$1,694,000

of supplies that should be identified in this allocation are printer paper, tapes, and toner and developer for laser printers.

The third complicated operations area is software. In today's environment, much of the software used by financial institutions (as well as in other industries) is purchased or leased.

This arrangement produces depreciation and maintenance expenses or lease expenses, which can be allocated to the resource unit pools by placing the expenses in one of three categories:

- Software directly assignable to a user or an operational area. This includes expenses such as the cost of a purchased application system (e.g., commercial loan accounting) that can be directly allocated to a loan processing area. Such expenses are *excluded* from computer operations costs.

- Software associated with a specific resource unit. This includes expenses such as the cost of tape librarian software, which could be directly allocated to the tape pool.

- Other software. This software, which includes data base management software, compilers, and operating systems, is most easy allocated to the CPU resource unit pool because it cannot be directly allocated to any other user or resource unit.

As mentioned earlier, the allocation of expenses for each organizational unit can be represented as a series of spreadsheets. Combining all of the columns from the individual spreadsheets makes it possible to determine the total pool of expenses associated with each resource unit. This is illustrated in Figure 9-4.

There also is a pool of general expenses that must be reassigned to the resource unit expense pools. For the sake of consistency, this allocation can be accomplished in a manner similar to that used for other general expense allocations. If computer operations costing is the first or only cost accounting being performed, these overhead expenses can be reallocated to the resource units on the basis of the percentage of other expenses directly allocated to a resource pool. The results of this allocation are shown in Figure 9-5 and are rounded for simplification.

Step 4—Development of Resource Unit Volumes

Several questions remain regarding the expenses being allocated. For example, are the expenses monthly or annual? Are they actual, historical, or budgeted? Answers to such questions are determined by the cost accounting philosophy to which the insti-

Figure 9-5—Resource Pool Expense Allocation (Including General Reallocation)

	Total Expense	CPU	Disk	Print	Tape	General
Salaries and Benefits	$1,398,000	$ 423,000	$	$ 76,000	$ 121,000	$ 778,000
Hardware						
Rent	1,750,000	722,000	600,000	58,000	370,000	
Maintenance	500,000	158,000	113,000	45,000	84,000	100,000
Depreciation	855,000	449,000	15,000	12,000	74,000	305,000
Software						
Rent	300,000	288,000		12,000		
Maintenance	250,000	209,000	15,000	8,000	18,000	
Depreciation	50,000	38,000	12,000			
Communications						
Voice	22,000					22,000
Data	2,000					2,000
Facility						
Occupancy	376,000	24,000	136,000	18,000	8,000	190,000
Furniture and Equipment	47,000					47,000
Other						
Supplies						
General	64,000					64,000
Printer	265,000			265,000		
Tape	65,000				65,000	
Disk						
Outside Services	105,000					105,000
Miscellaneous	81,000					81,000
Total	$6,130,000	$2,311,000	$ 891,000	$494,000	$ 740,000	$1,694,000
Percent of Total less General		52%	20%	11%	17%	
Reallocation of General		882,514	340,251	188,647	282,588	1,694,000
Total including General	$6,130,000	$3,193,514	$1,231,251	$682,647	$1,022,588	

tution subscribes. Steps 1–3 of the allocation process have not had to distinguish between costing methodologies, but in this step the development of resource unit volumes varies according to which of several costing approaches is employed.

Under one commonly used method—full absorption costing—the expenses used would be the actual expenses incurred for a certain time period. For example, if monthly full absorption were used, the current month's expenses would be allocated as described earlier. The total expense pool then would be divided by the actual resource unit usage for the same time period, in this example the month's actual resource usage. As with any full absorption costing technique, this procedure can lead to variations in the calculated cost because of period-to-period fluctuations in either the expenses or the resource usage.

Another common method of developing costs is to develop the expected cost (also called "average" or "budgeted" cost). This technique will be used in the following examples and discussions. In this method, the expenses for the total year's budgeted expenses and the expected resource usage for the budget year are used to develop a "standard" cost for each resource unit. This method smoothes the fluctuations from period to period and retains the advantage of full cost absorption since costs are absorbed by actual usage. This method is only as accurate as the expense budget and the projection of resource use. However, tools to help analyze and project both costs and usage have improved over the last several years, which has greatly increased the accuracy of both the cost and usage forecasts.

Many attempts have been made to determine usage based on a "theoretical capacity" model. This method has been generally discarded since it is greatly impacted by improvements in hardware, operating system technology, and variations in resource usage. A much more widely accepted method is to collect information on usage patterns over the last several years and to project the usage trends for the coming budget year.

This approach begins with analyzing historical resource usage data and normalizing the data for the effects of newer faster processors. An example can be seen in Figure 9-6.

Figure 9-6—Historical Resource Usage Data (in millions of seconds)

	FY90	FY91	FY92	FY93	FY94	FY Forecast
Recoverable CPU seconds	21.7	16.9	21.6	24.5	28.2	
Processor MIPS at FY start	100	150	150	150	300	
Normalized CPU seconds	21.7	25.4	32.4	36.8	42.3	

Figure 9-6 points out a couple of important concepts. Gathering information on recoverable costs is not as simple as identifying which processes serve users and which jobs are necessary to operate the data center, though this is a very important step. The chart points out that the effect of different processors is great and must be taken into account.

While a resource unit may be defined simply, the actual capacity of the unit can vary based on the specific equipment. For example, if CPU Model A is twice as fast as Model B, then a second on Model A can produce twice as much work as it can on Model B. If this fact were not incorporated in the development of a standard resource unit, there would only be a single cost for a "second" of CPU. All users then would want to process on Model A since it would take fewer seconds and therefore cost less than Model B.

To make this concept even more difficult, a CPU could be made twice as fast by one of two techniques, (A) doubling the speed of processor engine, or (B) doubling the number of processor engines. Either way, more work can be accomplished, but the method chosen has a dramatic impact on the amount of work accomplished in a CPU second. In Case A, a CPU delivers twice as much work (i.e., only half as many CPU seconds will be necessary to do the same amount of work). However, in Case B there is no change in the amount of work done in a CPU second. Rather, the number of available CPU seconds doubles.

Referring to Figure 9-6, the CPU upgrade in FY91 was a Case A type of upgrade, where the new CPU was 50 percent faster than the prior model. The CPU upgrade in FY94 was a Case B upgrade, where an additional processor engine doubled the number of available CPU seconds.

Based on the examples used and Figure 9-7, which was developed using available trending tools, the forecasted recoverable CPU seconds should be 48,500,000. Other resource units such as disk, tape, and print are much more straightforward. For example, DP should be able to manage disk storage at a 90 percent utilization level (900,000 out of every million bytes installed are actually used). If a total of 150 gigabytes (i.e., 150,000,000,000 bytes of storage) of disk were installed, then 120 gigabytes of disk storage would be available.

Step 5—Calculation of Resource Unit Costs

The next step in developing computer operations costs is dividing the resource expense pools determined in Steps 1–3 by the resource unit volumes determined in Step 4. Using the full absorption technique, this process normally would be completed by a cost accounting system that automatically allocates the period's expenses to the pools and then divides the pools by the resource unit usage. Using either the expected

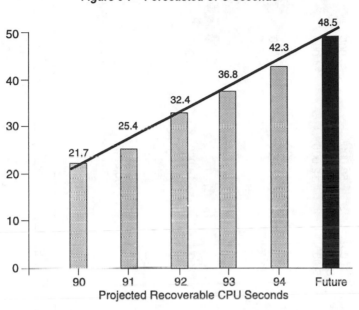

Figure 9-7—Forecasted CPU Seconds

Projected Recoverable CPU Seconds

or the standard cost method, this step typically would be performed by an analyst. The calculation for the example is shown in Figure 9-8.

Step 6—Reallocation of Costs

Although Step 5 appears to complete the process of developing computer operations costs, an additional step is required, especially for the development of standard costs. Certain resources are used by the operations organization itself in the normal operation of the system. Examples include disk space used by the system, CPU usage by systems and programming, and tape mounts for back-up files. This usage can be accounted for with a cross-allocation method that works as follows:

- The number of resource units used internally is extended by the costs determined in Step 5 to arrive at an expense to transfer from one resource to another.

- That expense is transferred.

- The volume used in the first calculation is removed from the original expense pool.

- Costs are recalculated after all expense pools are adjusted appropriately.

Figure 9-8—Standard Cost Calculation

	Total Expense	CPU	Disk	Print	Tape	General
Salaries and Benefits	$1,398,000	$ 423,000	$	$ 76,000	$ 121,000	$ 778,000
Hardware						
Rent	1,750,000	722,000	600,000	58,000	370,000	
Maintenance	500,000	158,000	113,000	45,000	84,000	100,000
Depreciation	855,000	449,000	15,000	12,000	74,000	305,000
Software						
Rent	300,000	288,000		12,000		
Maintenance	250,000	209,000	15,000	8,000	18,000	
Depreciation	50,000	38,000	12,000			
Communications						
Voice	22,000					22,000
Data	2,000					2,000
Facility						
Occupancy	376,000	24,000	136,000	18,000	8,000	190,000
Furniture & Equipment	47,000					47,000
Other						
Supplies						
General	64,000					64,000
Printer	265,000			265,000		
Tape	65,000				65,000	
Disk						
Outside Services	105,000					105,000
Miscellaneous	81,000					81,000
Total	$6,130,000	$ 2,311,000	$ 891,000	$ 494,000	$ 740,000	$1,694,000
Percent of Total less General		52%	20%	11%	17%	
Reallocation of General		882,514	340,251	188,647	282,588	1,694,000
A) Total including General	$6,130,000	$ 3,193,514	$ 1,231,251	$ 682,647	$1,022,588	
B) Usable Capacity		48,500,000	540,000,000,000	25,000,000	420,000	
A/B = Cost per Unit		.06585	.1900078900	.02731	2.43473	
Unit label		$/CPU sec	$/mbyte month	$/page	$/tape mount	

Figure 9-9 illustrates the principles used to remove and reallocate the costs associated with providing computer operations services.

COST ALLOCATION IN A NON-MAINFRAME ENVIRONMENT

The principles discussed in this chapter are focused primarily on cost allocation strategies in a mainframe environment. Dealing with non-mainframe environments frequently requires different strategies and techniques. Some of the non-mainframe platforms (such as some UNIX platforms or IBM's OS/400) have sufficiently robust accounting data to support the techniques discussed earlier in this chapter. However, many operating systems do not supply sufficiently detailed accounting data to support a usage based cost recovery system. Most network operating systems like Novell and personal operating systems like DOS or Apple System 7 do not keep the necessary detailed accounting data.

Several good alternative strategies to usage based cost allocations exist. Probably the most common method is user based chargeback. In this simple technique, all costs associated with a platform are accumulated and divided by the number of users. This is a particularly good technique for personal computing platforms where a machine is dedicated to each user and unused capacity is not usable by others.

Another more equitable and sophisticated technique is performance based user chargeback. This is similar to the user based chargeback above, but a higher charge is associated machines offering higher performance. For example, a loaded 486 PC might cost $350 per month while an older and slower 386 might cost only $200. This strategy may help extend the useful life of older technology. Inevitably, some users do not need the higher performance, particularly if they have to pay for it. Without price differentiation nearly every user will want the "latest, greatest, and fastest" system.

An interesting situation arises when dealing with truly infrastructure services such as LAN connectivity and file servers. In most cases this is best handled as a G&A overhead charge. In concept, this is similar to phone wiring and PBX costs. Rarely are these costs recovered directly by most businesses. However, some charges related to infrastructure services are appropriate to directly charge users, such as moves, adds, and changes. Charging controllable costs to users on a time and material basis encourages each business unit to use such services judiciously.

Figure 9-9—Reallocation of Computer Operations Costs

	CPU	Disk	Print	Tape
Total expense after general reallocation (A)	$3,193,514	$1,231,251	$682,647	$1,022,588
Usable units (B)	48,500,000	540,000,000,000	25,000,000	420,000
Cost per unit (C)	$0.06585	$0.19001	$0.02731	$2.43473
Units used by DP (D)	12,125,000	108,000,000,000	1,750,000	252,000
Cost after transfers (E=C×D)	$798,379	$246,250	$47,785	$613,553
Total Cost (F=A+E)	$3,991,893	$1,477,501	$730,432	$1,636,141
Usable capacity (G=B−D)	36,375,000	432,000,000,000	23,250,000	168,000
Cost per unit after transfers (F/G)	$0.10974	$0.28501	$0.03142	$9.73893
Unit label	$/CPU sec	$/mbyte month	$/page	$/tape mount

COMPUTER OPERATIONS COSTS ALLOCATION SUMMARY

The techniques presented in this chapter will yield recovery of all associated costs presented in the discussion as long as the budget and resource usage projections are accurate. However, in the real world this never really happens. Something unexpected always seems to occur. When it does, the recovered costs will not exactly zero out the computer operations costs.

There are several ways to deal with this situation. One way to address the variance is to ignore it if it is immaterial. Another method is to take the variance and add it to the allocated G&A account so that all areas share in the difference equitably. Probably the most common technique is to allocate the variance to each department based on their total contribution to the computer operations budget. Any of these techniques can be used to ensure that all operations costs are allocated to the remaining business units.

VARIATIONS ON COMPUTER OPERATIONS COSTING

In the last few years, several variations to the above cost recovery methodology have become popular. The variations fall into four major categories:

- Modifying pricing to help balance usage

- Adjusting pricing to cause better resource usage

- Service level adjustment

- Volume discounts

The first variation is used by the telephone companies. They offer substantial discounts to encourage people to use the phone during off periods. This technique has worked well and helped the phone companies lower their overall cost per unit by charging more for prime time usage. Computer operations costs are similar to those experienced by the phone companies, in that prime time usage drives cost, and very little additional cost is incurred to supply nonprime resources.

The second variation has been frequently used by electric and water utilities. Essentially they offer a rebate to users who install more efficient appliances. In the end, the utility company saves money by extending the useful life of equipment or by reducing repair/service costs. As an example, operations costs might be lower for tape cartridges than reel tape, as cartridges take less storage space and support greater automation.

The third variation deals with service levels. The best example of this is the overnight courier and mail service industry. Pricing is varied by the required service level, far beyond the actual cost impact of providing higher levels of service. Very high service levels cost many times what lower service levels cost. A letter by overnight air courier might cost $10.00, while second day might cost $5.00, next week might cost $.29. The premium collected for very high service levels helps to offset the cost of lower service levels. Operations costs can be modified in a similar manner. Examples include higher prices for express jobs, or high priority online services.

The final variation is offering volume discounts. We are all familiar with this model, but its applicability in computer operations costing may not be obvious. Economies of scale are significant in computer operations. If an operations organization services departments of widely varying resource consumption with a fixed standard cost, the big resource user will not gain the appropriate economies of scale. This has resulted in many departments starting their own operations units and the outsourcing of computer operations services. Both of these later techniques appropriately assign economies of scale to the proper users.

Use of these techniques is often worthwhile in very large and diverse organizations as the variations will tend to cause better equity in the allocation of costs, which in the long run usually results in more satisfied users. In small organizations, the cost of implementing these variations may be greater than the benefits gained. Whether a company is large or small, these variations should be evaluated and implemented based on a strong cost/benefit analysis.

DEVELOPING SYSTEMS AND PROGRAMMING COSTS

Systems and programming costs are developed according to the same approach used for computer operations costs. Once the costs applicable to systems and programming have been consolidated, a resource unit must be selected and a capacity determined for it.

The most common resource unit chosen for systems and programming is an hour of programming service. Since the basic skills and expertise of the programmers are the resources being utilized, an hour is a natural resource unit. Furthermore, like the units chosen in our computer operations example, an hour is a unit that users can readily understand. It should be noted, however, that while users understand this unit, they frequently do not comprehend the number of those units required to perform a task. This lack of understanding frequently leads to criticism of the credibility of the costs charged to users, but the validity of hours as a resource unit remains unquestionable.

The usable capacity of programming hours is determined through a methodology similar to that used for computer operations. Figure 9-10 illustrates a typical calculation of the capacity for programming hours. There, theoretical capacity is calculated using a full work year of 52 weeks (five days per week). Total nonchargeable time (analogous to downtime for the CPU) is then calculated for the average programmer; it usually reflects vacations, holidays, estimated sick days, administrative time, and education required to maintain technical skills. This time is deducted from the theoretical capacity to arrive at a usable capacity for the average programmer.

An analysis of the S&P staff is then performed to identify managers and clerical personnel who would not be expected to charge time. The total number of programmers is multiplied by the capacity for the average programmer. To arrive at the total capacity of chargeable hours, the result is added to an estimate for contract (outside) programming hours. This total capacity is divided into the total systems and programming expense budget to arrive at the cost per hour. Figure 9-11 illustrates the process.

Figure 9-11 uses just one resource unit, the programmer hour, but it is possible to have multiple resource units in the systems and programming area. Known by such terms as "analyst hour" or "senior programmer analyst hour," these units normally

---

Figure 9-10—Systems and Programming—Chargeable Hours Calculation

Theoretical		
Hours/Day	8	
Multiplied by Days/Week	× 5	
Hours/Week	40	
Multiplied by Available Weeks	× 52	
Theoretical Hours		2,080
Less:		
Holidays	(11)	
Sick Days	(2)	
Vacation	(15)	
Education	(10)	
Administrative	(8)	
Total Nonchargeable Days	(46)	
Multiplied by Hours/Day	× 8	
Total Unavailable Hours		(368)
Net Chargeable Hours per Average Programmer		1,712

Figure 9-11—Systems and Programming—Hourly Rate Calculation

Staff Analysts (Number of Individuals)	
Managers	8
Programmers	56
Administrative	4
Total	68
Total Chargeable Hours	
Programmers	56
Multiplied by Net Chargeable Hours/Programmer	
	1,712
Chargeable Hours (in-house)	95,872
Add Contract Programmer Hours	5,000
Total Chargeable Hours	100,872
Total Labor Budget	2,815,151
Total Chargeable Hours	100,872
Cost per Hour	$27.91

---

reflect the experience or skill level of specific programmers. Should an institution decide to develop these multiple resource unit costs, it would follow the single unit technique described earlier. All S&P expenses, however, would first have to be allocated to resource unit expense pools (similar to the process described in Step 3 of the development of computer operations costs).

DEVELOPING NETWORK COMPUTING COSTS

Network computing costs are developed using the same basic approach used for computer operations. Consolidating network computing costs is not a straight forward task. Costs typically will consist of a combination of hardware, software, personnel and external services and can be found in departmental, business and central IT units. Although it may be tempting to focus only on the costs within central IT units, this can lead to a situation of large "hidden computing costs" within an organization. In order for management to make effective decisions about managing information technology, it is highly desirable for the total cost of network computing to be identified, irrespective of organizational unit.

Network computing depends on an underlying technical "infrastructure" to function effectively. This technical infrastructure consists of hardware (network hubs, wiring, servers), software (network operating systems, productivity applications, network management software) and people to implement and maintain the hardware and software. Just as the national highway system is an infrastructure that has maintenance costs, so too does the network computing technical infrastructure. These infrastructure costs are identified separately from discretionary costs and potentially may require separate cost allocation methods. The most common cost driver selected is a per desktop or per user charge, assuming that all users have access to a similar set of network computing services, or a tiered pricing structure if different classes of service are available. Other issues should be considered, such as line charges, maintenance requirements, and customization.

As in the case with system and programming charges, a lack of understanding of the technical infrastructure support requirements frequently leads to criticism of the costs and the service providers. However, only by fully identifying network computing costs and adopting a standard resource unit—such as cost per desktop that allows comparisons with industry benchmarks—can management make informed decisions to manage the technology cost effectively.

In addition to fixed infrastructure costs, certain network computing activities are project-related and performed for the benefit of a specific user department. This may include an office relocation, a new network implementation, or a hardware or software upgrade. In these cases, the time in hours of the support personnel is an appropriate resource unit. The calculation of the standard cost per hour of technical support personnel is calculated in the same way as for systems and programming. However, certain technical resources may divide their time between project activities and infrastructure support activities, in which case all network computing expenses must first be allocated to appropriate resource unit expense pools. Activity based costing techniques (Chapter 8, Activity Based Costing) can be used in the allocation of time and costs to support processes. These processes or combinations of processes will define the appropriate expense pools.

DATA COLLECTION REQUIREMENTS

Up to now, the development of IT costs has been examined from a technical point of view. The costs, though informative, are useful only when associated with activities that can be managed or matched with revenue to provide some type of profitability information. Questions left unanswered by the costs alone are: "How much did we spend to develop the cash management system?" and "How much does it cost to support the branch network?" The answers require data regarding the usage of the resource units chosen as the allocation basis.

JOB ACCOUNTING SYSTEMS

The collection of resource usage information for the computer operations function typically is accomplished through a job accounting system. Such a system is usually capable of collecting data (such as CPU seconds used or pages printed) for each job that the system processes. By establishing standards for job names and accounting conventions, it is possible to collect virtually any data necessary. The actual selection of job accounting standards is beyond the scope of this chapter, but an illustration can be made of representative job accounting system conventions used to develop management information related to computer operations.

Suppose an institution wishes to monitor operations expenses on several levels. First, it would want to differentiate between operational or production costs, and development costs. It also would want to identify costs associated with the non-routine or casual use of the system. Such use might include the creation of one-time use programs or the development and production of special analyses. Furthermore, the institution would want to know how much it costs to support broad categories of products or organizations such as the branch system, installment loans, or commercial loans. To develop this information, it would need to collect resource usage data according to the costs it wishes to see. It therefore would establish job accounting system conventions such as the following for its computer operations unit:

- All names of operational jobs will begin with the letter "Z," all development job names will begin with "T," and all casual use will have a job name beginning with "X." This enables the institution to differentiate between the three types of work being run on the system.

- The second through fourth letters of all operational job names will be coded to indicate their relation to a certain type of processing. For example, all jobs associated with installment loan processing will have "ILS" as the second through fourth letters of their job names, and all jobs related to commercial loan processing will have "CLS" as their second through fourth letters. This enables the institution to collect information related to major processing groups.

- All jobs will require "accounting information" that contains the number of the unit that is responsible for the particular job. This enables the institution to charge the cost of the job to a responsibility center in its cost accounting system.

If conventions were established in this way, the job accounting system would collect data according to job names and the accounting information. (A simplified version of the output from such a job accounting system is shown in Figure 9-12.) The data could then be sorted and the computer operations costs developed previously could be used to determine various types of costs, as shown in Figures 9-12 through 9-15.

PROJECT CONTROL SYSTEMS

Just as computer operations relies on job accounting systems to collect resource usage information, the systems and programming area requires a method to capture data regarding programming hours and use of resources. Generally, this requirement is satisfied by a project control system.

The typical project control system collects programming hours by individual project (e.g., the development of a new cash management system). To accomplish this,

Figure 9-12—Job Accounting Output

Job Name	Cost Center	CPU Seconds	Disk	Tape Mounts	Pages Printed
ZILS123	5970	1200	20	0	5000
ZCLS123	5810	1450	100	22	450
ZDDA123	4960	1390	30	1	720
ZILS124	5970	2450	500	2	500
ZCLS124	5810	150	40	0	10000
ZCLS125	5810	980	90	0	3500
ZDDA124	4960	3790	75	0	80
ZDDA125	4960	5815	60	2	875
TDDA567	3210	250	80	1	5000
TCLS567	3310	850	50	4	500
TDDA567	3410	1200	500	2	780
TILS989	5970	1600	80	0	900
XFIN234	2340	550	90	0	1000
XFIN235	2340	900	125	0	5000

Figure 9-13—Job Accounting—Responsibility Center Cost: Center 2340

Job Name	Cost Center	CPU Seconds	Disk	Tape Mounts	Pages Printed	Total Cost
SFIN234	2340	550	90	–	1000	
SFIN235	2340	900	125	–	5000	
Total		1450	215	–	6000	
Cost/Unit		$0.10974	$0.28501	$9.739	$0.03142	
Cost		$ 159.13	$ 61.28	–	$ 188.50	$ 408.90
TDDA567	3210	250	80	1	5000	
TCLS567	3310	850	50	4	500	
TDDA567	3410	1200	500	2	780	
ZDDA123	4960	1390	30	1	720	
ZDDA124	4960	3790	75	0	80	
ZDDA125	4960	5815	60	2	875	
ZCLS123	5810	1450	100	22	450	
ZCLS124	5810	150	40	0	10000	
ZCLS125	5810	980	90	0	3500	
ZILS123	5970	1200	20	0	5000	
ZILS124	5970	2450	500	2	500	
TILS989	5970	1600	80	0	900	

each project is given a unique project number, against which programmers record time. Project numbers also can be incorporated into the "accounting information" required by job accounting systems to collect computer operations resource usage by project as well. Data collectively captured by the project control and job accounting systems can enable management to track and monitor all costs associated with each project number. Figure 9-16 shows an example of how this step could be accomplished.

Developing Product Costs

One of the major objectives of any cost accounting system should be to develop product costs. This objective holds especially true for IT services, since it is a function involved with virtually every product. The costs developed in preceding sections of this chapter are technically oriented (e.g., cost per CPU second), but those costs, along with the information provided by job accounting and project control systems, form the foundation for developing the IT component of product costs.

Figure 9-14—Job Accounting Processing Costs—Development Costs

Job Name	Cost Center	CPU Seconds	Disk	Tape Mounts	Pages Printed	Total Cost
TCLS567	3310	850	50	4	500	
TDDA567	3210	250	80	1	5000	
TDDA567	3410	1200	500	2	780	
TILS989	5970	1600	80	0	900	
Total		3900	710	7	7180	
Cost/Unit		$0.10974	$0.28501	$9.739	$0.03142	
Cost		$ 428.00	$ 202.36	$68.17	$ 225.57	$ 924.10
XFIN234	2340	550	90	0	1000	
XFIN235	2340	900	125	0	5000	
ZCLS123	5810	1450	100	22	450	
ZCLS124	5810	150	40	0	10000	
ZCLS125	5810	980	90	0	3500	
ZDDA123	4960	1390	30	1	720	
ZDDA124	4960	3790	75	0	80	
ZDDA125	4960	5815	60	2	875	
ZILS123	5970	1200	20	0	5000	
ZILS124	5970	2450	500	2	500	

If an institution established the job-naming conventions discussed in the preceding section, its job accounting system would collect data very much like the data shown in Figure 9-12. As Figure 9-16 illustrates, the same data then could be extended to determine the operational costs of a major application system.

If each such system were concurrently established in the project control system as a separate project number, the institution could combine the costs of systems and programming with those shown in Figure 9-16. To accomplish this, however, separate projects would have to be established for the maintenance and development for the system.

The combination of the three costs—computer operations, systems and programming, and networking computing, if applicable—in effect establishes a cost pool for the system. This pool can be divided by an appropriate product volume to determine the IT component of the respective product cost (see Figure 9-17).

A word of caution is necessary, however, concerning the selection of the appropriate product cost. While it may be desirable to obtain information technology costs on a very detailed basis, such as the computer operations cost of processing a loan

Figure 9-15—Total—Job Accounting—
Computer Operations Product Cost: CLS Costs

Job Name	Cost Center	CPU Seconds	Disk	Tape Mounts	Pages Printed	Total Cost
TCLS567	3310	850	50	4	500	
ZCLS123	5810	1450	100	22	450	
ZCLS124	5810	150	40	0	10000	
ZCLS125	5810	980	90	0	3500	
Total		3430	280	26	14450	
Cost/Unit		$0.10974	$0.28501	$ 9.739	$0.03142	
Cost		$ 376.42	$ 79.80	$253.21	$ 454.02	$1,163.45
TDDA567	3210	250	80	1	5000	
TDDA567	3410	1200	500	2	780	
ZDDA123	4960	1390	30	1	720	
ZDDA124	4960	3790	75	0	80	
ZDDA125	4960	5815	60	2	875	
XFIN234	2340	550	90	0	1000	
XFIN235	2340	900	125	0	5000	
TILS989	5970	1600	80	0	900	
ZILS123	5970	1200	20	0	5000	
ZILS124	5970	2450	500	2	500	

payment, it would require equally detailed project numbers in the project control and job accounting systems. Furthermore, most job accounting systems do not readily lend themselves to differentiating the specific function of a job. For example, if the cost of processing a loan were desired, only jobs that processed loan payments could be included in the cost, and all such jobs would have to be included in the cost. Since computer jobs typically perform multiple functions, this segregation is usually not feasible in job accounting systems. It is therefore normally acceptable to use a general product volume, such as the number of loans outstanding, to determine the product cost.

SYNOPSIS

Developing good cost accounting information, whether on a technical or a product-oriented basis, is no more difficult for information technology than it is for any other area of an institution. Several aspects of this function require special attention, but

Figure 9-16—Consolidated Job Accounting/Project Control—Total Information Technology Cost: Commercial Loan System

Job Name	Project Number	Cost Center	CPU Seconds	Disk Tracks	Tape Mounts	Pages Printed	Programmer Hours	Totals
TDDA567	D567	3410	1200	500	2	780		
TILS989	D678	5970	1600	80	0	900	120	
TDDA567	D987	3210	250	80	1	5000	340	
XFIN234	D999	2340	550	90	0	1000	40	
XFIN235	D999	2340	900	125	0	5000	40	
ZDDA125	M123	4960	5815	60	2	875		
ZDDA124	M123	4960	3790	75	0	80	500	
ZDDA123	M123	4960	1390	30	1	720	70	
ZCLS124	M345	5810	150	40	0	10000	45	
ZCLS123	M345	5810	1450	100	22	450	50	
ZCLS125	M345	5810	980	90	0	3500	120	
TCLS567	M345	3310	850	50	4	500	700	
Total			3430	280	26	14450	915	
Cost per Unit			$0.10974	S0.28501	$9.73893	$0.03142	$ 27.91	
Cost			$ 376.42	S 79.80	$ 253.21	$ 454.02	$25,537.65	$26,701.10
ZILS124	M567	5970	2450	500	2	500		
ZILS123	M567	5970	1200	20	0	10000	10	

Figure 9-17—Consolidated Job Accounting/Project Control—Information Technology—Unit Cost

Job Name	Project Number	Cost Center	CPU Seconds	Disk Tracks	Tape Mounts	Pages Printed	Programmer Hours	Totals
TDDA567	D56?	3410	1200	500	2	780		
TILS989	D678	5970	1600	80	0	900	120	
TDDA567	D987	3210	250	80	1	5000	340	
XFIN234	D999	2340	550	90	0	1000	40	
XFIN235	D999	2340	900	125	0	5000	40	
ZDDA125	M123	4960	5815	60	2	875		
ZDDA124	M123	4960	3790	75	0	80	500	
ZDDA123	M123	4960	1390	30	1	720	70	
ZCLS124	M345	5810	150	40	0	10000	45	
ZCLS123	M345	5810	1450	100	22	450	50	
ZCLS125	M345	5810	980	90	0	3500	120	
TCLS567	M345	3310	850	50	4	500	700	
Total			3430	280	26	14450	915	
Cost per Unit			$0.10974	$0.28501	$9.73893	$0.03142	$ 27.91	
Cost			$ 376.42	$ 79.80	$ 253.21	$ 454.02	$25,537.65	$26,701.10
Loans Outstanding								21,450
Product Unit Cost (cost per loan)								$ 1.2448
ZILS124	M567	5970	2450	500	2	500		
ZILS123	M567	5970	1200	20	0	10000	10	

the same costing techniques can be used for IT as are used throughout the organization.

Just as the techniques are the same, so too are the management issues. The institution must choose the appropriate compromise between accuracy and understandability of detail, as well as between level of detail and cost of developing that detail. Once those decisions are made, management must commit itself to the implementation and maintenance of an automated job accounting system and a project control system. Unlike other areas of the institution, there is no way to collect the data necessary for IT cost development without such systems.

However, once these steps have been taken, the IT function no longer need be the mysterious technical area it seems, and useful cost information for this function can be developed.

CHAPTER 10

Transfer Pricing of Funds

OVERVIEW

Funds-transfer pricing represents a series of management-accounting mechanisms that measure the value of opportunity costs of funds provided and used. If, in a manufacturing setting, materials costs are part of the profit and loss statement, funding costs in a banking setting are analogous to "cost of goods sold" (at least for asset-based products). Properly setting funds-transfer prices is important to accurately determining the profitability of business units, products, customers, etc. Also, the effects of funds-transfer pricing can represent the most material part of the income statement.

Funds-transfer pricing is closely related to a bank's overall asset/liability management (ALM) approach. Indeed, understanding how the various components of the balance sheet interact is essential to both transfer pricing and ALM. A well-designed funds-transfer pricing system can help banks identify, price, and manage interest-rate risk, create proper incentives for business unit behavior, and capture the effects of interest-rate shifts in a central funding unit.

By shifting interest rate risk to the funding unit, the funds-transfer pricing system focuses line managers' performance on fundamental business decisions (including credit risk), leaving rate speculation to the professional interest-rate risk managers. This concept of separating interest-rate risk from credit risk is one of the key objectives of the funds-transfer pricing process.

A number of general principles have evolved to guide design of funds-transfer pricing mechanisms, including which balances should be priced and how they should be priced. Specific issues in funds-transfer pricing approaches are less well evolved. These include the level of disaggregation to which funds transfer pricing should be applied, and whether to charge for liquidity or conversion options.

With the basics evolving, the future holds greater sophistication in funds-transfer pricing. Valuation and pricing methods will become more accurate. Information technology will allow greater use of coterminous matched funding at ever-lower levels of detail on the balance sheet. Finally, better links between funds-transfer pricing, ALM, and performance measurement will be developed.

In this chapter, the objectives of funds-transfer pricing are outlined. Then, some general principles are provided that should serve as basic "rules of the road." Subsequently, a number of specific transfer pricing issues are addressed. The chapter closes with observations on the likely evolution of transfer pricing techniques in the future.

FUNDS-TRANSFER PRICING OBJECTIVES

One of the great conceptual advances in the evolution of bank profitability measurement was the disassociation of asset and liability pricing. That is, profitability measurement was made more useful and accurate when bankers stopped trying to link individual assets on the balance sheet with a particular liability on the other side. Instead, a central focal point (commonly referred to as funds management or treasury) was created to act as a sort of clearinghouse for internal funds pricing.

Of course, besides serving profitability measurement needs, funds-transfer pricing is an integral element of asset/liability management. Although the ALM process is not within the scope of this book, it provides a contextual framework for many of the transfer pricing practices described in this chapter.

Ultimately, the objective of transfer pricing is the proper valuation of the provision or use of funds by the bank's organizations, products, segments, customers, etc., which are the subjects of profitability measurement. Funds-transfer pricing is a set of management accounting conventions and practices. It is not driven by GAAP or RAP.[1] Given its importance to the institution, numerous objectives may exist:

- Identifying the cost or opportunity value of funds to the institution.

- Facilitating the profitability measurement of various components (branches, products, customer, accounts) of the institution by relating appropriate costs to revenues.

- Isolating interest-rate risk from the business units and capturing it in a separate reporting unit.

---

1   However, where international funding transactions occur, which involve different tax jurisdictions, regulatory considerations may exist. Cross-border transfer pricing regulations could color the specific approaches used for these transactions.

- Enhancing asset and liability pricing decisions.

- Supporting asset/liability management and separating credit risk from interest-rate risk.

- Quantifying the net interest income impact of gap funding.

- Evaluating each component of the institution in a manner consistent with its economic impact on total earnings.

- Using funds-transfer pricing to set a course of action for employees whose activities are measured by financial reports.

It is difficult, if not impossible, to establish a transfer pricing mechanism that accomplishes all possible objectives, but it is critical to consider the most important objectives simultaneously. Different mechanisms encourage different behavior by an organization's managers; the mechanism selected therefore must seek to elicit the behavior desired. It is important that management remain cognizant of these behavioral ramifications. A fundamental proposition is that the transfer pricing system should reflect the true opportunity costs associated with funds provision and usage.

Figure 10-1 is an overview of the funds-transfer pricing process. Essentially, a central funding center "buys" funds from the parts of the bank that generate liabilities, and "sells" them to asset-generating parts of the bank, which require funding. It buys and sells at rates commensurate with the repricing characteristics of the asset funded or liability "bought," thereby match funding each transaction. Excesses or shortages of funds are handled through funding center transactions with the market.

In this manner, the impact of interest-rate gap risk is theoretically centralized within the funding center, and credit risk is held within the business units. The asset

Figure 10-1—Overview of Funds Movement and Transfer Pricing

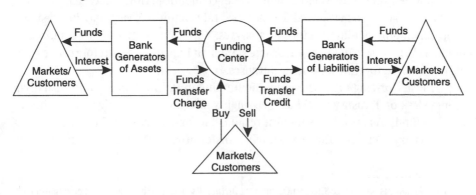

generators' net interest margin reflects the difference between the interest rates they charge to their customers on balances (less credit loss provision) and the funds-transfer price they pay to the funding center. The liability generators' net interest margin is, conversely, the difference between the interest rates they pay to their customers on balances, and the funds-transfer credit they receive from the funding center.

Funding-center net interest income reflects the net paid to and received from other bank units. It also reflects its transactions with market purchasers or providers of funds. These transactions do not necessarily perfectly offset the gap profit or loss inherent in the business units. Rather, the net result reflects the overall interest rate exposure the bank is willing to entertain, based on its expectation of future rate movements.

GENERAL PRINCIPLES

When designing a funds-transfer pricing approach, a number of basic "rules of the road" should be set in place. These should underlie the system; greater sophistication can be built on top of the foundation that they provide. A "transfer pricing manifesto" follows.

All balance-sheet items will be transfer priced. This means that all assets will receive funding charges and all liabilities and equity will receive funding credits. While seemingly straightforward, adopting this principle saves considerable debate. It sets the stage for an economically correct and useful performance measurement system.

GAAP will apply in the determination of the balances to be transfer priced. This principle simplifies the reconciliation of externally reported balances with internally used balances. It also short-circuits arguments about how to treat unrealized book value gains or losses: they exist if GAAP determines so. Of course, some institutions may view market values as more indicative of economic performance. And, for ALM purposes, changes in market value as interest rate conditions vary may increasingly supplement pure net interest income analyses. Yet, from a pure funding standpoint, nonbook balances do not have an income statement impact, and therefore can reasonably be ignored for transfer pricing purposes.[2]

Transfer pricing rates are set by the funding unit. The funding unit (usually a money desk or Treasury area) has the insights into the market values (opportunity costs) of funds. As a result, it should be responsible for determining the funds-transfer pricing charges/credits. However, funds-transfer pricing should be periodically re-

---

2   See the chapters on Balance Sheet and Capital for further discussion of book and market valuation.

viewed by the Asset/Liability Management Committee to see that they are properly determined.

Transfer pricing rates should protect the business areas from mismatch (i.e., gap risk). Gap risk should be centrally priced and managed by the funding unit. Business units should receive charges/credits that reflect the coterminous value of funds. Rates should be chosen from the transfer pricing yield curve to match the repricing duration of the assets being charged or liabilities being credited.

The funding unit will publish its funds-transfer pricing yield curve. Items booked on the balance sheet during the period covered by the yield curve will be priced using the rate corresponding to their repricing duration.

Various methods are used for deriving the funds-transfer pricing yield curves. Some banks use the Treasury (risk-free) yield curve plus a premium representing market and institution risk. Others use the swaps yield curve as a surrogate for a market-determined cost of borrowing. Conceptually, these approaches all attempt to quantify the bank's cost of buying and selling funds on the open market.

Pricing of funds used and provided should be as close to a true maturity (i.e., repricing and duration) match at the margin as possible. It should reflect the yield curve and rates obtained by the bank in the market. Using nonbank-specific reference rates sends improper pricing signals. It also obscures understanding the true opportunity costs to the bank of generating assets and liabilities.

Some banks book internal receivables and payables between business units and the funding center, in order to make the business unit balance sheets indeed balance. They then transfer price these receivables/payables to determine the aggregate charges or credits to a business unit. This approach is not recommended, as it precludes a more sophisticated pricing of classes of assets and liabilities based on repricing durations.

Further, business unit (i.e., profit center) earnings are "dividended" to the corporate center. They are not a funding source. There are no retained earnings in the business unit. The portion of business-unit funding represented by equity should be determined by the corporate capital allocation formulae. (This is discussed below as "funds value of capital" and in the section of Chapter 12 dealing with capital and its allocation.) Equity allocated to a business should, however, receive a funds-transfer pricing credit.

As much as possible, arbitrage opportunities should be removed from the system. That is, business units should avoid intrabank transactions, such as self-funding, that seek to bypass the funding center and escape the transfer pricing mechanisms. Further, business units should avoid disguising interest-rate risks in order to receive preferable funds-transfer credits. These actions destroy the integrity of the system and fail to provide the management tools to truly capture interest-rate risk.

SPECIFIC ISSUES

Most questions on the specifics of such a system can be answered with reference to the broad principles. That said, many specific questions exist. In fact, for each asset or liability on the balance sheet, it is likely that a considerable discussion on the proper transfer price could take place between the business unit responsible for it and the funding unit.

Repricing Characteristics

A problem to be avoided is to confuse the life of an asset with its repricing characteristics. For example, if an asset is expected to stay on the books for one year, it is tempting to transfer price it at a one-year rate. However, if the asset reprices on a monthly basis, transfer charging it at one-year rates would be in error. Determining the length of time certain categories of nonearning assets (e.g., cash) and "free" liabilities (e.g., demand deposits) will be on the balance sheet is important for transfer price determination.

Matched Funding

Advances in information technology have made it possible to identify and "match fund" individual assets and liabilities as they are booked. That is, each individual account receives a specific transfer rate based on the account type and such specific characteristics as duration and repricing points. However, for performance measurement purposes, it may be necessary in the case of certain classes of assets or liabilities to transfer price entire balances, such as cash or receivables.

Further, some assets and liabilities may reprice in maturity bands for which little interest rate distinction exists. As a simple example, a three-week rate may differ very little from a four-week rate. Trying to maintain a true "matched funded" system may not be worth the expense. As a result, many banks group assets and liabilities into separate "pools" with similar repricing characteristics.[3] The pools usually are for specific time periods (e.g., overnight, up to one month, one to three months, three months to a year, one to two years, two to five years, and over five years). Transfer charges and credits are driven by the pool with which the asset or liability is associated.

Core Deposits

Determining the proper transfer credit for such interest-free liabilities as compensating balances or demand deposit accounts poses problems. How long will the liability

---

3   The transfer pricing approach should mirror that used for ALM purposes.

be present on the balance sheet? What factors affect its volatility? Usually such questions are in the province of ALM. However, they have important profitability measurement implications as well.[4]

With respect to *core* deposits, the preferred practice is to determine the proportion of the balance in each line item (e.g., retail DDA, corporate DDA, and savings) that is stable over time. By using statistical models and evaluating the balance behavior over time and under varying interest rate conditions, the percentage of the balances that remain under most likely rate scenarios receives the longest-term funding credit. The remainder of the *noncore* balance is distributed across the pools as indicated by the modeling analysis.

Break Funding

"Break funding" occurs when a premature prepayment/redemption of an asset or liability takes place. The transfer price originally used differs from the one that would have been used had the actual maturity been known. For large-volume assets and liabilities, the statistically driven approach described above can determine what proportion of the balances is likely to be prematurely redeemed, and adjust the transfer pricing accordingly.

However, for larger-value instruments or transactions, deal-specific break funding arrangements should be established between the originating business unit and the funding center. These arrangements usually are incorporated into contractual agreements with the customer, as well.

Liquidity

The issue of liquidity is separate from funds-transfer pricing in its strictest sense. Recall that funds-transfer pricing deals with properly assigning credits or charges related to the repricing and maturity of balances with respect to interest rates. Liquidity relates to the manner in which balances contribute to or detract from a bank's ability to resolve claims (e.g., withdrawals by depositors or drawdowns on lines of credit).

However, because liquidity charges or credits are associated with different types of balances, and reflect a way of assigning a value to consumption and provision of a resource (similar to the way that transfer pricing assigns a value to funds) it is logically dealt with in this chapter. Further, because liquidity is a key element of ALM, it has another relation to funds transfer pricing, which also is an integral part of the bank's ALM process.

---

4 See, for example, Jeanne L. Warner and Jill M. D'Allesandro, "Funds Transfer Pricing for Retail Deposits." *Bank Accounting & Finance*, v.5, n.4, Summer 1992, pp. 22–32.

Specifically, how is liquidity provided or consumed? Consider core deposits, which provide stable funding under a variety of interest-rate conditions. The bank does not need to maintain high levels of liquid assets to redeem such balances beyond cash required for normal transaction, maturation, and withdrawal purposes. As a net result, core deposits provide liquidity.

On the other hand, loans, leases, and commitments consume liquidity. They require funds for drawdowns on lines. They also (in general) are not readily saleable in the market.

Certain assets, such as cash and short-term investments, are held in large measure to redeem expected and unexpected claims. Such "liquidity assets" are in essence an insurance policy against the volatility of other balances. If not for the volatility of other funding sources and the illiquidity of other assets, the bank would not hold the liquid assets in the quantities required for insurance purposes.

With respect to liquidity charges, the general principle that was articulated for transfer pricing on which balances to use does not hold. That is, while for transfer pricing purposes only GAAP on-balance sheet amounts are transfer priced, liquidity charges or credits can be assigned to off-balance sheet items. An obvious example are commitments to lend or consume liquidity, in that the bank may need to fund the commitment at a moment's notice.

Securitized receivables, if they may return to the balance sheet after a period of time, also could require a liquidity charge. Liquidity premium can be thought of in two ways. The first is to consider the opportunity costs of holding more liquid (hence lower yielding) assets to meet claims, and allocating the opportunity cost among consumers of liquidity. Concomitantly, the providers of liquidity would receive a credit which represents the value of not having to use other liquidity vehicles in their place.

A second method is to look to the market for a value of liquidity. For example, on-balance sheet assets, as demonstrated above, consume liquidity. Determining the yield differential between a liquidity consuming balance sheet asset and an off-balance sheet item with similar characteristics (e.g., a swap) could provide an estimated market value for liquidity.

Over recent years, liquidity has not been as dear as in some historical periods. Banks have used liquidity rates of six to 12 basis points, which is a relatively low price. However, as the size of a bank's balance sheet increases, the absolute dollar value associated with liquidity, even at six to 12 basis points, can be significant. Further, in the future, prices for liquidity may increase.

As a result, banks should consider building liquidity credit and charging capabilities into their performance measurement systems.

LOOKING INTO THE FUTURE

Banks have widely accepted and adopted the basics of funds-transfer pricing: rationales, principles, and mechanisms. Looking into the future, additional refinements will likely be put in place to build on the existing foundation. Areas that will see continued enhancements are disaggregated matched funding, pricing/valuation, and linkages to other systems, particularly other balance-sheet modeling systems.

As previously discussed, individual matched funding of assets when they are booked at their marginal opportunity costs provides the benefits of precision and timeliness. Yet the difficulty and expense of maintaining a system which does so for all balance-sheet items, particularly high-value retail accounts, historically have made this challenging.

However, such information technology capabilities as relational databases and client-server (integrated processing) are rapidly improving. These advances in technology will allow ever more refined transfer pricing to take place, especially in matched funding.

Further, advances in financial theory and practice will provide greater sophistication and rigor in valuing opportunity costs and transfer pricing balances. While this will be especially true of hedge pricing and embedded option charges, transfer pricing more traditional balances also will be improved. For example, using institution-specific swaps yield curves will provide better information on the true opportunity costs at the margin against which asset and liability transactions should be assessed.

Finally, greater integration among banks' various transaction, performance, planning and measurement, and risk management systems will take place. Transfer pricing will play an integral role in most of them. The greater degree of integration will provide more consistent information across multiple dimensions of measurement and decision making. It also will better enable planning at strategic (e.g., the business or balance sheet) and tactical (e.g., transaction pricing) levels.

SYNOPSIS

Funds-transfer pricing is an essential element of any performance measurement and profitability system. The signals sent to managers regarding the opportunity costs of booking assets and liabilities are powerful. Care must be taken to insure that proper (i.e., shareholder value enhancing) transfer prices are set.

As such, funding credits and charges should as closely as possible represent the marginal costs and benefits the institution faces. When combined with effective ALM processes and systems, this can create a high-performing and controlled net interest income margin.

PART III

Balance Sheet Components of Performance Measurement

CHAPTER 11

Balance Sheet Components of Performance Measurement

OVERVIEW

The financial performance of any financial institution is largely determined by the behavior of its balance sheet. The balance sheet is a wonder of dynamism and inertia. How assets and liabilities perform individually and in combination is critical.

Measurement of institution-wide profitability, and of the profitability of the institution's component parts, as driven by the balance sheet, is the focus of this section. The section contains two chapters. The first addresses allocation of balance sheet items, and conceptual and practical issues associated with balance-sheet performance measurement. The second deals exclusively with the allocation of a single balance sheet element: equity, or in common usage, capital.

How banks handle off-balance sheet items (e.g., swaps, commitments and options) is of increasing importance. Special reference will be made to off-balance sheet concerns at appropriate points.

Asset/liability management (ALM), the process by which institutions manage the interest rate and liquidity risks they face, will not be discussed in this section. Of course, the ALM process is intrinsically linked to performance and performance measurement. However, ALM is an especially complex and detailed topic in its own right, and one for which numerous other references exist.[1] Therefore, we have excluded it from the scope of this book.

---

1   See, for example, Pratt, Robert B., *Controlling Interest Rate Risk*, John Wiley & Sons, Inc., NY, 1986, 414 pp.

The balance sheet is a portrayal of the asset and liability accounts of a financial institution at a given point in time. In large measure, the behavior of such accounts—and increasingly of off-balance sheet items—drives the institution's performance. This chapter addresses issues related to the valuation of various on- and off-balance sheet items and their allocation or attribution to specific measurement units in support of organizational or product profitability. Funds transfer pricing and capital allocation are dealt with in separate chapters.

Similar issues exist with respect to the balance sheet as are presented by income and expense items. For example:

- When should deviations from generally accepted accounting principles (GAAP) be allowed in the determination of account values and balances?

- How should balance sheet accounts that result from shared or joint activities be attributed to individual measurement units?

- How deeply should the balance sheet be disaggregated for performance measurement purposes?

The answers to these questions are functions of the institution's management philosophy. This chapter discusses the issues associated with such questions so that each institution will be better able to decide which approach will work best for it.

Balance Sheet Management and Performance Measurement

Traditionally, an institution's Treasury function manages the balance sheet. That is, Treasury usually manages the funding components of the balance sheet, drives asset securitization strategies, and positions the institution with respect to interest rate movements, among other activities. These generally fall under the rubric of the institution's overall asset and liability management (ALM) process.

Of course, the way in which Treasury manages the institution's funding sources, securitization activities, and investment portfolio can greatly affect bank profitability. Further, balance sheet management and performance measurement are linked through funds transfer pricing mechanisms.

WHAT VALUE SHOULD BE USED?

A threshold issue is how the institution's balance sheet accounts should be valued. For most accounts, GAAP values are appropriate. However, GAAP treatment may not be appropriate under certain circumstances for specific accounts. In such cases, institutions may want to use other values, such as market value.

For example, accounts for which GAAP values are approximate or equal to market values (e.g., Cash, Due From, and Fed Funds) pose no problem. GAAP treatment does not lead to any distortion in results. However, GAAP value may not equal, and in fact may be substantially different from, market value for such asset accounts as Investment Securities Owned, Mortgage Servicing Rights and Premises, and such liability accounts as Long-Term Debt–Fixed Rate. Such GAAP versus market value differences in the portrayal of the balance sheet could cause distortions in performance measurement.

Of course, the distortion is not caused by funds-transfer pricing variations: only GAAP balances need to be funded. Instead, the distortion is caused by inaccuracies in period-to-period changes in value. GAAP values—typically historical-cost based—may not vary much from period to period. However, market values may fluctuate a great deal. Using GAAP masks such fluctuations.

Currently, few institutions use market values instead of GAAP for internal performance measurement purposes. Market values are more closely linked to external measures of performance (e.g., share prices) than are accounting values. Further, market values are increasingly being emphasized in financial and regulatory accounting pronouncements and interpretations, particularly for the items for which "fair value" can readily be determined. As a result, institutions will increase their use of market values for balance sheet and off-balance sheet items in the future.

ASSIGNMENT OF BALANCES

On the surface, the assignment of management responsibility for assets and liabilities, particularly loans and deposits, seems relatively straightforward. After all, every loan can be associated with an organizational unit such as a branch or line of business (for organizational profitability), with a customer (for customer profitability), or with a particular product (for product profitability). The same can be said of deposits.

However, as in the cases of revenue and expense, balance sheet assignments to organizations, products, and customers become less straightforward when several conditions exist, either individually or collectively:

- The balance sheet account spans multiple organizations, products, or customers.

- The balance sheet account includes amounts that are the result of actions taken by organizational units other than the unit that "owns" the account.

- The balance sheet account is held by a corporate or overhead unit.

- The balance sheet account balance is the result of a decision made by a previous management team.

In reality, although the direct assignment of assets and liabilities is in fact feasible in some cases, the multiple uses of profitability information frequently cause conflicts in this process. The assignment grows even more complicated when profitability information is used to measure managerial performance. Conflicts arise because many assets and liabilities are generated, serviced, or affected by more than one functional or organizational area. As a result, more than one area might claim a particular asset or liability if it improves the area's measured profitability, or deny responsibility if it detracts from that profitability.

Similarly, as in the thorny issue of allocating shared revenues and expenses among organizational units, no one method for attributing balance sheet items is appropriate for all institutions. The key is to select a method that:

- Sends correct signals and encourages managerial behavior that is aligned with the bank's strategy.

- Is consistent with allocation and attribution methodologies used for other purposes (e.g., revenue, expense, or capital assignment).

- Is relatively easy and inexpensive to administer.

A hypothetical case—a credit card business in a bank—illustrates some of the problems associated with balance sheet allocation when numerous organizations are involved in marketing and operations. The example has been simplified to make some of the points clear.

The credit card business usually consists of two distinct functions: the extension of retail credit to cardholders, and the processing of credit transactions from merchants. These two functions generally require the involvement of several organizational areas.

Branches may solicit potential cardholders and initially process credit card applications, or at a minimum serve as the normal depository and collection point for merchant deposits of the credit card slips. The back-office operations area (referred to here as "central credit card operations") probably is responsible for processing the credit slips. Finally, there is the commercial calling officer's relationship with the merchant.

Given this interaction of organizational areas, the question becomes how to assign credit card outstanding for various profitability measurement purposes.

From a product profitability perspective, the answer is that all of the assets, liabilities, revenues, and expenses should flow to a common endpoint: the product profitability statement. If we assume that two separate products have been defined— retail credit card for the credit portion and merchant processing for the commercial side—then the assignment of assets and the related revenues and expenses would be shown in Figure 11-1.

(Any associated deposits created by merchant processing are assumed to be in a product other than the two shown in this figure.) As shown in Figure 11-1, operating expenses flow to both products. However, the retail credit card product is credited with income from retail loans, while merchant processing is credited with revenues from fees.

Because products here are defined independently of organizational areas, product profitability can be determined separately from organizational profitability. As a result, there are no flows between organizations for product profitability.

In the credit card example, the product manager could use the resulting product profitability reports with little or no argument from either the branch manager or the commercial lending officer regarding the assignment of assets, liabilities, revenues, and expenses. This situation exists in a product-driven or matrix organization.

But in a functional organization the issue is more complicated. Here the asset, liability, revenue, and expense flows must cross from one organization area to another. The profitability reported for each area's manager is affected, and there may well be a considerable difference of opinion among these managers regarding which area should receive credit for which activity.

Typically, the branch manager believes that because he or she has established the relationship with the retail customer, he or she should receive credit for profits from

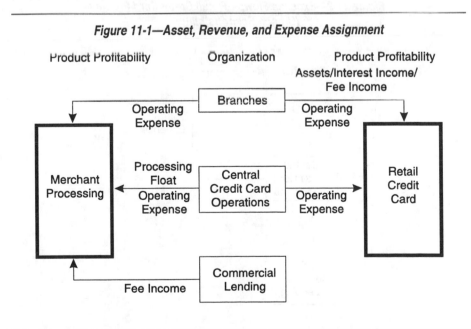

Figure 11-1—Asset, Revenue, and Expense Assignment

the retail credit card product. But the central credit card operations manager claims that because the relationship was established as part of a centralized solicitation, he or she should receive credit. Each argument is valid.

The key to solving this assignment problem is not case-by-case arbitration of the managers' arguments. With that approach, managers spend productive time resolving arguments instead of developing and using the profitability information.

Rather, the solution should differ depending on the institution's structure and the manager's basic responsibilities. If the branch is considered a profit center and the assigned responsibility of the branch manager is to profitably manage all retail relationships within a given geographic area, all profits from the retail credit card product in that area should be assigned to the branch. Assets, interest income, and operating expenses should flow from central credit card operations to the branch, as illustrated in Figure 11-2. (Figure 11-2 assumes that assets, interest income, and a portion of operating expenses already reside at the branch.)

If, on the other hand, the branch is viewed as part of the delivery system, and the responsibility for the retail credit card product is assigned to central credit card operations (as a substitute for a product manager), the situation is reversed. The branch should be a support organization for credit card operations. Central credit card operations should be the profit center to which assets and interest income for the credit card loans are assigned; expenses for processing cash advances and payments

---

**Figure 11-2—Expense Flows—Retail Credit Card Product
(Branch Responsibility)**

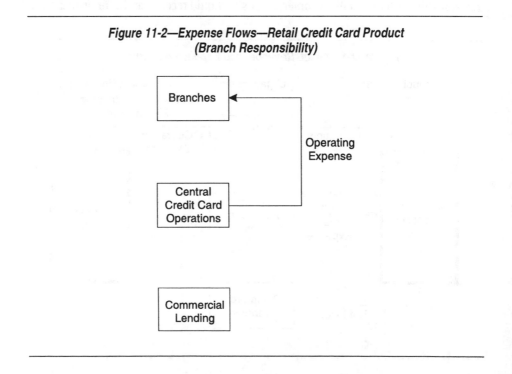

taken at the branch should be transferred to it. Figure 11-3 illustrates the flow under this arrangement.

RESPONSIBILITY ASSIGNMENT AND PERFORMANCE MEASUREMENT

In the credit card example, the development of profitability information rests with the assignment of responsibility. Concurrent with that assignment, the appropriate performance measurement of the managers involved must be carefully considered. Financial institutions frequently devote extensive resources to developing profitability information, only to find that divergent incentives have been created, producing organizational conflicts. Continuing with the credit card example helps to illustrate how this problem occurs. Figure 11-3 shows that assets for the retail credit card product have been assigned to central credit card operations. Presumably those assets are reported in the profitability measurement of the operations manager. His objective is to increase the profitability of the product, and his success can be directly measured by a product profitability statement. Thus the development of profitability

Figure 11-3—Expense Flows—Retail Credit Card Product
(Central Credit Card Operations Responsibility)

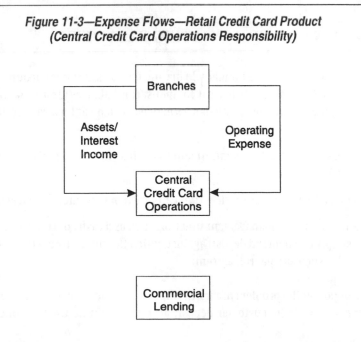

information has solved the responsibility issue for this manager. However, it has created an organizational conflict involving the branch manager.

The branch is an important element of the retail credit card product. It takes applications, processes payments, and so forth. Clearly, the central credit card operations manager needs the support of the branch manager to improve retail credit card profitability. In this case, however, the branch manager has little incentive to provide that support.

If the branch is considered a profit center for other items, it receives no profit from the retail credit card product. Instead, retail credit card profit is reported under central credit card operations. The branch nevertheless incurs the additional expenses associated with servicing the retail credit card product. If, on the other hand, the branch were considered a distribution system, its performance would be measured in part by the amount of its expenses. Any increased support the branch provides to the retail credit card product would probably cause these expenses to rise.

In either case, the branch manager has no incentive to support the institution's objective of increasing credit card volume and profitability. Nor has he or she any reason to support the central credit card operations manager in the objective of increasing the profitability of the retail credit card product. Clearly, the performance measurement for the branch manager must recognize this support role; otherwise, a critical link in the product strategy is weakened.

ASSIGNMENT OF COMPENSATING BALANCES

The same problem holds true for many loans and deposits, but it is encountered most frequently in determining how to treat compensating balances for profitability measurement purposes. Compensating balances may be on deposit for a variety of reasons, including:

- As part of a contractual commitment to the institution related to a loan (credit-related).

- In lieu of fees paid for services (typically cash-management services).

- As part of a cash-management function such as a cash concentration account, or simply as a demand deposit against which the corporate customer can write checks, such as a payroll account.

To compound the problem of identifying the specific purpose of the compensating balances, any single customer deposit account might be used for one or more reasons. More important, the institution may choose, for marketing reasons, to treat all of a company's deposit accounts as compensating balances even if separate deposit accounts exist. As a result, developing profitability information normally involves a single compensating balance that can be assigned to a variety of uses.

For customer and organizational profitability, the assignment of compensating balances typically does not present much of a problem. The balances belong to a customer, and their assignment for customer profitability purposes is based on the "ownership" of the accounts. By extension, if responsibility for each customer is clearly assigned either to a branch or to a calling officer, then the balances can automatically be assigned to the branch or calling officer organization responsible for that customer.

For product profitability, however, the assignment of compensating balances can dramatically affect the reported profitability. If, for example, the balances are required by contractual credit arrangements for loans, they should be assigned to the loan products; otherwise, the calculation of yield and spread will be inaccurate. Figure 11-4 shows the different results that can be arrived at by the assignment—or lack of assignment—of these balances.

In the loan situation shown in Figure 11-4, the requirement of compensating balances increases the institution's income. Alternatively, if the compensating balances are used in lieu of fees for noncredit services, earnings on the compensating

---

Figure 11-4—Comparative Loan Profitability Calculations (for a $100,000 Loan)

	With Compensating Balance		Without Compensating Balance	
Interest Income @ 10%		$10,000		$10,000
Average Loan Balance	$100,000		$100,000	
Compensating Balance @ 10% of Average Loan Balance	(10,000)		–	
Amount Funded	$ 90,000		$100,000	
Cost of Funds @ 8%		7,200		8,000
Net Interest Income		$ 2,800		$ 2,000
Yield—Interest Income ÷ Amount Funded	11.1%		10%	
Spread—Net Interest Income ÷ Amount Funded	3.1%		2.%	

balances become the primary revenue source for the noncredit products. Therefore, earnings on compensating balances must be accurately included in profitability measurement information.

Financial institutions rely on three basic methods of assigning compensating balances. The first method assumes that because compensating balances are common balances maintained for all uses, they should be distributed proportionately to products that have a claim on them. Any surplus or deficit balance is then distributed in the same proportion as the rest of the balance. Figure 11-5 shows how this process works.

This method has two major shortcomings. First, it does not recognize any contractual commitment related to loans. Assume, for example, that the contractual commitment called for a credit-related compensating balance of $10,000. If the compensating balances were deficient and the assignment method prorated only $50,000 to loans, the yield and return calculations for the loans would be misleading. They would make it appear as if reduced compensating balances were included in the loan-profitability measurement.

Second, this method disregards the typical commercial bank organization, in which the cash-management product manager and the calling officer are in different organizational units. Normally, the calling officer would be responsible for collecting

Figure 11-5—Compensating Balances —Proportional Distribution

	Required Compensating Balances	Percent of Total Required Compensating Balances	Allocation of Availabale Compensating Balances*
Loans			
Contractual Balances	$100,000	50%	$ 75,000
Fee Services			
Cash Management	40,000	20	30,000
Trust Services	10,000	5	7,500
Security Services	50,000	25	37,500
Total	$200,000	100%	$150,000

* Percent of Total Required Compensating Balances multiplied by available compensating balance of $150,000.

the compensating balances. If there were a deficit of $50,000 in those balances, the profitability of the cash-management products would be affected by the calling officer's failure to perform the collection. In either instance, the misleading information could induce management to make the wrong decision.

An alternative to the proportional method of assigning compensating balances is to determine a priority sequence for the application of the balances. For instance, the institution might decide that balances first would be applied to contractual agreements for loans, then to cash-management services. This method seems logical and simple, but it requires detailed decisions. For example, assigning first priority to loan agreements is insufficient; the decision must also specify the priority of loans. Similarly, the cash-management services must be specified at a level of detail consistent with the level of product profitability desired.

This second assignment method addresses some of the shortcomings of the first, but it merely shifts the location of deficient balances. The first method proportionately allocates the deficiency across all products, while the second concentrates the deficiency in products of lowest priority. Consequently, the profitability statements for those products can be misleading. In addition, both methods have the same problem of assigning responsibility. The profitability of certain products (for the second method, the cash-management products) is the responsibility of one manager—the product manager. But another manager—the calling officer—collects the compensating balances and controls the profitability measurement of the products.

A third method of assigning compensating balances uses a technique that isolates the collection of the compensating balances from the reported product profitability. Under this method, any compensating balances for contractual-credit arrangements are transferred first to the credit product. Using the example of a $10,000 compensating balance for a loan, the amount available for compensating balances would be reduced by $10,000. That amount would be considered a funding source for the loan.

This first step eliminates the potential for a misstated yield or return calculation. It ensures that the compensating balance is associated with the loan or credit. In the second step, the compensating balances are treated as a profit center, and all noncredit services that use compensating balances, such as cash management services, are considered services that support it. Under this step, the fees that should be collected— the volume of services times the fee per service—are assigned as income to the cash management services. The same fees are changed as an expense to the compensating balances. The collection of compensating balances is therefore isolated from the reported profitability of the cash management services.

This method has the ultimate effect of treating compensating balances as a separate product. It also removes the balances required for credit products, regardless of whether the balances have been collected. Likewise, the income of the cash management fees is attributed to the related area regardless of whether balances have been collected. Combined, these actions can produce negative balances or a reported loss, or both.

Negative balances are caused by the removal of balances for credit products and the reported loss by the expenses of the cash management fees. In either case, the reported profitability of demand deposits would indicate whether sufficient balances are being collected. Just as important, if the responsibility for the demand deposits were assigned to the calling officer, the control of collections would match the

Figure 11-6—Example of Compensating Balances Treatment

	Loan Profitability	Demand Deposit Profitability		Cash Management Profitability
Interest Income	$ 10,000			
Interest Expense	—			
Transfer Credit/(Charge) for Funds @ 8%	(7,200)	$ 7,200		
Net Interest Income	2,800	7,200		
Other Income			Step 2:	$4,000
			Compensating Cash Management	
Operating Expenses	(1,000)	(3,000)		(2,000)
		(4,000)		
Operating Income	$ 1,800	$ 200		$2,000
Outstanding Balance				
• Assets	$100,000			
• Liabilities		$100,000		
• Transferred Balances	$ 10,000	$ (10,000)		
		Step 1: Loan Compensating Balances		

reported profitability of those collections. Figure 11-6 illustrates the third method of assigning compensating balances.

ASSIGNMENT OF CORPORATE DEMAND DEPOSIT BALANCES

Another frequently encountered assignment issue involves corporate demand deposit balances. Often these deposits are accounted for in branch offices. In those cases, the earnings on the balances are generally used as compensation for branch services provided in support of the corporate customer, such as payroll-check cashing, deposit acceptance, and cash handling. This cost accounting treatment causes problems for profitability measurement, for the following reasons:

- Development of a profitability figure for the institution's corporate business segment correctly requires inclusion of corporate demand deposit balances. When assigned to the branches, the balances may initially be aligned with the retail business. If so, they must be realigned.

- From a branch manager's perspective, any measurement that includes corporate demand deposits entails a function that he or she does not control. In many cases, the branch manager's reported profitability then is dependent on the actions of the corporate calling officer. This situation violates the premise that a manager should be assigned responsibility only for balance sheet components he or she controls.

For these two reasons, branches normally do not receive credit for corporate demand deposits. Accepted though it may be, this practice can create a counterproductive situation similar to that of the branch manager in the retail credit card example. Specifically, if corporate demand deposits do not provide earnings for the branch, there is no incentive for the branch manager to provide service to owners of those deposits; it would produce expense without any corresponding benefit or earnings.

Motivating the branch manager to service these accounts without assigning corporate demand deposit balances to the branch can be accomplished in one of two ways: by transferring the cost of servicing the corporate demand deposit by the branch, or by using shadow income or shared income techniques. This situation further reinforces the idea that profitability measurement alone cannot measure all aspects of the branch manager's performance. Therefore, other measures probably will be needed.

ASSIGNMENT OF WORKOUT LOANS

Workout loans represent a third balance sheet component of profitability measurement that comes under the general category of assigning responsibility. Although workout loans are defined differently from institution to institution, as a generic asset group they may include nonperforming loans, loans past due, and loans that fail to meet the letter of the loan agreements but still are considered current.

Assignment of workout loans rests with the issue of who is responsible for them. If the responsibility lies with the originator of the loans—the calling officer—their assignment is handled the same as for any other loan. Once they are assigned, their workout status is automatically incorporated in the profitability measurement because the asset is assigned, but little or no interest income is associated with these loans, thereby reducing the reported profitability. Any operating or recovery expenses also would be assigned to the originator, as would any actual recoveries.

Many institutions, however, have decided that responsibility for workout loans should be assigned to a group of workout specialists. This step is taken for a variety of reasons, but most often the institution expects better long-term results. Furthermore, with responsibility assigned to a workout group, lending officers can concentrate on developing new accounts and managing existing business. Regardless of the reason, once the institution assigns responsibility for workout loans to a specialist, a series of issues arise with respect to the profitability measurement concerns involved. For example:

- Should the asset be transferred to the workout division, or should it continue to be assigned to the area that originated the loan?

- Who should be assigned responsibility for operating or other expenses incurred in attempts to recover the value of the underlying assets, if any?

- Who should receive the benefit of any recovery?

As an example, assume that a commercial bank has a $10 million dollar credit with a past-due status. The decision has been made to classify the loan and to assign it to a "special credits" workout division. (The same situation arises if the special credits division is part of the credit policy or credit review area of the bank.) At the time of the transfer, the loan was secured by a building (which was then acquired by foreclosure) with a market value of $8 million, resulting in a $2 million charge-off.

Figure 11-7—Workout Loans—Special Credits Division as a Profit Center

	Year 1	Year 2	Total
Charge for Funds ($8,000,000 × 10%)	$ (800,000)	$ (800,000)	$(1,600,000)
Operating Costs	(500,000)	(500,000)	(1,000,000)
Gain on Sale ($10 Million Sale – $8 Million Asset)	–	2,000,000	2,000,000
Total Profit/Loss	$(1,300,000)	$ 700,000	$ (600,000)

Figure 11-8—Workout Loans—with Reassignment to Originator

	Year 1	Year 2	Total
Charge for Funds ($8,000,000 × 10%)	$ (800,000)	$ (800,000)	$(1,600,000)
Step 1 — Operating Costs	(500,000)	(500,000)	(1,000,000)
Gain on Sale ($10 Million Sale - $8 Million Asset)	—	2,000,000	2,000,000
Total Profit/Loss	$(1,300,000)	$ 700,000	$ (600,000)
Step 1 — Reassigned to Originator	$(1,300,000)	$ 700,000	$ (600,000)

The bank then operates the building for two years, at a total cost of $1 million, and eventually sells it for $10 million.

The issues surrounding the treatment of these profitability components adhere to the same basic principles used for assigning other balance sheet components. In this case, the special credits division can be a cost center or a profit center.

If the division is viewed as a profit center, the loan is considered completely removed as far as the originator is concerned, and the profitability measurement of the special credits division is determined by its related resources. Under this approach, the division assumes responsibility for the $8 million current value of the credit, and pays any funding costs for that current value. The $2 million charge-off is treated in a manner consistent with other charge-offs. The special credits division also incurs all operating and recovery expenses for the property, and receives credit for any actual recovery. The division's profitability statement under this approach is shown in Figure 11-7.

If the special credits division is considered a cost center, the same principles are followed as a first step. A consolidated report on the state of the workout loans and the effectiveness of the division is generated by comparing the expenses versus the recoveries. However, as a second step, the net recovery for the workout loans is reassigned to the originator, as shown in Figure 11-8.

Because the profit-center approach assigns the responsibility of the workout to the special credits division, not to the originator, it normally is the preferred method when an institution wants to restrict the originator's profitability measurement to ongoing business. The profit-center approach also proves useful in situations where large workout loans can have a dramatic effect on reported profitability. The cost-center approach is preferable if management wishes to incorporate all business factors—past and present—into the profitability measurement of the originator.

A variation of the profit-center and cost-center concepts can provide the benefits of both methods. Separate profit/cost centers can be established for the originating source of the special credit. This step makes it possible to assign the responsibility for workout loans to the special credits division (typically through hierarchy tables on a reporting system). It also provides a source of the credit. The profit/loss for workout loans is then included as a footnote or memorandum item in the originating source's profitability report.

ASSIGNMENT OF INTEREST PAYABLES AND INTEREST RECEIVABLES

Interest payables and interest receivables are two other balance sheet components that require a management decision on responsibility assignment. Historically, these items had little bearing on an institution's profitability. However, as interest margins narrowed, these items began to affect profit dramatically. Their assignment is a pervasive management issue.

Assigning these two balance sheet items should follow the assignment procedure used for underlying interest-earning assets or interest-bearing liabilities. The accrued interest receivable for a loan, for example, should be assigned to the same organization, product, or customer as the loan itself. This is an appropriate way of assigning these assets and liabilities, and has the added attraction of creating management incentives for profit improvement.

The typical commercial loan provides an example of this procedure. The interest receivable represents the interest income accrued on the loan but not yet received from the customer. Assuming the loan is current, the resulting receivable is a direct function of the loan's payment structure. Only a negligible interest receivable results if the interest is paid monthly. However, if interest accrues monthly—as it does for financial reporting—and is paid quarterly or annually, the receivable accumulates.

Such accumulation creates an asset that, like the loan itself, must be funded. More important, the receivable is an asset that requires capital to meet capital-adequacy regulations. If the receivable is assigned and included in the profitability measurement, then the lending officer is held accountable for funding the asset. He or she probably would structure the loan to keep the receivable as low as possible, or to reflect the funding cost of the receivable in the interest charged.

Although it is desirable to base the assignment of the receivable in the underlying asset or payable on the underlying liability, most data-processing systems in financial institutions are incapable of maintaining interest receivables and interest payables at the level of detail necessary for profitability measurement. The measurement of customer profitability, for example, requires the commercial loan and deposit systems to maintain the receivables and payables at the loan or deposit account level. Even if this maintenance were possible, many institutions would not be willing to track and maintain the data at this level for fear of the extensive processing requirements that would result.

An approximation method often is used to overcome these difficulties. This method bases distribution of the receivables on the interest income or interest expense assigned to a particular profitability measurement statement. For example, if the loan interest for a certain category of commercial loans represented 1 percent of total loan interest income, then 1 percent of the total interest receivable would be assigned to that category of commercial loans. A weighted allocation also may be used. For instance, because international loans are typically paid less frequently than domestic loans, different weights may be appropriate for each.

While the approximation method is far from accurate, it does serve the useful purpose of bringing to management's attention the issue of interest payables and interest receivables and their effects on profitability.

ASSIGNMENT OF FEES RECEIVABLE

Fees receivable (excluding loan fees) is a balance sheet component that resembles interest receivables and interest payables. Like the interest receivables, historically it has had little impact on institutional profitability. With the increasing emphasis on generating fee income, however, fees receivable are assuming greater importance throughout the financial-services industry.

Fees receivable could be directly assigned in the same way as underlying fee services. For example, fees receivable for a testamentary-trust service could be associated with the testamentary-trust product. But special care must be taken under this methodology with respect to fees for cash management services. If compensating balances are treated as profit centers the fees receivable also should be associated with the compensating balances, not with the cash-management services. The general rule is to assign responsibility for fees receivable to the area responsible for collection. Following this rule, cash-management fees would be assigned to the lending officer, because he or she collects those fees (albeit in the form of balances).

This assignment method assumes that responsibility for fees collection can be tied to the same customer or product whose profitability is being measured. An alternative view is that the collection of fees is more a function of the way the particular fees are processed and collected than of the product or customer itself. For example, the billing and collection of fees for safe-deposit boxes is typically an accounting function rather than a safe-deposit box function. As an accounting function, the fees receivable are not assigned to safe-deposit-box profitability.

ASSIGNMENT OF FIXED ASSETS

Fixed assets are the final balance sheet component in the discussion of responsibility assignment. Assignment of these assets usually depends on three criteria:

- *Practicality*—It is unrealistic and far too expensive to track every fixed asset in the institution.

- *Measurement Objective*—The ultimate objective of the profitability measurement is a major determinant of how the fixed assets should be assigned.

- *Material*—It is unlikely that the precise assignment of the cost of a single piece of furniture, for example, will dramatically alter any profitability being measured.

In most cases, establishing a reasonable lower limit for the assignment of fixed assets is a practical way to meet these criteria. For example, every asset over $5,000 could be specifically assigned, and all assets under $5,000 could be assigned to a central responsibility center, typically within a division.

If this takes place within the operations division, then any responsibility center within that division is assigned the minor fixed assets of less than $5,000. The expense of tracking transfers of every minor fixed asset is thus avoided, diverting more resources to identifying and assigning specific responsibility to the fixed assets with a significant effect on profitability, such as computer and telecommunications equipment.

LOAN LOSS RESERVE AND
LOAN MIGRATION ANALYSIS[2]

A substantial shift in bank management thinking is occurring with respect to allocation of loan loss reserves. Historically, loan loss reserves were set primarily through a "top-down" method, and allocated out to business units or products using some type of broad method (e.g., proportionally to the loan balances attributed to that unit). The new thinking employs a "bottom-up" approach, concurrent with managing the loan book as a portfolio.

The emerging method for determining the total loan loss reserve balance for the bank, and for measurement units, is the same one employed for determining the bank-wide provision (allowance for loan loss) and attributing it to organizations, products, and customers. It employs a technique known as "migration analysis" to build up required levels of provision and reserves.

A key principle of leading performance measurement approaches is to capture credit risk at the business-unit level. This requires that a consistent, objective methodology be developed and applied to determine loan loss provisions and reserves across all reporting units. Loan loss migration is a method which meets several important objectives:

- Reflect economic substance, be analytically sound and scientifically based.

- Withstand regulatory and financial accounting scrutiny.

- Provide for the determination of loan loss provisions and reserves across all discrete reporting units of the bank.

- Support shareholder value-based management reporting while recognizing the current state of technology.

Loan migration analysis accomplishes these goals. By framing the problem as an absorbing Markov chain, advanced mathematics can be used to calculate needed

---

2   This section draws from Meyer, Douglas, "Loan Migration Analysis, Expected Losses, and Adequacy of Reserves," *Bank Accounting and Finance*, Fall, 1994, v.8, n.1 (Institutional Investor, Inc., New York, NY).

provisions and reserves based on current and expected loan balances. The methodology is outlined below.

The Methodology

Step 1—Segregate the Portfolio

Loan migration analysis is the examination of groups of similarly classified loans to determine the level of credit losses. The first step in quantifying these expected credit losses is to disaggregate the loan portfolio by risk rating and understand how balances change from one period to the next.

For example, an institution may have $100 million in loans with a risk grade or rating of 3(RG3) in one quarter and $110 million next quarter. The net change of $10 million actually masks a wide range of movement, or migration, in the portfolio. Figure 11-9 illustrates the various movements which make up the net change:

- Increases in balances

- New Loans; new credit balances booked at risk rating 3

- Upward and downward migration; loans improving to risk rating 3 from lower classifications, or degrading to rating 3 from higher grades

- Decreases in balances

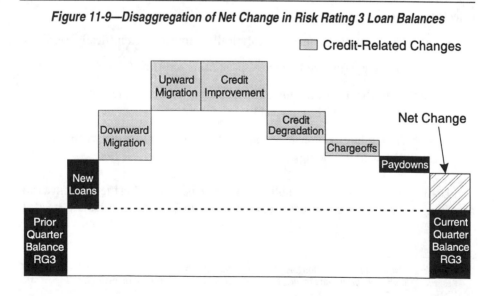

Figure 11-9—Disaggregation of Net Change in Risk Rating 3 Loan Balances

- Credit improvement and degradation; loans which were risk rating 3, which have improved to a higher classification or degraded to a lower one

- Pay downs; risk rating 3 balances that were paid off

- Chargeoffs; risk rating 3 balances that were written off

Step 2—Create the Transition Probability Matrix

Capturing the change in balances for each period is performed at least on a quarterly basis, and can be an automated process. Changes in loan balances are used to calculate probability vectors for each risk rating. Probability vectors are percentage estimates of how loans within a particular risk grade will migrate from an initial state (t_0) to a subsequent state (e.g., t_1).

For example, of the balances rated 3 last quarter, what percent remained on the books as risk rating 3, what percent improved to risk grades 1 and 2, what percent degraded to 4 and lower, what percent was paid off, and what percent was charged off? Figure 11-10 shows the probability vectors for the risk rating 3 loans of a hypothetical bank.

Probability vectors can be calculated from historical information, and should be periodically adjusted for changes in estimates resulting from current information.

The probability vectors for all risk classifications are assembled to a transition probability matrix. Figure 11-11 shows an illustrative transition probability matrix for an institution with 5 risk grades.

Step 3—Calculate Expected Losses

Given a particular transition probability matrix, it is mathematically possible to calculate expected losses. A Markov process is a system of potential outcomes of which the probability can be readily determined. If the loan portfolio changes each period in accordance with the transition probability matrix, how will the portfolio be affected when the number of transitions approaches infinity? A Markov chain is used to model the expected behavior of the current portfolio.

Figure 11-12 is a schematic illustration of a Markov chain using just 2 risk grades. Each period, a certain percentage of risk grade 1 balances remains the same, another portion degrades to risk rating 2, and the remainder either is paid off or is charged off. The same situation exists for risk grade 2 balances. Paid-off and charged-off balances are considered absorbing states. Because absorbed balances exit the system, each period the remaining loan balances become smaller and smaller. As the number of transitions approaches infinity, the loan balances approach zero.

The Markov chain analysis uses matrix algebra to calculate the total expected losses by risk rating. The end result of the calculation is the percentage of each initial balance paid off and the amount charged off, by risk grade. This latter figure—the total

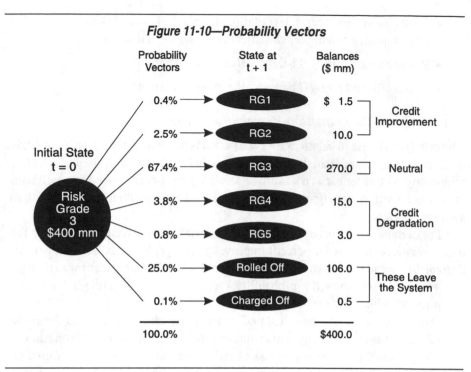

Figure 11-10—Probability Vectors

Probability Vectors	State at t + 1	Balances ($ mm)	
0.4% →	RG1	$ 1.5	Credit Improvement
2.5% →	RG2	10.0	
67.4% →	RG3	270.0	Neutral
3.8% →	RG4	15.0	Credit Degradation
0.8% →	RG5	3.0	
25.0% →	Rolled Off	106.0	These Leave the System
0.1% →	Charged Off	0.5	
100.0%		$400.0	

Initial State t = 0 — Risk Grade 3 $400 mm

Figure 11-11—Loan Transition Probability Matrix (%)

Risk Grade This Quarter

		1	2	3	4	5	Rolled Off	Charged Off
	1	65.0	8.8	0.3	0.0	0.0	25.8	0.0
	2	1.7	66.7	4.5	1.1	0.0	26.1	0.0
Risk Grade Last Quarter	3	0.4	2.5	67.5	3.8	0.8	25.0	0.1
	4	0.0	0.1	3.0	69.0	9.4	17.9	0.6
	5	0.0	0.0	0.3	2.3	89.5	4.3	3.8

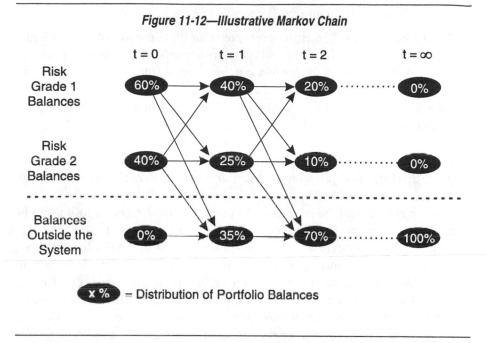

Figure 11-12—Illustrative Markov Chain

percentage of initial balance ultimately charged off—is the expected loss by risk grade.

Note that it is not necessary to have direct chargeoffs in a risk rating in order for there to be expected losses. The Markov chain calculates the amount that starts at a given level and ultimately degrades to the point at which loss occurs.

Step 4—Calculate the Required Provision

The required loan loss provision can be compared to an insurance premium that amortizes the cost of a loss over the period of time in which the loss can be expected to occur. The analysis provides the total expected loss over the life of the portfolio. In order to determine the pro rata periodic risk charge, it is necessary to know how long the current balances by risk grade will remain on the books.

Markov chain mathematics provides the answer. It is not the number of transitions until all balances are either charged off or paid off (which is infinite), but rather the balance-weighted average number of transitions that counts. Taking this number by risk rating, which comes out of the matrix algebra, and dividing it into the total expected losses by risk rating, provides the needed periodic provision as a percentage of outstanding balances.

Step 5—Calculate the Required Reserve

If actual losses (chargeoffs) occurred evenly over the life of the portfolio, there would be no need for a reserve. However, real losses are unpredictable. Losses tend to occur later rather than sooner in the life of a loan portfolio. As the portfolio ages, certain credits degrade to the point where they are written off. Each period, the reserve balance is increased by the proportionate share of the total expected losses, and decreased by actual chargeoffs.

For example, consider a loan portfolio with a life of four years. Each year, 25 percent of the total expected losses will be provided for and added to the reserve. Suppose that in the first year no actual losses are charged off. At the end of the period, the reserve balance will be 25 percent of the total expected losses.

In the second year, an additional 25 percent of total expected losses will be provided for. If chargeoffs of 6 percent are taken, a net 19 percent will be added to the reserve, increasing its balance at the end of Year Two to 44 percent. In Year Three, another 25 percent of total expected losses is taken. Given chargeoffs of 26 percent of total losses, a net 1 percent will be subtracted from the reserve, leaving the balance at the end of Year Three at 43 percent of total expected losses. In the final year, 25 percent of total expected losses is provided for, and the remaining 68 percent of total expected losses is charged off. The net subtraction from reserves is 43 percent, leaving zero balance in the reserve at the end of the fourth year.

During the life of a single portfolio the reserve balance increases in the early years and declines in the later years. In this example, the ending reserve balance as a percentage of total expected losses for each year is 25 percent, 44 percent, 43 percent, and 0 percent. In a steady state model, a new portfolio is added each period. At the end of the second year, the reserve consists of 44 percent of the expected losses from the original portfolio, plus 25 percent of the expected losses from the second portfolio.

With successive years, additional layers are added to the portfolio and to the reserves. In such a steady state, a reserve balance builds up and maintains a certain level because new loans are constantly being booked as old ones roll off. Continuing that logic, it can be determined that the steady state level of needed reserve expressed as a percentage of total expected losses is the average of the ending reserve balances for each year of the life of the portfolio. In this example, 28 percent—the average of 25 percent, 44 percent, 43 percent, and 0 percent—represents the level at which the reserve must be maintained.

Analysis of a cross-section of the institution's actual chargeoffs—where they occurred in the life of the individual credits—can be used to determine the needed reserve as a percentage of total expected losses.

Implementation Issues

Periodic Process Overview

All of the elements are now in place for a full-scale implementation of the system. Each quarter, prior quarter loan balances, tagged by industry classification, geographical distribution, organizational group, and other appropriate indices, are downloaded according to their current risk rating, or whether they have been paid down or charged off. These balances are downloaded from the various mainframe loan systems to a workstation-based analysis and reporting system within the credit risk division.

The credit analysis software creates a transition probability matrix. Using this matrix, an absorbing Markov chain calculation is performed to derive total expected losses and weighted average number of transitions by risk rating. Needed provision by risk grade is determined by dividing total expected losses by weighted average transitions. Needed reserve by risk grade is determined by multiplying total expected losses by the bank's appropriate loss pattern. All of these factors are multiplied by current balances by risk rating to achieve a first-cut provision and reserve. Management, using a top-down perspective, reviews the calculations and makes adjustments for specific large problem credits, LDC loans, and other exception items

Various standard reports can be created to show expected losses, chargeoffs, needed provision, and needed reserve, based on the current quarter versus a weighted average range of prior quarters. Reports also can be created for the entire portfolio or subsets selected by industry, geography, organizational unit, or other parameter.

Regulatory Issues

Banking Circular No. 201 specifically mentions the use of migration analysis as a permissible reserve methodology for use with pools containing a large number of loans and related balances. The circular lists five portfolio components that banks should use, as a minimum, when analyzing the adequacy of their loan loss allowance. Migration analysis is possible with three of these groups:

- Nonsignificant problem credits—C&I loans, real estate loans.
- All other loans and commitments—C&I loans, standby letters of credit.
- Homogeneous uncriticized loans—Consumer loans, credit cards, mortgages.

Reserves for the other two loan categories—significant credits individually analyzed (including at a minimum, all large credits classified doubtful) and transfer risk from cross-border lending—must be determined with regard to specific credits.

Retail Loans

Retail credits not categorized by risk rating can be analyzed by account payment status. Most retail credits are ranked current, 1–30 days past due, 31–60 days past due, etc., with chargeoffs occurring after 120 or 180 days. The transition probability matrix is calculated according to these categories, and the calculation proceeds as described above.

Shareholder-Value-Based Reporting

The methodology described here is easily embodied in a shareholder-value-based management reporting system. The needed provision and reserve factors can be applied against business-unit and product-level balances each period to support the creation of value-based income statements and balance sheets at each discrete reporting unit within the institution.

Even when using advanced loan-loss migration techniques, general or unallocated reserves often are calculated and included on the institution's balance sheet. For performance measurement purposes, these can be handed in one of two ways.

For institutions that prefer not to fully allocate all items, the loan loss reserve can be held in a corporate or reconciliation unit. The impact of such corporate (e.g., institution-wide) decisions can be gauged by looking at the profit or loss. The second method, for institutions that prefer to fully allocate, is to assign the general loan loss reserve in a method proportional to the reserves developed by using the migration analysis.

Of course, care should be taken to ensure that internally used provisions and reserves closely reconcile to externally reported provisions and reserves. Given the importance of these categories in determining an institution's profitability and assessing its financial health, management should not be perceived as running two sets of books for such accounts.

FLOAT

Float is another category of assets that is maintained and controlled in a way that makes profitability measurement difficult. Because float basically is the amount of money in the process of being collected, it is normally accounted for in due from accounts in the central item processing area. That area balances, reconciles, and keeps track of the float. While this method is appropriate for handling the float, some technique must be used to assign this asset to the various levels of profitability measurement (e.g., organization, product, or customer).

A basic float issue related to profitability measurement is which float to use. The traditional accounting approach measures actual float incurred. In other words, if it takes three days to collect a check, the accounting shows the actual three days of float. Unfortunately, the primary source of float assignment—the demand deposit account system—cannot capture actual float. Instead the system captures what is normally referred to as "scheduled float." For scheduled float, the demand deposit system operates on an assumed collection schedule.

With that three-day check, for example, the system might assume a two-day collection. The demand deposit system can only associate this two-day float with a particular customer, product, or organization. The difference between the assumed two-day collection and the actual three-day collection is not assignable in most systems.

Although the ideal profitability measurement method would assign actual float, it is virtually impossible to do. Therefore, most profitability measurement systems use scheduled float to assign float assets to the appropriate business segment. In some cases, the difference between the total float assigned from the demand deposit system, and the actual float as measured by the due from accounts, also is assigned. This assignment uses a proportion of scheduled float. For example, if a product such as retail NOW accounts had 12 percent of the total scheduled float, it would also be assigned 12 percent of the total difference between the actual and total scheduled float. This reassigned float is sometimes referred to in profitability measurement as "allocated float" to differentiate it from scheduled float.

In some cases, the demand deposit system either does not or cannot assign the scheduled float. Periodic sample surveys can be used, however, to determine the typical float for such broad categories of liabilities as corporate demand deposits or correspondent bank deposits. These average float percentages can be used as weighting mechanisms—along with average balances—to allocate the total actual float. Or, they can be applied directly to the balances to determine float. In the latter case, there still would be a difference between the float assigned to the respective liability categories and the total bank float. That difference could be handled in a proportional manner similar to that described above.

A second issue related to float is determining which side of the balance sheet should reflect it. Because float normally is included in a due from account, financial reporting dictates that it be listed as an asset. For profitability measurement, however, float usually is reported not as an asset but as a contraliability.

Such reporting allows the profitability report to show ledger balances (from the basic accounting systems) reduced by the amount of float (from the assignment method) to report collected funds. This representation of the balances is essential, particularly for product-profitability reporting of liabilities, because it permits the use of transfer pricing to calculate earnings for those collected funds (adjusted for deposit reserves, if required). If the float were reported as an asset, this advantage might not be possible.

A third, frequently overlooked, aspect of float is that a wide variety of products and processes generate it. For example, float can be created by payment of a mortgage loan or an installment loan with another institution's check. Absolute accuracy of product-profitability would dictate that management assign the float resulting from this transaction to the mortgage loan or installment loan product's profitability measurement.

Practicality, however, suggests that information regarding this float is virtually impossible to collect, is likely to be more expensive to collect than it is worth, and does not in general materially affect profitability measurement. For these reasons, miscellaneous float either is ignored in the development of profitability information or is roughly estimated on the basis of periodic samples. Internal float, however, should be reviewed occasionally, not only to ensure more accurate reporting but also to improve float management.

DEPOSIT RESERVES

Deposit reserves constitute another class of assets maintained and controlled one way that require a different treatment for profitability measurement. Deposit reserves consist of an institution's vault cash and Federal Reserve deposits. The amount of deposit reserves required is centrally calculated, and the proper maintenance of these reserves usually is the responsibility of the institution's asset/liability manager.

Like float, deposit reserves must be assigned to various liability products to determine the amount of funds available (and therefore credible, from a funds transfer pricing perspective) for the products. This assignment normally is accomplished in one of two ways.

In the first, the institution allocates its actual deposit reserves to the appropriate products, using regulatory reserve requirements as weights. Under the other method, the institution applies regulatory reserve requirements to the respective collected funds to arrive at a deposit reserve requirement. For example, if commercial demand deposits required a 12 percent reserve, then the collected balance (ledger balance less float) for commercial demand deposits would be multiplied by 12 percent to determine the reserve assignment. This method, like the similar methods for float and loan loss reserve, typically produces some difference between the total assigned deposit reserves and the institution's total actual reserve. The discrepancy results from timing and other minor calculation differences between the assignment method and the method used to meet regulatory requirements. This "residual" also can be reallocated, using the assigned reserves as the basis.

DUE FROM ACCOUNTS

Due from accounts form another asset category that is frequently overlooked in developing profitability information. In many cases, due from accounts are viewed as float accounts; in actuality, many of them represent compensating balances for services provided to the institution.

A good example is a compensating-balance account maintained at another institution to clear security transfers. Because these due from accounts are not float, they should not be aggregated into the float accounts and ignored. Such treatment results in overstated profits for the specific area benefiting from the due from account and understated profits for the demand deposit accounts.

Two basic methods can be used to assign due from accounts. One method establishes a separate due from account to segregate the compensating-balance account from the float accounts. Once separated, the compensating-balance due from account can be treated like any other asset. Management can establish responsibility for the account and assign the asset to the segment of profitability being measured.

The second method requires periodic studies (annual or semiannual) to determine the amount of due froms that should be assigned to a particular segment of the business. Once the institution determines this number, it can assign the due froms to the appropriate segment and keep them there until the next study.

SYNOPSIS

For the lion's share of the balance sheet, attributing assets and liabilities to organizational units, products, and customers is straightforward. However, as with revenue and cost assignment, problems develop when balance sheet accounts are shared or when they reflect the impact of one unit's behavior on another's performance. Using methodologies that reflect the following principles can help guide institutions through such issues:

- The actual assignment of an asset or liability should be focused where responsibility for that asset or liability rests.

- Once an assignment is made, the behavioral effects of that assignment must be considered, including the effects on other areas and other managers within the institution.

- Management's overall objectives and goals must be incorporated into the resolution of the issues.

Special attention needs be paid to the impact of balance sheet accounts on performance when market values differ significantly from GAAP. As GAAP evolves over time to reflect more a market valuation perspective, such differences will decrease. However, in the near term, institutions should adopt a consistent viewpoint of when market values will be used in place of GAAP and, how such differences will be reconciled for performance measurement purposes.

CHAPTER 12

Capital Issues[1]

OVERVIEW

Banks increasingly use risk-adjusted return on capital (or return on risk-adjusted capital) to measure business-unit, divisional, or product performance. As a result, properly allocating equity has become a critical issue. While methodologies for assigning equity are evolving, some aspects of leading approaches have been defined:

- Economic capital, rather than regulatory capital, is used.
- Portfolio effects are captured.
- Hurdle rates specific to business are used.

Special attention needs to be paid to off-balance-sheet items and non-asset-intensive businesses. At first blush they may appear to require minimal capital. However, upon closer examination they often require significant capital allocations.

WHY ASSIGN CAPITAL?

The increasing focus on shareholder-value maximization has changed the way institutions plan and operate. Combined with the international guidelines on risk-adjusted capital, it has increased bank executives' attention to business-line, divisional, and product use of and returns on capital. Senior management is demanding a disag-

---

1 This chapter incorporates "What's Wrong with Capital Allocation Methods?" by John Karr, published in the Summer 1992 issue of *Bank Accounting and Finance*, (John Colet Press, Boston, MA,).

gregated view of the institution, with an eye toward identifying which components contribute to or detract from its value.

The emphasis on shareholder value has greatly affected management reporting, particularly financially oriented management information systems (MIS). Internal systems for measuring financial performance have evolved through several stages. Top-line revenue generation and net-interest income as primary measures gave way to direct and often fully allocated contribution (including transfer pricing of balances), initially for sectors or business units. Fully allocated contribution analysis is increasingly being carried to lower levels of the organization (e.g., products or branches).

Another change in MIS is the move toward reporting rate-of-return information, as opposed to pure bottom-line measures. This requires institutions to allocate assets to organizational units, business lines, or product groups, similar to the revenue and expense allocations necessary to arrive at meaningful net profit figures. Return on assets was a substantial advance over pure bottom-line results; however, it proved insufficient.

Executives have become more comfortable thinking of their institutions as collections of individual businesses and products, each with its own impact on profitability and capital use. This new way of thinking demands that MIS provide data about return on equity (ROE). Moreover, regulatory risk-adjusted capital guidelines reinforce the notion that different activities have different capital requirements. Therefore, allocating equity to products or business lines on a risk-adjusted basis has become important in developing strategy and measuring financial performance.

The practical and theoretical challenges to setting up such ROE-focused, or value-based, reporting systems are daunting for most U.S. banks. Institutions are only now developing cost-allocation methods that appropriately and consistently treat direct and overhead expenses. Funds transfer pricing mechanisms, which were adequate for highly aggregated views of the institution, are being made more sophisticated and granular. And choosing whether to show ROE by business line, legal entity, product family, distribution channel, place in the value chain, or some combination has been problematic.

Allocating equity to business lines and determining the appropriate hurdle rate also pose substantial challenges. Institutions' managers, eager to implement value-based systems, have taken shortcuts that contain substantial theoretical failings and undermine accuracy. There are four major shortcomings in the ways institutions allocate equity to business lines.

- They usually allocate equity using the regulatory risk-adjusted capital adequacy guidelines, rather than a true, economic derivation.

- Equity allocations to lines of business generally do not embed the portfolio effects provided by covariance of returns among transactions, products, or businesses.

- Institutions usually set a single hurdle rate for all lines of business, with different capital allocations used to capture individual business line variations in equity costs.

- Businesses that are non-asset-intensive (e.g., trust and custody) and off-balance sheet items (e.g., swaps) usually do not receive capital allocations that reflect their true risks.

ECONOMIC ASSIGNMENT

The regulatory risk-based capital adequacy standards provoke institutions' management to consider how various businesses consume equity. The regulatory concept of segmenting assets and off-balance sheet activities by their underlying risk profiles neatly parallels an emerging shareholder-value method for analyzing and developing the institution's strategy. This method separates the institution into business lines and calculates their individual profitability, required rate of return, and contribution to the institution's total value.

A key problem is determining the equity that should underlie each business line. Institutions must determine the appropriate equity-to-assets ratio—or leverage—for each business line. The regulators face a similar challenge in determining capital adequacy guidelines.

In theory, in a world without taxes or the costs of financial distress, capital structure would not matter. That is, the value of the institution would be invariant to the degree of leverage employed. No equity level would be more appropriate than any other.

In the real world, capital structure does matter, especially for such highly leveraged entities as financial institutions. The tax shield on debt, given taxes on corporate income, offers an incentive to increase leverage (that is, less equity and more debt). Conversely, the prospective cost associated with bankruptcy, especially for institutions possessing illiquid, not-marked-to-market assets, creates an incentive to decrease leverage.

Such a framework views equity as both a recipient of residual value (after payments to debtholders and needed investment) and a buffer, or insurance, against unexpected loss. To maximize the institution's equity value, leverage must be set at that point where the marginal dollar of tax benefit received equals the marginal dollar of expected (that is, probable) cost of bankruptcy or financial distress.

Of course, accurately determining the probability of bankruptcy (defined as a situation in which the market value of liabilities exceeds the market value of assets or for which required payments to debtholders exceed available cash in any time period) is difficult. But by examining the volatility of earnings over time, institutions can establish a probability distribution of profits or losses and set equity levels on the basis of that distribution, which reflects risk.

To avoid bankruptcy, entities should set equity capitalization to cover some large percentage of probable losses. In other words, assuming a normal distribution of profit or loss outcomes, equity should cover losses at least two standard deviations from the mean. Or, equity could be set to capture 99 percent of all expected outcomes, approximately three standard deviations from the mean.

Institutions can use this volatility-driven method to allocate equity to each business line or activity. In fact, the regulators used this basic concept to establish the risk-based capital rules. However, institutions should not attempt to use the regulatory risk-adjusted capital levels to set business-line equity-to-asset ratios for three reasons.

First, the regulatory guidelines do not cover all risks. The regulators address only credit risk in the bulk of guidelines[2] (the rules for off-balance sheet activities may incorporate a broader view of risk). Other risks, such as market (price), liquidity, interest rate, and operations also affect volatility and capital requirements. Therefore, the risk-adjusted capital guidelines are probably inaccurate measures of true economic risk.

Second, the regulatory segmentation of asset classes is too broad to be useful, even if all risks are calculated properly. For example, all corporate loans receive a 100 percent risk weight, implying the need for 4 percent equity (Tier I capital) capitalization. However, the volatility of corporate-loan returns varies greatly with the size, type, and geographic location of the borrower. Using a constant equity percentage across all corporate-lending business could be a mistake.

Third, the characteristics of each individual institution's business may differ from those of the industry as a whole. So while the required equity percentage for corporate loans may be 4 percent on average, the volatility—and resulting capital requirement—of a specific institution's corporate-loan business may be greater or less. Using a national regulatory standard for all institutions ignores bank-specific business-line risk profiles.

---

2 New regulatory guidelines cover capital required for interest rate risks and the risks of "nontraditional" activities.

Some argue that because institutions must comply with the regulatory capital standards, they should use these standards to evaluate each business line. Under this argument, regulatory requirements drive true capital consumption. However, this belief is flawed when it comes to allocating capital for business-line planning, reporting and valuation.

The institution as a whole does need to maintain capital to meet regulatory standards, which is the ticket to enter and stay in the industry. And the new risk-adjusted capital guidelines do build up total capital requirements as the sum of the capital specified for each risk class. However, the actual quantity of capital needed by an institution's business line—reflecting the trade-off between taxes and bankruptcy costs—is based on its own specific volatility profile, not the regulatory standard. Keeping the institution in compliance with regulatory guidelines is intrinsically different from allocating capital in order to make decisions.

Suppose the risk profile of an institution's business line suggests that a 2 percent equity-to-assets ratio is appropriate, but the regulatory rules stipulate 4 percent equity capitalization. The institution that uses the regulatory standard will systematically understate return on equity and, in turn, could allocate resources away from this line of business, ultimately harming its institution. Similarly, if the regulatory standard were below the actual risk of the business line, the institution would overestimate the business line's return and potentially overinvest in it.

Institutions can meet regulatory capital standards and still be over- or undercapitalized in an economic sense. If overcapitalized, the surplus equity required for regulatory purposes should not be notionally allocated back to business lines, which would cloud accurate measures and comparisons of returns. Instead, it should be held at the corporate level to recognize its drag on overall profitability.

If the institution meets (or exceeds) the regulatory standards but is undercapitalized in an economic sense, it also should recognize that it is overleveraged. It should recognize the excess returns caused by the economic overleveraging at the corporate level, not at the level of the business unit.

While a seemingly attractive shortcut, using regulatory risk weights to establish business-line capital requirements is inferior to deriving equity allocations from the institution's actual experience. Before allocating equity, institutions should analyze the volatility of their own business lines rather than rely on the capital adequacy rules.

PORTFOLIO EFFECTS

Most institutions exclude a portfolio effect, or correlation/covariance of returns among transactions, products, or business lines, when determining capital requirements. To improve their capital allocations they must ask two questions:

- How should portfolio effects be taken into account in determining capital requirements?

- At what level of the organization should such effects be included?

While business-line volatility drives institutions' capital requirements, business-line correlation (measured by covariance of returns) also influences capital requirements. Because business-line (or transaction or product) returns are not perfectly correlated (that is, they do not move by the same amount at the same time due to the same causes), diversification can reduce the volatility of the institution's returns as a whole. Because of this portfolio effect, the overall economic capital requirement by a single institution with two different business lines is less than the sum of the capital each business requires separately.

Therefore, it is inappropriate for institutions that encompass activities with independent distributions of returns to rely solely on volatility estimates to derive capital levels. For example, if the institution trades two currencies—dollars and sterling—with a correlation coefficient of under 1.0, the capital required for the overall currency-trading business should reflect the covariance of returns between them. In essence, the combined distribution of returns is less risky than in each individual currency's distribution of returns alone.

The same general principle holds true for all banking activities, such as capital markets, lending, deposit-taking, trust, and processing. However, most institutions find the ratio difficult to establish, and therefore returns are not captured very well for illiquid assets or for liabilities not marked to market. As a result, tracing correlations among loan returns or between a lending business and a securities processing business can involve much effort and many assumptions.

Assuming that an institution can correctly approximate these correlations, it must decide where to include the diversification effect: at the level of the individual element (business line, transaction, or product), or at the level that reflects the combination of the individual elements. In the currency-trading example, the institution could reduce the capital required for the dollar and sterling desks individually or reduce the capital required for the currency-trading business overall.

Each alternative has merit. By incorporating the correlation effect at the level of the individual element, the institution shows the contribution to its overall return of an incremental unit of volume in that business line, as long as the covariance with other elements remains constant.

But capturing correlation effects at a level above the individual elements that exhibit covariance of returns is the better alternative. Correlation is corporate property, not the property of the discrete unit. Benefits from correlation can accrue only to an entity that consists of two or more subunits that have return covariance. To give a stand-alone transaction correlation benefits understates the capital it alone consumes.

For example, if the institution decides to exit a business, product, or transaction, it loses the correlation effect, and the remaining entity is instantaneously undercapitalized. Moreover, the incremental contribution of the next unit of volume to the overall correlation may differ from historical patterns. If the incremental volume is large, the effects may be substantial.

Given the rudimentary nature of most institutions' capital-allocation methods (which generally employ regulatory standards), factoring in the correlation effect still is worth the effort. Clearly, if faced with a choice between determining economic capital attribution by business line or analyzing correlation impacts, an institution should develop accurate estimates of volatility first. In fact, an institution can produce volatility estimates and derive correlations simultaneously, if it structures its analysis properly.

The portfolio effect is greatest for institutions that conduct a wide range of activities across broad regions and for a variety of different customers and markets. Institutions should consider this rule of thumb when deciding whether or not to invest in developing the variance-covariance matrix for their business lines.

HURDLE RATES

Another common error is to use a single, institution-wide hurdle rate (cost of equity) to measure all business lines. Institutions that use a single rate often base their choice on two assertions:

- Differences in equity allocations across business lines implicitly create appropriate hurdle-rate differentials.

- Determining business-line-specific hurdle rates is almost impossible because no observable market comparables, or pure plays, exist.

Differences in equity allocations do not create different hurdle rates. Using different equity allocations across business lines to create different hurdle rates implicitly confuses two types of risk: pure volatility and systemic-market covariance.

The risk captured in setting the appropriate equity level (that is, properly levering the business) is the risk of bankruptcy, driven by business-line volatility. Alone, it tells us little about the required rate of return on the equity needed to lever the business.

Recall that in the ideal world, one without taxes or the costs of financial distress, capital structure is irrelevant to the institution's value. In actuality, however, the appropriate equity-to-assets ratio for a business line is in part a function of the stand-alone volatility of that business (leaving aside the discussion of where to incorporate inter-business-line correlation effects). As a result, stand-alone business-line volatility merely defines the proper degree of leverage. It does not provide the full array of information needed to determine the business line's required rate of return on equity, or hurdle rate.

In fact, another dimension beyond stand-alone volatility is needed to determine the proper hurdle rate for each business line: the systemic risk embedded in that business line, for example, as measured by its beta coefficient, based on the capital asset pricing model (CAPM). Beta is a measure of the risk of the business relative to overall market risk, based on patterns of business-line and market return covariance. (Risk-return measures other than beta also exist, for instance, those based on arbitrage pricing theory (APT). This book does not discuss the relative merits of CAPM and APT.)

Because equity investors can diversify their own portfolios, they will not compensate for the nonsystemic, or stand-alone, risks of particular businesses. Instead, they will require a rate of return based on systemic risk only, equal to the current risk-free rate plus a market premium. The market premium reflects the long-run market return over the risk-free rate, multiplied by the business's beta coefficient.

Individual banking businesses have their own patterns of covariance with the market, and they result in different betas. While the historical beta of the banking industry as a whole has been estimated as more than 1.0– (suggesting a risk higher than the overall market), discrete components such as specific institutions or businesses can show higher or lower betas. Therefore, determining the business line's covariance with market returns, as indicated by its beta, is an integral step in establishing its true hurdle rate.

Where does this leave the discussion about leverage? As it turns out, betas reflect both business risks and financial (leverage) risk. Market-observed betas may embody a leverage ratio that differs from the one deemed appropriate for the specific institution's business line. If the businesses are similar in all respects except leverage, their betas cannot be directly comparable. So, the market-observed beta must be adjusted to reflect the actual leverage of the business line, as determined by the volatility-estimating process discussed above.

Keeping decisions about leverage separate from decisions about required rates of return gives management more insights into the institution's risks and return profile. By explicitly differentiating required rates of return by business line, the institution can better measure performance and value the contribution of each business to the value of the bank as a whole.

MARKET COMPARABLES

A number of publicly traded companies, funds, or trusts concentrate the bulk of their activities in a small set of identifiable business lines, so it usually is possible to find observable market betas for banking businesses.

These can be related to similar products or services, which may be bundled together within an institution. For example, publicly traded credit card-backed assets can indicate the credit card business's beta and required rate of return. Similar comparables exist for retail financial businesses, mortgage banking, and transaction-processing businesses. And as markets emerge for corporate loans, their required rates of return will also be discernible.

Meanwhile, institutions can use regression or factor-analytic techniques to estimate the imputed return-on-equity requirements by major business segments. By including a large enough sample of financial institutions and categorizing the range and scale of their activities, business line (as opposed to institution-wide) equity costs can be developed.

NONASSET-INTENSIVE BUSINESSES

The fact that equity levels are derived as some percentage of assets has led some institutions to conclude that businesses or products that are nonasset intensive require little, if any, capital. As a result, rates of return calculated in such a manner approach the infinite.

In fact, nonasset-intensive businesses and products do require capital. The capital they require should be determined in the same manner that required equity levels are set for asset-intensive businesses, and through an analysis of the economic risk they entail. Regulatory guidelines on capital requirements for off-balance sheet items reflect this type of approach in broad terms. Internal performance measurement methodologies should reflect it as well.

For example, the trust/custody business typically does not generate large amounts of assets to put on the balance sheet. Therefore, it has traditionally received little equity allocation—perhaps 4 percent to 8 percent of the asset balances attributable to it. When returns are calculated using such low equity amounts they can exceed 100 percent ROE. This alone suggests that something is amiss with the calculating methodology.

Such an approach does not capture the full extent of the business risks. In fact, the volatility of returns, which drives capital allocation using an economic framework, can be high. Trust/custody businesses generally have high fixed-cost structures and variable revenue streams. They also are subject to operations risk. Such factors imply that considerable "insurance" against unexpected losses (i.e., capital) be allocated.

Using a market view confirms this line of thinking. Capitalization ratios can be observed for comparable, non-asset-intensive, fee-generating businesses that are publicly traded. Indeed, the market requires them to carry substantial amounts of equity on their balance sheets. For such businesses, leverages of $20 in assets to $1 in equity are rare; capital ratios in the 25 percent-plus range are more common. A similar business operated by a financial institution should not require significantly less capital simply due to its ownership.

OFF-BALANCE SHEET INSTRUMENTS

Off-balance-sheet instruments result in economic exposure to the institution, primarily though not exclusively through credit risk. Volatility can be calculated and a fractional value derived that represents the economic capital that should back the off-balance sheet transaction. While required capital levels are usually mere fractions of the notional transaction value, when aggregated they can represent significant sums.

LINE-OF-BUSINESS RESULTS

In recent years, some institutions have provided line-of-business results in their annual reports, and some have expressed their performance in terms of return on equity. Using this information can show the amount of equity required by lines of business, defined at a very high level.

Of course, interpreting such information is difficult because:

- Differences can exist in how institutions define the business lines. Some institutions include mortgage banking and credit cards in their retail line of business while others do not.

- Differences can exist in their institution's capital allocation methodologies. For example, some build capital requirements from individual transactions, while others use a more "top down" approach.

Figure 12-1 and Figure 12-2 show examples from two banks' 1993 annual reports. Equity-to-asset ratios for each line of business are shown, along with some of the information included in the annual report.

Figure 12-1—Line of Business ROE

	Retail and Community Banking	Commercial Banking	Trust and Investment Group
ROE	15.2%	22.5%	29.5%
Average Assets	$18,615m	$6,209m	$751m
Average Equity	$1,388m	$435m	$134m
Implied Equity/ Assets Ratio	7.5%	7.0%	17.8%

Source: 1993 Annual Report, First Bank Systems, p.13.

Figure 12-2—Line of Business ROE

	Retail Banking	Corporate Banking	Investment Management and Trust	Investment Banking
ROE	21%	17%	53%	29.5%
Average Assets	$27,489m	$12,866m	$480m	$751m
Average Equity	$1,401m	$ 1,706m	$130m	$134m
Implied Equity/ Assets Ratio	5.4%	13.2%	27.1%	17.8%

Source: 1993 Annual Report, PNC Bank, p.28.

SYNOPSIS

More institutions are adopting shareholder-value-based planning, analysis, and reporting. Their underlying conceptual foundations and implementation approaches are becoming better understood and increasingly sophisticated. A wide variety of industry participants and analysts are debating and addressing basic methods. In the next several years, a rigorous set of capital-allocation and required-rate-of-return conventions are likely to become accepted at most institutions. At the same time, solid information will be developed on the risk-return profiles of disaggregated business lines, products, and perhaps even transactions. These will put capital-allocation decisions and performance measurement processes on more sound analytic foundations.

PART IV

Implementation Issues Related to Performance Measurement

CHAPTER 13

Getting Started

OVERVIEW

An understanding of measurement methods and techniques is critical when constructing a performance measurement system. In the remaining chapters of this book we lay out a road map to implementing a system at an institution.

Throughout the book, we have emphasized the importance of matching an institution's philosophy and structure with its performance measurement system. When an institution defines its performance measurement needs, management's objectives must be clearly identified and numerous policy decisions made. Only through such an exercise can the link between objectives and measurements be firmly established.

The first step in actually developing a performance measurement system is to translate these objectives and policy decisions into a conceptual design. This chapter details the design process.

APPROACHING THE DEVELOPMENT OF PERFORMANCE MEASUREMENT INFORMATION

Performance measurement is above all a management tool, intended to support and assist management in tactical or strategic decision making. It follows that management understanding plays an important role in resolving the complex issues surrounding performance measurement and the successful use of the information. For example, if management places a premium on business lines meeting ROE targets, then it needs to be fully informed of how capital is being allocated at the business-line level.

But the most effective role for management in developing performance measures extends beyond just obtaining an understanding of its inner workings. Management must be actively involved in the development. It has been noted that performance measurement is evolutionary in nature. As management's information needs evolve and grow more complex, the means for generating that information must advance accordingly. Chapter 4 describes the most common evolutionary stages of this development along what is termed the Performance Measurement continuum. Without management involvement in initial design of each phase along the continuum, and without ongoing management attention as each phase progresses, the process will evolve inefficiently, if at all.

Overall system design should reflect a high-level perspective and should provide for collaboration among senior executives, line management, and the accounting staff responsible for implementing the system. Each group has a critical role to play in developing a performance measurement system. Project staffing issues are discussed in detail in Chapter 14.

STATING OBJECTIVES

The first phase of the conceptual-design process is to lay out management's objectives for the performance measurement system—including definitions of the entities to be incorporated in the system—and to determine the implementation approach (i.e., phased or comprehensive).

A statement of management's objectives should indicate the data to be produced and their intended uses. Line and business-unit managers need to understand up front what senior management expects from performance measurement and how it will use the resulting information for decision making. In this way, any middle-management misgivings or confusion about senior-management intentions can be put to rest.

A detailed and appropriate assignment of responsibility should be developed and clearly spelled out in the statement of system objectives. Essentially, management must determine who it intends to measure and the entities for which that person or business unit will be held responsible.

For example, should a credit card operation be viewed as a lending (consumer loan) or a payment-processing (corporate fee) product? Is a branch manager responsibile for bottom-line branch performance or just for deposit generation? If commercial loans are defined as a product line for analysis, how will they be categorized—by interest-rate sensitivity (repricing characteristics), by collateral (secured versus unsecured), by funds use (equipment financing versus working capital), by market segment (oil and gas versus government), or by some combination of these perspectives?

The end result of this design exercise is a detailed list of the products, centers, or customers, etc. for which performance measurement information will be generated, together with a description of the components of each of these elements.

How these definitional issues are resolved will largely determine how the performance measurement system drives management behavior. If a branch manager, for instance, is indeed held responsible for bottom-line branch performance, then an incentive exists for becoming involved in loan marketing and pricing. Through behavioral incentives, seemingly inconsequential decisions made during the design of a performance measurement system can have complicated and far-reaching strategic implications. Also, these decisions can dramatically affect a system's design, development, and required lead time. For all of these reasons, senior management should have the final say in any such definitional issues.

DETERMINING PROJECT SCOPE

Defining performance measurement scope first involves listing the business units, affiliate banks, subsidiaries, products, etc., to be included in the analysis. Decisions regarding which entities to include primarily hinge on management's span of control, information needs, and the the feasibility of meeting the scheduled deadline for project completion.

For example, the lead bank in a large holding company may have little incentive to investigate the performance of unrelated business units under the holding company; it may have little ability to influence decisions regarding these entities.

The second step of scope definition entails mapping out an approach for implementing performance measurement. The performance measurement continuum described in Chapter 4 shows that total-bank performance can be broken down into a number of component parts—such as organizational, product, or customer—each providing a different perspective on performance. While the range of decision making flexibility may be greater for customer-performance information than for organizational information, customer-measurement systems require more time to implement and involve greater complexity.

Decisions about which level of measurement to undertake first, second, or third (or whether to build a comprehensive, integrated system at one time) depend on what level is of greatest interest to management and how soon it needs to see the information. Obviously, it is critical for senior management to play a key role in this aspect of scope definition.

A final scope issue sure to arise is the amount of measurement detail required (see Figure 13-1). For product-performance measurement, management must choose between individual product information and aggregate product-line data.

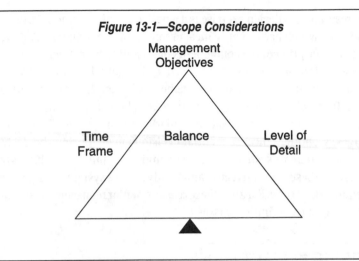

Figure 13-1—Scope Considerations

For example, if individual product information is desired, should recurring wire transfers be differentiated from nonrecurring transfers? Also, how detailed should unit-cost information on functions or activities to support those products be? Are separate costs of statement processing, checks cashed, checks cleared, and address changes needed, or will a simple total cost for the average account suffice? For customer-performance information, will the differentiation between wholesale versus retail, or high net worth versus middle market provide satisfactory detail?

ACCOUNTING THEORIES

Management's approach to several accounting issues serves as a foundation for generating and analyzing performance measurement data. For example, in the case of customer or product performance measurement systems, product costs are as essential as revenue information, not only for historical analysis but also for modeling.

There is no "right way" to approach cost accounting, yet the choice among methods will have a significant impact on performance results. Decisions about such issues as the types of costs that will be used for allocation purposes and the level of detail in gathering cost data are critical. In fact, management buy-in to the measurement data derived from the system cannot be assured unless it has significant input into the selection of—if not the final say in—cost accounting methods. The issues that should be reviewed and defined during the conceptual design phase include:

- *Actual versus Standard Costing*—Will full absorption costing be used for unit costs determinations or will unit costs be standardized for allocation and reporting purposes?

- *Treatment of Fixed and Variable Costs*—Should fixed and variable costs be broken out for allocations and reporting, or are the barriers to doing so too great for the institution?

- *Allocation Development Techniques*—Will elaborate work-measurement methods be used to develop unit costs, or will more heuristic, less costly methods such as interviews be selected?

- *Allocation Sequence*—Are hierarchical allocations, for example from one cost center to another, appropriate or should simultaneous allocations take place to account for reciprocal relationships between support centers which provide services to one another?

- *Sampling Approach*—In cases where time constraints prevent cost studies at every branch location, how can sampling techniques be employed to adequately represent the remaining branches?

ALLOCATION METHODOLOGIES

Determination of relative performance results at any level along the "continuum" are affected by how the institution resolves several key allocation and measurement issues. Senior management should be responsible for deciding among a number of alternative approaches based on their objectives for the system and on other factors particular to that institution.

Those banks that have undertaken performance measurement efforts of any type will recognize some of the following as controversial topics which had to be addressed at an early juncture of the project, normally prior to the implementation phase:

- *Funds-Transfer Pricing*—Should a pooled or matched-funded approach be employed (normally based on the degree of accuracy and complexity desired), and how should the associated transfer-pricing issues be resolved?

- *Overhead*—How should the components of corporate overhead be determined, and how should it be allocated to business units, products, customers, etc. (if at all)?

- *Advertising and Marketing*—What is an appropriate allocation method for bank "image" advertising and marketing department expenses, neither of which normally has a measurable impact on specific products or centers?

- *Capital*—How much bank capital should be allocated, and what method for doing so is most appropriate? (This issue is particularly important when ROE measures are given high priority by management.)

- *Loan Loss Reserves and Provisions*—What allocation method should be selected for general and specific reserves as well as provisions?

- *Compensating Balances*—How should fee income/compensating balance credits be spread among cash-management products and activities?

- *Float*—What definition of float is most appropriate for allocations, and how can float distributions at various levels be determined?

COMMUNICATIONS AND DOCUMENTATION

The actual mechanics and operational procedures of the conceptual design and implementation projects must also be addressed during the early stages of systems design.

During the design phase, issues arising or resolved, and assumptions or decisions made, must be documented and subsequently communicated to those involved in implementation. This process better enables the conceptual-design phase to provide a foundation for implementation of the performance measurement system.

For example, a list of performance measurement and cost-accounting terms (with definitions) should be created for institutions/managers unfamiliar with measurement systems and the accompanying terminology.

A conceptual design document, summarizing the results of the systems design process, may be put together to serve as an important vehicle for transferring this knowledge from design to implementation.

Tools developed during design to facilitate comprehensive communication/documentation during implementation may include allocation documentation, report-user reference guides, user training sessions, and periodic update meetings with senior management.

REPORT FORMATS

Developing report formats during the design stage forces the team designing the performance measurement system to define at the project's inception the desired level of reporting detail, frequency, and to some extent the intended distribution. Because each element influences system complexity, the choice of reporting level depends on the resources and skills available and the scheduled time frame for implementation.

Assume, for example, that reporting requirements consist of only periodic reports of product-line profitability for senior management. High-level product-line contribution reports prepared quarterly and distributed to senior management may be all that are required. However, if product managers need monthly data on the performance of individual products across the institution, the effort to build and maintain the system will increase. Having this knowledge up front may significantly improve the efficiency with which the system is built.

During report design, management must decide what key qualitative (nonfinancial) information to include. For instance, average account size, break-even balances, activity volumes, or total deposit costs (interest and operating expenses) could be valuable system outputs. Management must not only decide which qualitative data to incorporate in reports—which will vary depending on who receives them—but must also format reports to portray this information appropriately.

Detailed formats for the performance measurement reports to be produced should be determined early in the design stage for several reasons.

First, early completion of this step will further reduce the effort needed to build the system. Formats let system builders graphically demonstrate the new information the reports will provide. A line-by-line determination of the information to include highlights the allocation methodologies and data requirements that will need particular attention during the remainder of conceptual design. In this way, early report design focuses the team on the most critical design issues.

Second, early report formatting will improve the chances for eventual management acceptance of performance measurement results. At the beginning of this chapter, we emphasized the importance of conceptual design in selling measurement results to line and upper management. Report design provides an early opportunity to generate management interest and buy-in to the system. By illustrating the effect of policy decisions made during design, report formats help management better understand the interaction between performance and design decisions. For example, in developing branch performance measurement, if management decides to allocate shareholder's equity to branches and transfer price it as a source of funds, management could better envision the impact of such a decision on branch performance.

Finally, permitting management to determine the content and appearance of reports gives it full responsibility for ensuring that reports help tie performance measures to overall system objectives. (For additional information on the implications of report formats for system design and for sample formats, refer to Chapter 15.)

DATA MANAGEMENT

At an early stage in conceptual design, the data-management process within the system should be defined. Some institutions may find this most easily illustrated using such vehicles as data-flow diagrams. The overall process is normally described in terms of data inputs, system production, and the outputs (reports) generated by the system. (This process is discussed in detail in Chapter 15.)

SYNOPSIS

This chapter describes several key issues arising in the conceptual design of a financial institution's performance measurement system. A critical factor in designing a successful system is ensuring that management's objectives for performance measurement are reflected in system implementation and reporting. Only when the system meets senior management's information needs, bearing in mind the relevant time frame and available resources, can management's commitment and buy-in be assured.

Establishing a clear tie between management's objectives and system specifications requires management involvement in the design process. Not only should senior executives be responsible for laying out performance measurement objectives, but also the scope of the units, products, customers, etc., to be measured. Other areas requiring senior management attention due to their importance for performance measurement include accounting theories, allocation methodologies, report formats, and systems and data issues.

Equipped with this base of knowledge about getting started along the performance measurement continuum, institutions should be better able to understand and use the implementation details (i.e., project staffing and technology) provided in the remaining chapters of this book.

CHAPTER 14

Organizing and Staffing

OVERVIEW

How does performance measurement information come into existence? Chapter 13 offered some suggestions for getting started in the development and use of performance measurement information. This chapter comments on some of the organizational structure and human resource issues related to developing and maintaining performance measurement information.

Because performance measurement and management accounting are interrelated, we will start by reviewing some of the management accounting activities that may be considered within the performance measurement framework. The balance of the chapter will be devoted to such organizational issues as staffing requirements, key roles and responsibilities, and reporting relationships. The chapter concludes by suggesting some general concepts related to organizing and staffing the performance measurement effort.

Throughout this chapter, ideas are illustrated by descriptions of organizational arrangements in use at major financial institutions. In addition to showing the ideas at work, these examples help demonstrate the diversity that exists in organizing performance measurement responsibilities. They reinforce the idea that there is no one "right" way to get the job done.

Performance Measurement/ Management Accounting Functions

The role of the management accounting or profitability analysis department is often to produce internal management reports, develop budget data and monitor performance against the plan, develop cost-accounting information, and design and develop organizational, product, and customer profitability data. These responsibilities are undertaken during the conceptual-design phase, implementation phase, and in the reporting, analysis, and maintenance responsibilities going forward.

CONCEPTUAL DESIGN

During conceptual design, the department's role is often as a high-level advisor, overseeing the key conceptual-design issues discussed in Chapter 13. Its responsibilities include building executive and management consensus, organizing task forces to help discuss and resolve issues, and preparing documentation for Steering Committee approval. The department also may be responsible for developing the conceptual design for the Steering Committee to review and approve. In essence, management accounting's role is to provide a "blueprint" for a successful implementation.

IMPLEMENTATION

During the implementation phase, management accounting personnel are actively involved in executing the plan. Execution can be addressed in light of several distinct tasks.

- *Performance measurement analysts* are responsible for allocating noninterest expense to organizational centers, business lines, or products. In most cases, analysts visit each responsibility center to determine the proper cost-allocation methodology (see Chapters 7 and 8). The cost-allocation process is often the most time-consuming task associated with implementation.

- *Source data* is a process of allocating interest income, interest expense, fee income, and assets and liabilities to the proper reporting level. All interest income and interest expense accounts must be allocated to reconcile to total organization income statements. Assets and liabilities must be allocated in order to apply a funds-transfer charge or credit for each balance sheet item (see Chapter 10).

- *Volume and data collection* involves tracking and collecting all required volume data. This includes documenting all volume requirements, coordinating programming efforts with computer operations or systems personnel, and ensuring the accuracy and availability of volumes on a timely basis.

- *Funds-transfer pricing* responsibilities include developing and maintaining the necessary algorithms for executing funds-transfer pricing, including the rate and data collection. In organizations with evolving funds-transfer pricing systems, this may mean coordinating with outside vendors or internal systems personnel to integrate funds-transfer pricing data into the measurement system. For organizations using the pooling approach, this role may include developing appropriate pools for balance sheet items and designing the measurement system to incorporate the pooling approach.

- *Systems maintenance* includes developing and maintaining the necessary hardware and software for automating the process, as discussed in Chapters 15 and 16. This includes coordinating installation, configuring the systems, establishing data gateways and delivery methods, etc.

STAFFING REQUIREMENTS

Designing and implementing a performance measurement system is often time consuming and labor intensive. The resources required depend upon the sophistication of the measurement system, level of systems expertise, analytical ability, cost accounting principles, scope of project, and number of responsibility centers, among other factors.

Some institutions use personnel from other functional areas to assist with selected roles. Others turn to consultants experienced in performance measurement systems, who supplement the institutions' experience with industry best practices. The following section discusses how organizations can match their resources with several of key implementation needs and create a viable workplan.

Key Roles and Responsibilities

Successfully implementing a performance management system requires top management and line managers to comprehend and support the project in order to integrate the new system into existing information systems and allow it to meet its intended purposes. To accomplish this, several cross-functional teams should be established as shown in Figure 14-1.

STEERING COMMITTEE

In order to be successful and effective, the objectives of a performance measurement system must be properly documented and communicated. Overall management buy-in and participation are key determinants of success.

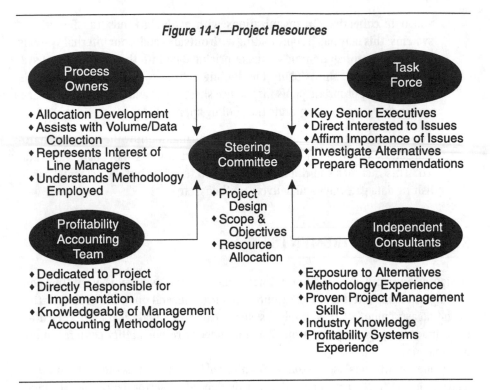

Figure 14-1—Project Resources

A steering committee of key institution executives should be established to oversee the system's design and implementation, guiding implementation to meet the organization's strategic and tactical needs. The steering committee should provide high-level direction for each of the conceptual-design issues discussed in Chapter 13.

The committee should resolve outstanding issues and approve resource commitments and the overall project workplan. And it must approve all findings and recommendations of the task force (discussed below). The committee's primary role does not end with the conceptual-design phase, however. It should continually assess the organization's information needs and fine tune the performance measures as its strategy changes.

TASK FORCES

Developing task forces can be an effective way to review and resolve specific measurement issues. Several key tasks forces are discussed below; any number may be found. Overall, their role is to review assigned issues, evaluate options, and recommend appropriate solutions to the steering committee.

Funds-Transfer Pricing Task Force

The funds-transfer pricing task force reviews current methodologies and designs an approach tailored to meet the institution's objectives. Its goal is to resolve such issues as overall funds-transfer pricing methodology, and other concerns discussed in Chapter 10. The funds-pricing task force also should explore the "make versus buy" decision about the system as a whole.

Capital Task Force

The capital task force reviews needs and issues related to capital, and defines a mechanism to allocate capital to the various reporting levels. The task force's objectives are to affirm the importance of capital allocation and review related industry trends. Capital issues that must be addressed include the amount of capital to be allocated, the frequency of allocations, and how to respond in over- or undercapitalized situations.

Systems Task Force

This task force is responsible for designing and developing the systems architecture that will best support the methodologies selected for the performance measurement system. The systems task force reviews all system requirements and reviews implementation alternatives, develops overall systems architecture, and makes recommendations to the Steering Committee for all required software purchases. It should work closely with the performance measurement staff to assist with volume collection requirements, data gathering, and programming efforts.

Loan Loss Task Force

The mission of this task force is to adopt a common methodology for allocating the allowance for loan loss provision to the proper reporting level. The loan loss task force affirms the importance of consistent loan loss allocations and investigates alternative allocation methodologies. It also should address all issues related to loan loss, including general and specific reserves, chargeoffs, negative provisions, and frequency of allocation calculations.

Product Profitability Task Force

A well-designed performance measurement reporting system should have the flexibility to perform multidimensional profitability reporting at the organizational, business line, product, and customer levels. Although many institutions implement these reporting levels one at a time, it is important to design the performance measurement system to meet future profitability reporting requirements.

Unit cost information derived from the product profitability system can be used as a basis for customer profitability. The product profitability task force should define the institution's overall objectives regarding product profitability and draft an initial list of products, product lines, and activities.

Process Owners

As mentioned earlier, implementing a performance measurement system touches on virtually every area of an institution. In order to properly develop income and expense allocations, dedicated staff known as "process owners" can be used. Process owners understand the process or activities being analyzed and have a working knowledge of the operational, financial, and lending activities performed.

Process owners' roles include reviewing allocation methodologies, updating the reporting staff about significant organizational changes, serving as a communication link between the reporting staff and responsibility centers, and organizing the volume and data collection efforts.

Finally, process owners provide a link between the reporting staff and the responsibility centers, helping facilitate better communication and "buy in" among line managers. Unlike the task forces, process owners are primarily used during implementation and can be an effective communication device after implementation is complete.

Independent Consultants

Developing a system without the necessary in-house expertise can be a huge drain on an institution's resources. Independent consultants experienced in all the facets of performance measurement systems can accelerate the design and implementation process, share best industry practices, identify potential obstacles and barriers, and provide solutions. Most importantly they can assure the institution that the system is developing in line with industry norms. Consultants can add a great deal of credibility to the development process, as they have proven experience and no "turf" to protect.

Workplan

Successful implementation depends heavily on a well-designed workplan and dedicated, available resources. Two workplans should be developed: one for conceptual design and another for implementation.

The conceptual-design workplan should integrate all conceptual design issues with the appropriate resources. The workplan should include the scheduled start and completion of each appropriate task, and the resources responsible for resolving each one. The workplan also should include the percentage completion for each task, so that the document can be used as a dynamic status report throughout conceptual design.

The length of conceptual design will vary depending on several factors, including the scope of the project and availability of resources. However, in most financial institutions it averages between two to four months.

The implementation workplan should be developed during conceptual design and incorporate all resolved conceptual design issues. The format should be resemble that of the conceptual design workplan.

Implementation time frames are considerably longer than those for the design phase. But once again, this depends on the scope of the project, number of responsibility centers, and complexity of methodologies chosen.

Reporting Relationships

In the most common organizational approach, the management accounting function and much of the performance measurement function are located within the controller's division. This approach has grown out of management accounting's need for access to the financial data, as well as out of the controller's traditional role as overseer of all financial information.

Because the management accounting function exists in part to objectively measure the performance of various aspects of the business, the linkage with an independent department such as the controller's division is natural. However, the objectives of management accounting can be at odds with those of financial accounting. Internal reporting has reporting formats that often differ from those of financial reporting. Also, internal reporting accepts approximations rather than precise measures for allocations.

Many financial institutions have therefore started to "break out" all or part of the management accounting function. It is not uncommon to find this function reporting to the chief financial officer (CFO), the director of management information systems or, in rare instances, directly to the chief executive officer. The most common situation finds the overall management accounting function reporting either to the controller or the CFO, with a direct link to a steering committee for direction setting. For instance, the commercial bank illustrated in Figure 14-2 assigns performance measurement functions among three groups: financial accounting, management accounting (reporting to the CFO), and operations.

The situation grows even more complicated for multibank holding companies and other multidimensional financial institutions. One organization, for instance, divides the performance measurement functions as shown in Figure 14-3. Functions such as budgeting, cost development, product, and organizational profitability are performed in the management accounting area at the holding company level. Each institution then relies on its own accounting staff for financial accounting, regulatory reporting, and special analyses. Customer profitability is handled within each institution's line organization.

KEYS TO SUCCESS

As an institution analyzes the organization and staffing of its performance measurement function, it should keep in mind some general guidelines without which successful organization and staffing would be difficult, if not impossible.

Sensitivity to Management Needs

For example, producing excessive detail when management prefers limited detail can prove an expensive and pointless inconsistency.

It is imperative that performance measurement personnel contrast management's needs and desires with those of the entire organization. A determination then must be made as to what can be accomplished within planned time frames.

Building on Strengths

The institution must capitalize on current strengths. Some institutions allow areas to "borrow" personnel from other areas to assist with allocations in their respective area. For example, one institution's management accounting group had access to employees from trust, bankcard, and commercial lending who were trained in performance measurement methodologies. They, in turn, were responsible for determining cost allocations for their respective areas.

Education of Management

The performance measurement group must take the lead in educating management about any and all performance measurement systems. On an ongoing basis, the group should coordinate training programs so that performance information is appropriately used. This instruction and communication is the only way to ensure understanding and acceptance of the systems. In many institutions, process owners and responsibility center managers are trained before to the implementation phase. As a result, user expectations and commitment can be developed prior to the results being published.

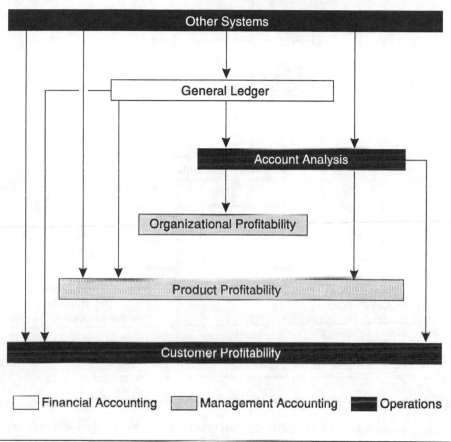

Figure 14-2 — Typical Reporting Alignment

Reporting Frequency

Performance measurement information must be frequently reported. Without credible information, the function will lose all effectiveness. Many institutions produce organizational reporting monthly while product profitability is reported quarterly. Customer profitability usually is reported quarterly, and viewed as an analytical rather than a production tool.

Responsibility for Actions

The various performance measurement functions must assume ownership of and responsibility for the systems they use. This responsibility includes the control of access, input, and uses of the information.

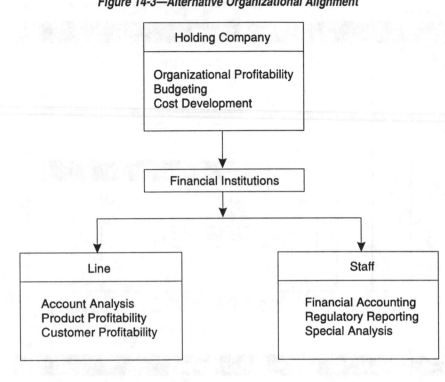

Figure 14-3—Alternative Organizational Alignment

Communication with Information Technology Personnel

Performance measurement specialists must maintain effective contact with information technology personnel throughout the institution. The heavy reliance on various systems makes this link crucial to the performance measurement function's success.

Staff Commitment

An adequate, appropriately trained staff must be committed principally to the development and ongoing production of performance measurement information.

SYNOPSIS

Through proper organization and staffing, financial institutions address the human element in the performance measurement system. Even state-of-the-art information systems may fail if these structural and human resource issues are not addressed.

Among the issues that must be addressed in the organizing and staffing of a performance measurement effort are: management accounting's roles and responsibilities, staffing requirements, task force roles and participants, and creating workplans. Institutions need to determine how they will amass the necessary resources and organize them to most efficiently perform the tasks specified by the workplace and assume the necessary roles and responsibilities.

Attention to organization linkages is also important. Reporting relationships must be clearly and logically designed, and working relationships must be carefully cultivated to ensure that the performance measurement effort works smoothly with all other impacted organizations.

A final and basic concern involves the skills required for the performance measurement staff. Experience in the financial services industry, knowledge of information systems, analytical ability, and familiarity with cost accounting are some of the qualities essential to performance measurement project staffing.

CHAPTER 15

System Design Considerations

OVERVIEW

Performance measurement systems vary in scope, functionality, and objectives. There are no perfect designs, but general approaches can be followed to help insure that systems are developed to meet management's information objectives. As in most information systems designs, there are four major phases: conceptual design, detailed design, development, and implementation of the basic input, processing, and output functions.

It is important to stress that one group in the institution should clearly "own" the design of the performance measurement system. Preferably, this should be the group that will be responsible for the operation of the system once it is placed in production. Other groups will likely be involved with some aspects of implementation, especially the more technical tasks. Because performance measurement systems usually involve data inflows from several organizational areas, this group should be centrally positioned in the institution in order to effectively manage and coordinate all aspects of system development and operation.

CONCEPTUAL DESIGN—FOUNDATION

When an institution defines its performance measurement needs, management's objectives must be clearly identified and numerous policy decisions made, linking critical success factors to their measures. The first step in actually developing the *system* is to translate these objectives and policy decisions from the conceptual design, which acts as the foundation for the detailed system design. As discussed in Chapter

13, the conceptual design reflects high-level perspective and should provide for collaboration among line management, the group designing the system, and the group actually developing it.

Developing comprehensive output formats (screens, reports, graphical displays) early in the conceptual design process is extremely important to the accuracy of the detailed system design and eventual acceptance by management. These formats let the system builders graphically demonstrate the new information the performance measurement system will provide.

In addition, a line-by-line determination of which information to include helps identify problems or concerns about how specific data elements should be gathered. Simulated outputs also illustrate to senior management the effect of policy decisions made during the design process. In developing branch profitability, for example, if shareholders' equity were to be allocated to branches and transfer priced as a source of funds, management would see the effect of the policy on each branch's earnings reports.

Today's technology offers the opportunity to quickly develop prototypes of reports and screen displays, using test data that will bear a strong resemblance to real conditions. This technique can be very valuable, especially with systems that emphasize electronic delivery. It speeds the refinement of the conceptual design into more detailed specifications that can be quickly programmed and will require minimal modification during acceptance testing.

Developing report formats at this stage offers the added benefit of forcing the system's designers to define, at the project's inception, the details and content of the reports desired and, to some extent, the intended audience. Both elements influence the system's complexity.

Typical report formats are illustrated in Figures 15-1, 15-2, and 15-3. There are no standard formats in the industry, as each institution has its own style and information needs. Many institutions are now supplementing their basic reports with ratio analyses graphs and trends.

Definitions are another important facet of the conceptual design. For instance, if policy decisions require an organizational performance reporting system to allocate equity, loan loss reserve, float, and deposit reserves to individual responsibility centers, written definitions of these policy decisions should supplement the sample report formats. Such definitions clarify for senior management the key policies that will be in effect, before detailed system design and development commence. These policy documents should detail the issue, the policy decisions, the affected performance measurement reports, and include line item descriptions.

The conceptual design also will include descriptions of essential information required to produce the reports, flow charts, and descriptions of the flow of data from the source applications.

Figure 15-1—Sample Organization Profitability

Interest Income	$3,000
Interest Expense	(6,000)
Credit/(Charge) for Funds	5,000
Net Interest Income	2,000
Provision for Loan Losses	200
Interest Income after Provision for Loan Losses	1,800
Other Income	300
Net Revenues	2,100
Operating Expense	850
Operating Income	$1,250
Overhead	90
Income before Taxes	$1,160

For example, suppose senior management wants large loans, such as fixed-rate money-market loans, to be match-funded (see Chapter 10 for a discussion of funds-transfer pricing). The loan accounting system, however, does not provide for a match funded rate field. The performance measurement system still must include a native match-funding capability because the source application system cannot currently provide that information.

To ignore the feature would be to sacrifice management's objectives without exploring any possible solutions. Before the system design is complete, research must be done to determine whether the match-funding capability can be cost-effectively built into the design, and if all the necessary source data (in this instance loan type, origination date, maturity date, and repricing date) can be gathered.

Regardless of how well the conceptual design is conceived, the system should be implemented in a manner that is as adaptable as possible, given resource and timing constraints. Reorganizations, acquisitions, changes in products, and changes in operations all potentially have an impact on the processing and credibility of performance measurement information. Even a relatively minor organizational change can result in numerous changes in responsibility hierarchies, roll-up levels (how centers are aggregated), input procedures, expense allocations, standard costs, and report distributions.

The designer has several tools to enhance overall flexibility. They include table-driven maintenance and support for powerful ad-hoc access and reporting tools.

Figure 15-2—Sample Product Profitability

	Total	Lines and Commitments	Commercial Loans	Fee Services	Retail Loan	Deposits
Interest Income	$3,000		$2,000		$1,000	
Interest Expense	5,800					$5,800
Credit/(Charge) for Funds	5,000		(1,700)		(1,500)	8,000
Net Interest Income	2,200	—	300	—	(500)	2,400
Provision for Loan Losses	200		200			
Interest Income after Provision for Loan Losses	2,000		100		(500)	2,400
Other Income	100	$70		$20		10
Noninterest Expenses	850	5	20	15	50	760
Contribution	1,250	$65	$ 80	$ 5	$(550)	$1,650
Overhead Expense	90					
Income before Taxes	$1,160					

Figure 15-3—Sample Customer Profitability

	Total	Lines and Commitments	Loans	Fee Services	Deposits
Interest Income	$50		$50		
Interest Expense	10				$10
Credit/(Charge) for Funds	(10)		(40)		30
Net Interest Income	30	—	10	—	20
Provision for Loan Losses	1	—	1		
Interest Income after Provision for Loan Losses	29		9		20
Waived Fees	(29)			$(29)	
Other Income	42	$10	2	30	
Noninterest Expenses	39	2	1	35	1
Contribution	3	$ 8	$10	$(34)	$19
Overhead Expense	4				
Income before Taxes	$ (1)				

Because all reporting requirements cannot be anticipated in advance, data downloads allow users to manipulate the data using spreadsheets to perform calculations and word processing to format the output to suit current needs.

As part of the conceptual design process, senior management should be encouraged to describe its view of system flexibility. This can be done by identifying measures or reports that are "sacred," and those that present more opportunity for tradeoff. This information will help the designer to better understand just how flexible management requires the system to be and what areas are vital to its needs.

It also is important to incorporate planning and historical data into the conceptual design at the outset, because most performance reporting has little meaning without benchmarks to serve as a basis for evaluating current results.

DETAILED SYSTEM DESIGN

Once management has approved the conceptual design, the next step is to develop detailed system requirements, often referred to as a functional specification. This action should translate the conceptual design into specific input, processing, and output elements. It should show how the gap between information requirements and availability will be bridged (again, see Figure 15-1).

During this phase of development, detailed system objectives and requirements are defined involving numerous decisions. For example, how often will funds transfer pricing rate changes be made? If the yield curve is static, monthly quotes may suffice. However, weekly or even daily quotes may be required in times of rapidly fluctuating interest rates. Other issues to be resolved during this phase include the required frequency of reporting, reporting media, and the distribution of the report formats to the various levels of management.

Input

After detailed system requirements and objectives have been identified, the data elements needed to develop the desired information must be defined. These elements vary according to whether the objective concerns are organization-, product-, or customer-related (they also vary with management policy). For example, customer identification is required to develop and report customer profitability, but it may not be necessary to analyze product or organizational profitability. Ultimately, however, it becomes very useful to capture customer, product, and organizational identifiers simultaneously.

A list of data elements commonly required to provide basic performance measurement information is provided below. This list is not exhaustive, and the elements included are not necessarily part of every institution's system. They are generally obtainable, however, and can satisfy most performance measurement needs. The discussion of these data elements assumes the system design depicted in Figure 15-4, in which information is derived from individual source applications, including general ledger, and merged into a repository database.

The database is used to house the results of transfer pricing calculations, provide the basis for all allocations, and prepare detailed performance measurement reports. This data repository approach is growing in popularity, primarily because it relieves the production systems of the burden of producing integrated performance measurement information.

Many of these data elements are required to perform funds-transfer pricing and may come from a variety of sources, usually spanning several systems. For instance, some transfer pricing systems require balance data directly from the customer application systems, but they rely on general ledger input for noncustomer-related balances. Therefore, it is important not only to identify the data elements but also to identify their source, and the integrity of those sources:

- Institution identification for report consolidation purposes in multibank holding companies or in banks with nonbank subsidiaries.

- Branch/location identification for branch profitability reporting.

- Responsibility center identification for responsibility center reporting. Depending on the organization structure, these data also may be used to report business line profitability.

- Customer identification for customer profitability reporting. Care must be taken here to obtain consistent customer identification across all systems that provide input to the performance measurement system. A centralized customer information file best provides that consistency.

- Product identification for product profitability reporting. This identification can be either a fixed product code or, for more flexibility, a combination of one or more existing fields used to identify loan or deposit types (e.g., Fed line/call codes for loan systems or type/series codes for deposit systems).

- Loan or deposit number for audit trails when funds-transfer pricing occurs at an individual loan or deposit level of detail. This data element also is necessary for ad hoc analysis at the individual loan or deposit level.

- Average daily balance for reporting period for funds-transfer pricing calculations of yields, and reporting of profitability information. This data element often is the most difficult to accurately capture. Potential problems include the

Figure 15-4—Integrated View of Systems and Information Flows

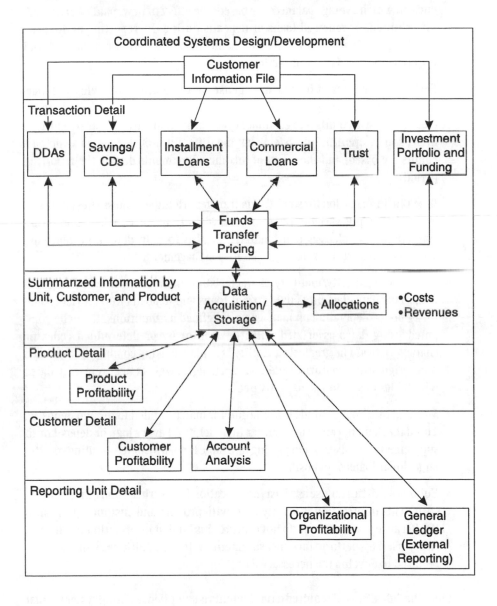

existing average balance fields being on a customer cycle rather than on a financial reporting cycle; source application systems having different month-ends on which average balances are based; the effect of new, paid-off, charged-off, matured, or renewed loans or deposits during the reporting period; the effect of participations; the effect of unamortized discounts or premiums; and the effect of back-dated transactions.

- Period-to-date interest income or expense for calculations of yields and margins and for reporting profitability information. Potential problems here include interest accounts on a customer cycle rather than on a financial reporting cycle; source application systems having different month-ends on which accounts are based; and the effect of income adjustments during the reporting period.

- Base-rate information for some funds-transfer pricing schemes. These data can be used to apply variable rates to average daily balances when computing transfer pricing charges and credits, and also to help determine repricing sensitivity of portfolios for asset/liability management.

- Repricing sensitivity/maturity characteristics for funds-transfer pricing systems. This data element is used to slot loans and deposits into repricing/maturity pools, depending on management-defined assumptions. It can be computed using dates associated with the loan or by predetermined codes or characteristics. The greatest flexibility is achieved using combinations of current, origination, maturity, and last repricing as well as next repricing dates with tables to slot into sensitivity pools.

- Matched rate/cost of funds information for match-funded loans and deposits. This data element can be used either to match-fund every loan or deposit or to supplement a funds-transfer pricing rate table for use in match-funding specific large dollar loans or deposits.

- Volume statistics for use as a basis of allocation for overhead and other indirect costs. This information is mainly used with product and customer profitability. Because many systems do not capture this kind of information in a format easily used by performance measurement systems, additional work often is required to develop the necessary data.

Once the "ideal" list of required data elements is compiled, existing systems must be researched to determine whether the elements are available. If not, tradeoffs may be necessary between accuracy and the cost of developing the needed information.

For instance, many thrift institutions do not maintain average balances on their general ledger systems. For these institutions, a new general ledger system or substantial changes to their existing systems may be required to add average balance capability. As an alternative, they may choose a simple averaging methodology as an imprecise but cost-effective way to provide average balance information. After choosing such a simplified solution, however, most institutions would strive for more precise information by including average balance capabilities in their long-range systems plans.

Today's sophisticated activity-based costing methodologies rely on the availability of a wide range of detailed statistical data. Often these data are available only from product delivery/application systems that are optimized for maximum throughput and efficiency, without regard for management information requirements. If the desired statistics are captured at all, they are in a form that is very difficult for anyone to use without extensive technical knowledge of the system.

Another factor often overlooked is the fact that processing systems often are not used by back-office personnel in the manner in which they were originally intended. This often creates data corruption that can stymie the most diligent data analyst. Specifically, let's say a consumer loan application is enhanced to include a data element for customer segment code. It then appears as a required field on the input screen. Unless an effort is made to maintain the integrity of what is entered, the information is useless. Moreover, this condition will not be revealed until someone (often the management accountant) tries to use the information, and it yields meaningless results. Often, a time and resource-consuming data "scrub" is the result, along with project delays.

Processing

Processing logic is an integral part of any information system. It is especially important in management reporting because of the many data input systems and organizations involved in preparing the information. Management reports, for example, often include yields, cost of funds, and other rate information. Depending on the complexity of the system being developed, the underlying information may consist of several different rate calculation methodologies.

Commercial loans may use a "month/year" convention such as 30/360, actual/360, or actual/365 to annualize interest rates. Installment loans may use a similarly wide variety of methodologies, depending on the loan types. But when totals are aggregated and combined yields/rates are calculated, which annualization method should be used? For this reason and others, institutions must be careful when making decisions and designing system logic such as rate annualization. The effect on reported yields and margins could significantly affect individual line managers' reported profitability.

Processing logic in a funds-transfer pricing (FTP) system should receive special scrutiny during design and development, especially when precise methodologies such as duration adjustments and match-funding are employed. Transfer pricing systems calculate charges for funds used and credits for funds provided by organizational units, products, and customers. As discussed in Chapter 10, these charges and credits determine the net interest spread of assets and liabilities.

Over the last several years, many software vendors have introduced sophisticated FTP systems with the flexibility to be tailored to most performance measurement system designs. Given the overall significance that FTP plays in profitability and in the time to implement, many institutions are turning to these commercially available programs for their FTP solutions.

However, designing and implementing a custom FTP system can be done with proper planning, time, programming abilities, and a clear design. Because FTP calculations require detailed information from source systems, it is often preferable to build this capability directly into these source systems, especially the larger ones such as commercial loans and time deposits. For the rest of the balance sheet, a native FTP capability is necessary that can perform the proper rate assignment, charge/credit accrual, summarization, and posting to the management accounting ledger.

Several other calculations are performed in funds-transfer pricing that may not be verifiable elsewhere (because data are pulled from several places, such as commercial loan and certificate of deposit systems). Examples include grouping transactions by repricing sensitivity, calculating margins after charges and credits, and instrument/product summarizations. Extreme care must therefore be exercised to ensure that the logic is well designed and that the design is communicated to the intended recipients of the reports. This communication will facilitate the recipients' understanding and acceptance of the system.

Tables should be used wherever possible to enhance processing and operating flexibility. For instance, as part of organizational profitability measurement, the reporting of responsibility center roll-ups should use tables to deal with the organizational changes that are bound to occur. Or, in a transfer pricing system, expense pool assignment and historical rate tables can give management the flexibility to change key assumptions later without necessitating major systems revisions.

Operational characteristics of the system also must be included in the detailed design. Report distribution, report media, processing schedules, reconciliation procedures, rerun criteria, and other elements all must be addressed at this stage of the development process. Some institutions defer decisions on such operations until late in the process, but the more complex the system, the more important it is to settle these matters early on.

Consider, for example, a situation in which a sophisticated transaction-oriented funds-transfer pricing system must run before product profitability reports can be produced. Management may be expecting product profitability reports on the eighth workday after month-end, but funds-transfer pricing may have to run on the second weekend after month-end for volume reasons. That will delay the delivery of product profitability reports.

An important reason for defining report distribution early in the development process is to help management decide who really needs to receive each report, and when and how. Management systems often are developed with only a rough idea of who must have reports and how the reports will be used to measure performance. Forcing the decision early may reduce the number of reports required, or at least cause a change in the production and distribution schedule. It may be decided, for example, that detailed product profitability reports will not be distributed to individual line managers until final adjustments are made, and then only via electronic media in lieu of paper.

Output

With the new emerging technologies and electronic platforms being developed, the output from performance measurement systems may actually be through a terminal or workstation rather than on hard copy. Executives today are more equipped to use computers, and are interested in obtaining the information they need directly electronically. With this capability comes the need to have the ability to "get at the information they want to see." Regardless of the media, the raw data must be organized and produced in a structured manner, and ad hoc report writing capabilities factored in.

Report formats are another important element of a detailed system design. Although most of the work in defining these formats will have been completed during the conceptual design stage, changes may now be required because of other system design decisions. In such cases, project management should review the changes before development is continued.

Balancing and reconciliation reports usually are defined at this stage of system development. These are important for control purposes (as is true of any information system) but they are critical to the acceptance and credibility of the performance measurement system.

It is extremely important that any management reporting tool remain credible in the eyes of the line managers whose performance it measures. Balancing reports serve that function in a performance measurement system. These reports should be designed to allow information to be verified, where possible, against existing information sources with which managers are already comfortable. This may seem obvious, but many institutions spend considerable time and money on sophisticated performance measurement systems only to have them rejected or discredited by line managers who could not verify the reported results against such other information sources such as general ledger, or externally reported results.

Output, however, is not restricted to reports. Data can be made available via decision-support software or Executive Information Systems (EIS) so that managers can perform ad hoc and "what if" analyses. Some institutions, in fact, favor ad hoc reporting and analysis capabilities to such an extent that they largely dispense with production reports.

SYNOPSIS

The design and development of a performance measurement information system consists of four basic steps: conceptual design, detailed design, system development, and implementation. Each of these steps should be followed just as strictly for management systems as it is for customer accounting or transaction processing systems. Particular attention must be paid to defining the data elements, verifying the data's validity, designing the output formats, defining significant calculations, and developing procedures to balance and verify results against other information sources.

Because many systems and organizations are usually involved in developing performance measurement information, the design and development process works most effectively with centralized coordination. Most important, however, is that senior management participate in and approve all facets of the process.

CHAPTER 16

System Implementation Issues

OVERVIEW

Many factors must be taken into account when planning the implementation of a system to drive performance measurement reporting. First, the scope must be clearly defined, along with the relative priorities within that scope. Understanding the scope will help in choosing the appropriate technological platform for the system. The rapid pace of change in technology forces the design to be a forward looking solution, because the institution must consider what new capabilities will become available over the course of the development cycle. Subsequently, the requirements for financial and technical resources will emerge, along with the necessary human resources. Matching availability of resources to physical needs will determine the final schedule, so that preparations can be made for the delivery tasks of installation, documentation, and training. Projecting these dates may identify inherent process conflict with such cyclical activities as the fiscal year close and budgeting. This may, in turn, force schedule adjustments to accommodate necessary participants from outside the project team who are critical to system acceptance and ultimate adoption. As is the case with all systems development projects, developing a good plan and sticking to it will keep the effort on schedule and under control.

NO TWO PERFORMANCE MEASUREMENT SYSTEMS ARE EXACTLY ALIKE

All business information systems must reflect the management process they support as well as the environment in which they will operate. They also must fit within the constraints the business environment imposes on them with regard to both development and ongoing operation.

Although the basic system processes are generic, various management styles, cultures, and needs make it very difficult for a commercial software developer to market a management accounting application that would appeal to a wide range of financial institutions. Contrast this with the world of financial accounting, where the rigor of externally defined reporting standards makes the general ledger almost a commodity item. The few management accounting systems on the market are really "shells," consisting of a basic data model, a generic reporting capability, and processing engines that support the commonly used allocation and funds-transfer pricing methods.

Even if one of the commercially available packages becomes a part of the solution, the user must expend a considerable degree of effort to provide the necessary data interfaces and customize the processing and output to the institution's unique requirements. As such, all performance measurement implementations, regardless of whether they are bought or built, will require a significant development effort in order to be successful.

ASSESSING INFORMATION NEEDS AND DESIGN IMPLICATIONS

Before an institution actually begins designing a performance measurement system, it needs to examine its information network from a business perspective. That is, it needs to look at its information systems not individually but as components of an overall business information support mechanism.

This seems obvious, but is often a difficult step to take. It can involve many different organizations within the institution, each with a different perspective on what information the systems can and should provide. For example, lenders need marketing and customer relationship information, tellers need individual customer account information and transaction detail, and internal auditors and credit review groups need loan classification and credit risk information.

Looking at information needs in this broad sense, a financial institution will find many options available for developing a performance measurement system. These alternatives range from simple "high-level" PC spreadsheet-based systems to comprehensive client-server and integrated mainframe-based systems. As illustrated in Figure 16-1, this range of systems possibilities mirrors the range of an institution's information needs (the performance measurement continuum). The arrow at the top represents the performance measurement continuum (as described in Chapter 4),

Figure 16-1—Developing Performance Information

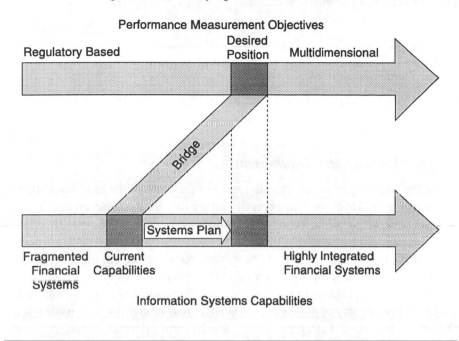

Performance Measurement Objectives

Regulatory Based   Desired
                          Position   Multidimensional

Bridge

Systems Plan

Fragmented   Current
Financial   Capabilities   Highly Integrated
Systems   Financial Systems

Information Systems Capabilities

while the arrow at the bottom represents the information systems continuum. Performance measurement information system designs include both short-term solutions ("bridging" the two arrows) and longer-term approaches that move capabilities along the bottom arrow.

Although institutions generally move from left to right along these continua, that movement is not necessarily sequential. For instance, an institution that regularly uses basic organizational profitability information may at the same time develop high-level, ad hoc product profitability information. The institution thus begins to develop some form of product profitability information without actually moving from left to right along the information systems continuum.

As with all systems development, the information approach management decides on will eventually require tradeoffs between objectives, resources, and time frame. For instance, management may be willing to settle for product-line profitability information (with many associated assumptions) for an initial phase until more detailed product profitability measurement systems can be developed. PCs and LAN servers can be ideal tools to help provide such interim information while more comprehensive systems are in development. In fact, some institutions find that interim solutions provide most of the information they need and never actually pursue a more comprehensive solution.

IMPLEMENTATION PLANNING AND SCOPE

Many factors determine the scope of an implementation effort in terms of the amount of time and resources that will be required. Among the most important are:

Interface Development Requirements

By far the most important driver with regard to the scope of the implementation is the effort required to acquire the necessary source data from product application and delivery systems as well as financial and administrative systems. The extent to which such data are already available through an existing interface, or can be acquired through a new one, requires careful analysis and cooperative planning, often involving resources not under the direct control of the project team.

In some cases, changes or enhancements to the processing sequence within the target application may be required. Such changes may or may not be feasible within the overall scheme of enterprise system development priorities. If not, near-term "work-arounds" may be necessary.

Source Data Analysis

The conceptual design (see Chapter 13) will indirectly set the requirements with regard to the scope and granularity of the necessary source system data. A critical task during implementation planning is to precisely match and map these requirements against the availability of data elements from the product delivery systems (e.g., loans and deposits), administrative systems (e.g., general ledger), etc. This is often a "reverse engineering" process that begins with the reports, traces back through the management accounting processes, and finally results in a list of required data elements to support those processes at the requisite level of detail. In most cases, the analyst will have to enlist the aid of those who maintain and use the source systems, because they best understand the system's contents beyond what is documented or widely known.

For example, if the conceptual design calls for allocated human resource or personnel expenses to organizations based on active headcount, with varying rates for full-time, part-time, salaried, and executive staff, there is an implied requirement that headcount data by type must be available at the organizational level for each center within the institution.

Another common example involves the requirement to use monthly average balances. Many existing loan and deposit systems do not maintain this information, necessitating the collection of daily information at the instrument level in order to generate monthly average balances and perform detailed funds-transfer pricing calculations. For larger institutions, the prospect of efficiently handling such a large volume of data on a daily basis can pose a daunting technical challenge.

It should never be assumed that the data to support the desired methods and reporting conventions will be readily available, or that the process of seeking them out will not consume a significant amount of time and effort. Nor should it be assumed that the integrity of such data will hold up under the intense scrutiny commanded by performance reporting. Data analysis and interface development are invariably the most demanding phases of the implementation process.

The project team must always be aware of the cost of the incremental level of precision and make informed decisions on a case-by-case basis. It is also important to consider that the precision of the overall calculation chain is only as strong as its weakest link; that is, the most detailed transaction volume information has little value if the method used to arrive at unit costs is imprecise.

Processing Implications of the Methodology

Some reporting conventions require custom processing that can add complexity. For example, the use of multiple day-basis calculations in the application of FTP rates or the application of adjustments for tax-advantaged investments can create subtle distortions in the results, unless enough time is allowed for thorough development and testing.

Retention/Restatement of History

If an institution attempts a conversion from an existing application, a considerable effort may be needed to capture and convert the history to a comparable basis. In many cases, this is a task best avoided unless it can be accomplished without compromise.

Delivery Requirements

Traditionally, fixed-format paper reporting was the accepted delivery mode for these applications. Many institutions now demand that results be delivered electronically, through an existing automated office infrastructure. Such an approach can yield considerable efficiencies, but will entail a systems integration task that can easily be underestimated, especially if the effort is inconsistent with the institution's overall office systems direction and timing.

Experience of the Project Team

Generally, management accountants are not specialists in systems design and development disciplines. They often must learn these skills as they go, which can add to the duration of the effort. It is good practice to include specialists on the project team with considerable experience in this kind of work.

Enterprise Management Model

Institutions that intend to grow must include the effect of anticipated consolidations and/or acquisitions in their planning. With new companies come new accounting systems, new operations, and new procedures and standards. Incorporating these into the framework without corrupting the resulting information is key to overall success. An important consideration here involves the level of autonomy the management of the individual legal entities have within the holding company structure.

In some cases, the management model treats these as semi-independent entities and merely attempts to measure their performance along a consistent set of high-level benchmarks. In other cases, acquired companies are completely assimilated, both operationally and philosophically, into the existing structure and become part of a monolithic whole. This model features combined source applications, common information standards, and performance measurement methods that assure a consistent financial "language" and comparability of results in all dimensions.

Each of these approaches implies a very different strategy for systems implementation. In many cases, there is a slow progression from a legal entity view to a line of business view that must be reflected in all performance reporting. As a result, the system design must support both.

Data Dimensions and Views

A truly comprehensive solution must be able to identify all the multiple business dimensions separately. But it also must allow construction of separate hierarchical views in each dimension, and provide flexible access to results both within and across these dimensions and views:

- Dimensions
  - Organization
  - Account
  - Product
  - Customer/Household/Relationship

- – Market Segment
- – Time/Period
- • Views
  - – Legal (external)
  - – Managerial (span of control)
  - – Line of Business (market)
  - – Actual/Plan/Forecast (benchmark)

Tradeoffs and Phasing Strategies

Once the ideal scope of the ultimate implementation is determined, the desired features must be rank-ordered, both in terms of their absolute necessity and the time and resources required to put them into place. This will often result in tradeoff decisions, which must be arrived at through thoughtful discussions between developers and users.

One commonly used phasing approach is to implement the entire functionality of the system for one organization at a time. This is often used in bank holding companies comprised of several semiautonomous legal entities of comparable size. It has the effect of "containing" the implementation by limiting the number of interfaces, the amount of data to be processed and delivered, and the number of users to be affected. It works so long as comprehensive results can be reported for the portion of the enterprise that is included. For integrated organizations, carving out such a pilot group can prove more difficult. In these instances, a phasing strategy that implements the most valuable aspects of the design first and rolls out other features over time will keep the scope of the effort attainable, and effectively manage expectations within the user community.

A vital consideration here is the enhancement and replacement plans already in place for the source applications as part of the performance measurement system implementation plan. For instance, it makes little sense to develop a comprehensive interface to a loan accounting system that is due for replacement in the near future. A temporary high-level interface can be put in place until the new system is installed, at which time a complete data stream from the new system can be designed. This also gives the designers of the new source system the opportunity to include the data requirements of the management accounting system in their plans. In this way, progress along the performance measurement continuum can advance in sync with advances along the overall systems development continuum.

This notion of building external MIS requirements into delivery system design is vital to the institution's overall information system strategy.

PLATFORM SELECTION CRITERIA

Once the scope of the implementation is determined, a technology platform consistent with that scope must be selected. The system must have the capacity to support the information technology and storage requirements of the functional specification. It may also have to support direct on-line access for many individuals/users at once.

During platform selection, the designer must provide for sufficient capacity, not only for the initial implementation, but for the inevitable growth of any successful system, and all successful enterprises. For this reason platforms where capacity can be added incrementally without changes to the basic system architecture are desirable.

Today, many more technology platform options are available than ever before. They range from stand-alone desktop systems to large-scale enterprise networks, each having specific implications with regard to functionality, cost, and support requirements..

The following factors must be considered when making a selection to ensure a proper fit:

Organizational Size and Detail Requirements

These will drive the absolute amount of information the system will process. The sheer volume of data that must be acquired, processed, reported, and stored can be accurately estimated and used to assemble a capacity plan. This plan will determine which system components can reside on the desktop, and which may have to be relegated to larger departmental server or mainframe computers.

Organizational Model

A centralized, monolithic organizational model is more consistent with a centralized system architecture, operated by a single group at a single site that emphasizes control and consistency. Decentralized institutions prefer a distributed architecture that emphasizes flexibility and responsiveness over efficiency and control.

Number and Location of Users

This will determine the role which telecommunications must play in the implementation. In some cases, enhancements in this area must become part of the project scope.

Flexibility of Scheduling: Need to Control Computing Resources

If flexibility and speed of the closing cycle are high priorities, it is desirable to perform as much of the processing as possible on dedicated computing resources. A management accounting application that must compete with the time deposit accounting system for computing resources will not be available on demand for a reconsolidation.

Opportunities for Process Integration

If integration with such other related processes as planning and forecasting is part of the implementation strategy, this may be more easily achieved if those systems should reside on the same platform as performance reporting.

Availability of Technology Support Resources

Whatever platform is chosen, it is imperative that the necessary resources be available to support it from a technological perspective, both during installation and for the life of the system. This support should be included in the overall project resource projec tions.

System Usage Expectations

A proper system design will always be the direct outgrowth of the conceptual design, because this is the functional specification in its purest form. One question the conceptual design must answer is who the real users of the system will be. This may seem obvious, but often is not.

Some systems are designed to be used almost exclusively by the administrative reporting function, usually within the financial organization, which, in turn, produces the presentations that line management ultimately sees and acts on. These users require data that is "actionable" (i.e., that can be used as input to modeling/analysis and presentation tools that are used to add decision-supporting value).

Other systems are designed to bring the information directly to the desktops of executive management, which is empowered to manipulate the information directly as required. In this scenario, the provider's role is to ensure that the information is credible, reliable, and timely. This approach is gaining favor, as the technology has become more user-friendly and managers are learning the advantage of removing the information "filters" from the management process.

What is the physical nature of the audience? To how many people, how often, and in what medium will performance data be delivered? Will the recipients be in the office or on the road? The answers to these questions will drive the delivery mode of the design. Systems that provide for predominantly electronic delivery with ad-hoc data access are quite different from those that rely entirely on fixed-format paper delivery at a fixed point in time.

Flexibility and Capacity

Another attribute that must be taken into consideration is flexibility. Changes in system requirements will be ongoing and frequent as the institution changes management strategy and focus. Because performance measurement systems are only as effective as they are relevant to their environment, they must have the ability to adapt easily and quickly. Generally, a technology platform that facilitates end-user computing will prove superior in this regard, because it puts more of the maintenance directly in the hands of the users. For institutions that are growing quickly, the ability to rapidly increase system capacity can best be served with "scalable" platforms that can be expanded simply by adding additional processors and disk storage, without changes to other system components. The increasingly popular client-server platforms tend, by their nature, to be very strong in these areas. As a result, they quickly are becoming the most popular platforms for building decision support applications.

Technological Constraints

All system designs must fit within the overall information technology context of both the institution and the intended users. Leading-edge technology that is incompatible with, or cannot be supported by, the existing technological infrastructure will fail, unless it is considered part of an explicit experiment into new technologies, and is intended to help set a new direction.

This "pioneer" work is distracting but necessary. Performance reporting applications cannot be considered end-user computing exercises that run independently of the traditional IT organization, because they depend on data from the rest of the enterprise, and are considered mission-critical upon acceptance by the executive community.

Resource Constraints

The design of any such application cannot outgrow the resources that have been allocated to it. Overly ambitious designs that outgrow their budgets often fall behind schedule, lose precious credibility, and die of their own weight long before final implementation. It is imperative that a well-thought-out design drive an equally well-considered project plan. The plan must make reliable estimates of the technology and human resources necessary for development, testing, and installation. Any attempt to expand the scope of the project after initiation should be resisted, unless it is mandated and funded by executive sponsorship.

As is always the case in proper information systems planning, it is vital that the designer build in the capacity to accommodate anticipated growth and change in functional requirements. Decision-support systems in general, and performance reporting systems in particular, are dynamic in nature. After successful implementation, there inevitably comes the demand for expansion of scope. The best defense against premature obsolescence is a forward-looking design, constructed on a flexible platform, allowing for incremental expansion that fully leverages the initial investment.

NEW TECHNOLOGIES: CHANGING THE ECONOMICS

For decades, the computer processing capacity required to maintain a sophisticated management accounting capability within any sizable financial institution was the exclusive domain of the central information technology function. This function's primary task was to support the product delivery applications that generated revenue. MIS applications, which were not perceived to directly impact the bottom line, were often given little or no priority.

The arrival of powerful desktop and departmental-level processors that can be purchased, maintained, and programmed directly by staff support organizations has had a profound effect. End-user computing has proliferated the enterprise, in many cases putting performance reporting applications entirely within the technological and budgetary reach of the user institution.

The amount of data that can be processed for a fixed amount of money will continue to grow exponentially. The perceived economic value of decision support data also is also growing, as line executives' demands for timely, credible, and thoughtfully presented information become integrated into the management process. This, combined with the trend toward downsized, streamlined organizations, puts the onus on support organizations to achieve very high efficiency levels in their business processes.

Manually assembling and collating data, most often exemplified by the task of rekeying data from reports to spreadsheets, has no place in this scenario. The task of adding value through analysis and presentation has become the primary focus, and the market has responded with technologies that enable the user to operate effectively in this role. For the management accountant, these technologies include:

- Powerful end-user programming tools that can access and manipulate data without a long learning curve, eliminating much of the cost of specialized programming talent.

- Packaged software for cost allocations, funds-transfer pricing, and reporting functions, which has reduced the need for custom programming.

- Scalable client-server processing platforms that combine the flexibility of desktop-level data manipulation with central data storage for efficiency and control, at far less cost than mainframe-based solutions of comparable capacity.

- "Open" systems standards that enable the transfer of data between applications and hardware platforms, which has allowed the interoperability of competing vendors and driven down prices.

- Wide-area networks that economically support the transfer of large volumes of data between physical locations.

- Database gateway technology that makes data from existing mainframe-based "legacy" systems available to the desktop, in many cases without the need for extensive custom programming and maintenance.

- Electronic delivery through office automation networks that eliminates most of the cost of printing and transporting paper reports.

PERFORMANCE REPORTING DATA ARCHITECTURE

A financial services industry standard has emerged for the basic data architecture behind integrated performance reporting systems. It has several elements which are detailed in Figure 16-2.

Workstations

The financial analyst workstation concept provides a single point of integration for all data access, analysis, manipulation, and presentation functions. Through the use of consistent graphical interfaces, applications are kept easy to learn and use. Open systems standards assure seamless transfer of data between tools and applications. This approach yields opportunities for improving the reporting process.

Executive Information Systems (EIS)

Workstations also can be configured to serve as an executive information system, through the use of specialized tools that generate user interfaces suitable for the executive audience. If the other architectural components are in place, implementing an EIS is as simple as changing the emphasis of the workstation application from analysis to presentation.

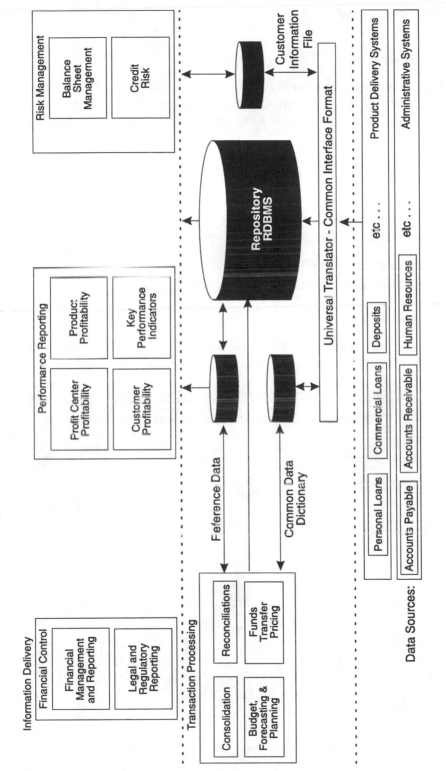

Figure 16-2—Financial Systems Architecture

Common Interfaces

Many decision support applications have the same elemental needs. Therefore, combining them has many benefits, including assuring consistency of timing and content, reducing overall processing, and cutting down on maintenance through the elimination of redundant feeds.

Inclusion of External Data

A fully integrated strategy also must support the current and projected data requirements for other related MIS, such as:

- External and regulatory reporting
- Marketing and external data
- Balance sheet (asset-liability) management

Common Structures

Use of common data definitions and structures, such as hierarchies and report titles, ensures a common reporting language throughout the enterprise. This greatly facili-

Figure 16-3—Financial and Cost Analysis Workstations

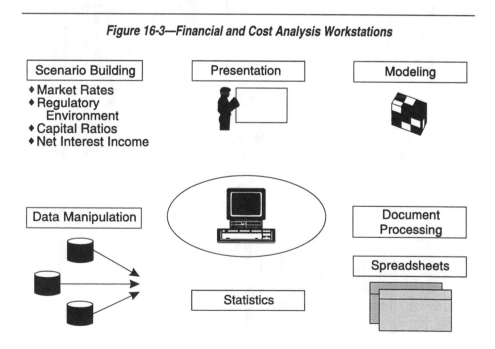

tates the data analysis task for the developer, and the data interpretation task for the user.

Central Data Repository

The most important component of the architecture is the use of a data repository that spans all the applications and houses all the common data elements. This is vital to assure consistency and credibility, and produce operating efficiency. Because flexibility is an essential requirement of the system, this repository is almost always built upon a relational database platform.

Transaction-Level Data "Warehouse"

This option is particularly useful when data are required at transaction level detail that would otherwise not be retained over the course of a reporting period by the source system. The warehouse captures these data, usually on a daily basis (weekly is also an option), and acts as a staging area where the data can be normalized and summarized at the end of the cycle. It thus removes this burden from the source applications and makes it easier to perform any custom processing required.

BUILD OR BUY (AND MODIFY)

The decision whether to build or buy a performance reporting system often becomes difficult, but need not be. None of the commercially marketed packages aimed at the financial services industry is usable "out of the box." All demand a certain degree of customization during the implementation process to incorporate the institutions' reporting hierarchies, charts of accounts, and other necessary structures.

Data interfaces will have to be constructed regardless of whether or not a purchased solution is involved. Some packages, however, provide specific support for the interface process that can make it easier to implement. Although custom-developed solutions are always most faithful to the conceptual design, few financial services organizations have sufficient development resources available for design, development, and testing of such a complex application. Moreover, as a rule, these disciplines are not supported within the user organization.

For the vast majority of institutions, purchased software will play a significant role in the overall solution. Some of the most important factors to consider when evaluating a purchased solution include:

- The software must be able to support the conceptual design, including the basic management accounting methodologies.

- Custom development nearly always costs more than a purchased solution, due to the effect of "reinventing the wheel."

- Vendor solutions require less time to implement, through the elimination of most coding and testing tasks.

- Implementation support for commonly used packages is readily available in the marketplace, either through the vendor or through third-party consultants and value-added resellers.

- Reputable vendors can provide reference clients who are a source of much valuable experience and expertise.

- The overall project expenditures are easier to predict and control with a vendor solution.

SYSTEM DEVELOPMENT AND IMPLEMENTATION

Once the detailed design is completed and approved, systems development efforts can begin in earnest. During this stage, there must be close coordination between the system designers and developers, because design changes often occur due to system or cost constraints unforeseen during the conceptual and detailed design stages. Management should review and approve design changes and resolutions before the affected aspects of the system are developed.

For instance, if a matched-maturity funds-transfer pricing system is being developed and a repricing information field used to define the term of the instrument turns out to be unreliable, another field or methodology for funding rate assignment may have to be chosen. This change could significantly alter the information included in the final managerial reports, and that possibility should be communicated promptly to management to avoid unrealistic expectations. If possible, the implementation team should include people who will eventually be using the system, to help them better understand it and to help establish its credibility.

Testing

Performance measurement systems are data-intensive by nature and require exhaustive test cycles. Each interface must be tested as a unit, along with each of the calculation processes and reports. Once these have been certified, they must be tested as a group in what is known as an integration test. This is accomplished by having the development team run the entire production cycle, using a test "script" with relatively small amounts of data manufactured for the purpose, much as it would occur in production. Because the desired results are known in advance, the outputs from the test are compared to the benchmarks from the test script. This is always an iterative process because the resolution of one error often reveals the presence of others.

System performance testing calls for processing large volumes of usually meaningless test data to see whether the application can handle the stress of full production volumes, while remaining within the production scheduling windows called for in the system requirements. In this case, the numeric results are ignored, because the test is meant only to measure processing speed, efficiency, and system stability. The overall "usability" (from the administrator's point of view) and flexibility should also be evaluated at this time.

Once these tests are successfully completed, the next stage is what is generally called user acceptance testing. This is where "live" or real data are processed through a normal production cycle by the organization that will administer it in production. This is the first attempt to operate the system exactly as it will be when delivered. It amounts to a "dress rehearsal," except that the output is not distributed outside of the group. It is at this stage that the high-level results are reviewed against external sources and basic integrity reviews of the FTP and cost transfer processes are performed. For example, the FTP process will create a profit or loss condition within the internal treasury unit that must fall within an established range. The same holds true for the residual expenses that remain in processing and support organizations subsequent to cost allocations.

The output functions must also be tested to ensure that they accurately represent the content of that database. One common method is to verify that any two reports or screens with common content show equivalent results. Another method is to use ad hoc query functions to verify the data on reports and screens. This capability is extremely helpful when testing the integrity of large data stores such as those inherent to a management accounting system. Often, the same data access and work station facilities offered to system users can be employed for this purpose.

The last major testing function involves the documentation of the system, which should be made available, in draft, to selected users. The users should review it to ensure that it is clear, informative, and easy to use. This should be done early enough to incorporate any necessary changes in time for scheduled system delivery.

Documentation

The documentation process actually begins during the conceptual design phase (see Chapter 15), when the management accounting methodologies and policies are reviewed and approved. Subsequent activities, such as functional and detailed specifications, build on that foundation. If all of the relevant policy and procedure assumptions, along with the specifications for input, process, and output functions, are maintained in a central library with consistent formats, preparing the final delivered documents requires little more than assembly and packaging on the word processor. Electronic media are preferable, because, as we have noted, these systems tend to be highly dynamic and the manuals end up becoming "living" documents. If they reside on a network, up-to-date versions are always available to users without a labor-intensive publishing process. For systems with electronic delivery, custom help screens can be integrated right into the application.

Orientation and Training

It was once pointed out that there are "lies," "damn lies," and "statistics." And in fact, without a proper understanding of the data, and a context within which to interpret them, the numbers produced by a performance measurement system are, at best, merely accurate quantitative measures of the state of the business at a point in time. At worst, they can be misleading, and can direct management toward courses of action that are counterproductive.

For example, a bank that was allocating capital based on asset volume was giving funds credit on that capital at a high long-term rate. The bank's senior executives realized that they could raise their divisional net income, as well as their ROA (which formed the basis of their incentive compensation formula) by booking large volumes of low-spread Acceptance assets. From an external perspective, this proved to be a marginal use of scarce capital resources and the bank's stock suffered in the market.

In order to realize the value of an investment in performance measurement systems, careful thought must be given to communicating the management process assumptions inherent in the conceptual design both to the decision makers that are the real users of the system, and to their financial support organizations. Particular attention must be paid to carefully explaining the management accounting methods and policies, as well as the manner in which the results are displayed in the tables and graphs. Any compromises made with regard to the completeness and accuracy of the data or the precision of the calculations should be completely documented.

It is well documented that MIS applications that are not well understood or perceived as mysterious "black boxes" will not be accepted by the executive community. In these instances, the information provided will be ignored, or even openly challenged and subverted by a distrustful audience. This danger always exists, because performance measurement systems are, by their nature, used to evaluate their users, and users who do not fare well often will seek to discredit the data.

In many firms, a formal orientation session is scheduled to prepare the users just prior to the delivery of the initial results. This is used to announce the availability of the new information, distribute the documentation, explain any changes from previous reporting conventions, and answer any questions that may arise. If the important policy and methodology issues are continuously reviewed by the project sponsors during the development period, the users will be well prepared to accept the new system and quickly use it to advantage.

SYNOPSIS

When developing an implementation plan for a performance measurement system, particular attention must be paid to defining the ultimate scope of the effort, establishing the priorities, and choosing the appropriate technology platform. It also is vital to make sure that all of the proper resources will be available to accomplish the necessary tasks on schedule, including allowance for a complete testing and documentation regimen. Until the system has established the necessary credibility, accessibility, and flexibility, it will not be accepted as a prime source of information to support critical business decisions by the executive community. And without this, even the best system designs provide little or no value to the institution.

PART V

Using Performance Measurement Information

CHAPTER 17

Managing and Using Product and Customer Information

OVERVIEW

Successful performance measurement systems supply management with the information it deems valuable to make informed decisions around the products and services the institution offers and the customers it serves. The uses of performance measurement information are not limited to expense control, and budgeting and planning. One of the most valuable uses is in the effective and efficient design and delivery of products to a defined customer base. By combining performance information with product management and customer profitability, institutions can better tie the relationships between product development and customer targeting in their quest to virtual banking.

Product management and customer profitability are multifaceted processes, and performance measurement information enhances different parts of these processes to varying degrees. Product management processes may be seen as: a product's overall concept, design, marketing, training, monitoring, pricing, and delivery (which includes packaging, launching, distribution, and monitoring). Key decisions are being made during each of these processes.

Customer profitability processes may be viewed as: targeting and defining the customer group, setting financial goals and expectations, customer pursuit, packaging of services and products, closure (including customer pricing, customer start-up conversion, training, and other tasks to fulfill the customer contract), and finally monitoring.

Performance measurement can facilitate the decisions made during each of these processes by providing valuable financial and nonfinancial feedback. The types of feedback include origination cost, payback periods, break-even volumes and balances, and average transaction volumes, just to name a few. This feedback will aid performance management by directly influencing the behavior of employees or by providing insight into how to influence the behavior of customers. This chapter discusses the many uses of performance management information and suggests several ways to use it to provide valuable feedback. Although the discussion uses product as examples, services offered to customers can utilize these concepts.

MANAGING THE INFORMATION

Key Elements of Product Management

With the rapid changes in the industry today, bankers are faced with ever-increasing demands on product management. In the last 25 years, institutions have more than doubled the number of products and services offered, rarely eliminating one. With the changing regulatory climate, institutions are facing new product competition and even introducing once-prohibited products and services. All this change gives rise to the need to more formally define the key elements of winning products.

Defining the Right Mix of Products and Customers

For many financial institutions, the traditional strategy of being a full service bank by "being all things to all customers" is no longer effective. As the array of potential customers and products increases, the ability to select products that serve a market and also capitalize on the competitive strengths and weaknesses of the institution becomes all the more essential to success. Pinpointing profitable market/product combinations is vital, and product profitability, along with customer profitability, is key to that process. In addition, deciding both how and to whom to provide products and services is key to developing a virtual strategy. Institutions must define the right mix of products and services, targeted to the right customers within the right market. The challenge lies in understanding what is "right," because it can mean different things for different organizations with differing strategies.

The Definition Process

Both product management and customer profitability require a mature organization, capable of setting and measuring profitability goals across traditional organizational boundaries. Because both product management and customer profitability are information-intensive functions, a mature technology infrastructure is required. At times, the analytical information supporting product management and customer profitability will be contradictory—customer profitability and product profitability will be at odds with each other. This highlights the need for integrated views of the information.

Organizationally, an intermediary is needed. The sales, customer service, or product management organizations may be suitable to fit this role. The sales function is aware of customer needs and demands. However, sales may be biased because its compensation would be impacted if the customer/volume were dropped. The product management organization could serve as the intermediary as long as it did not take a singular, product focused view, ignoring the value of customer relationships. The customer service group is, organizationally, separate from the interests of the other two groups and has little expertise in the design and delivery of products and services. The ultimate process owners of this information must, however, be empowered to make decisions which will have a profit and loss impact on the institution as a whole.

The Integrated Solution

Satisfying both product and customer views calls for an integrated information solution. This solution should cross all product lines and services used by customers. Product management systems cull information from "vertical," or singular delivery systems. The customer view is a summation of product information across these vertical products and systems. Hence the customer profitability view is a much more comprehensive view of the institution's total operations, production, etc., based on the product view.

Integrating Data into Information Tools

Systems supporting product management and eventually customer profitability are essentially decision support systems. To create decision support systems, institutions need to know where their data is and what type it is. With this knowledge they can integrate the data for decision support application systems. Following is an example of a growing customer relationship and the product manager's issues with the growing customer relationship.

As mentioned previously, product management systems will be "vertically" oriented application systems. These systems will meet the performance measurement needs of a single product, or possibly two closely related products supported by the same or similar organizations. Regardless, as the customer begins to use more products under differing legal names (Widget Part A Co.; Widgets Part B Co.), for various diverse operating divisions (domestic, international), the product manager will need to identify and understand these various customer accounts as belonging to the same customer relationship. Hence, a single product manager will come to understand the need for tracking volumes, costs, pricing, etc., not only at the transactional, account level, but also at the summary points of customer legal entity relationships and customer organizational relationships. Eventually, the product manager will need to track and understand the volume drivers across even joint venture entities of existing customers—and perhaps even as far as affiliate relationships. The value of a relationship should always be quantifiable to a product manager.

The issue becomes how to track a single relationship across several individually opened, operated, and maintained relationships. One method of bringing a measure of order to the institution's data is a process known as data modeling. Data modeling attempts to link similar relationships based on redefined types of information, for instance linking relationships across different applications based on last names with the same address.

Gathering data, however, is only half the battle. The other half is converting these data into useful information, organizing them, and making them accessible to the right people at the right time—and most important, keeping them current to reflect changes to customers, products, services, costs volumes, and revenues. Customer information files (CIF) should help do that by aggregating data from many vertical, product-account-based databases into a single customer-oriented picture of behavior and profitability.

Many institutions maintain one central CIF that helps to unify customer information from selected areas. A few have one or more CIFs that serve one business. Some large institutions maintain dozens of CIFs for each line of business, a state of affairs that can be worse than having no CIF at all.

Institutions striving to improve their customer information should build an integrated view of the data based on the total customer relationship across all relevant locations, products, and account types, ensuring that the data are complete and all-encompassing. Building and maintaining the data is a process, not an event. Additionally, there should be a concentrated effort to build analytical capabilities that support marketing and management decision-making. For instance, management needs to know which customers are buying which products when, which age groups are most likely to buy, which products and services to link, and which branches are best at generating new savings accounts. A maximum of flexibility is required, because the factors that are relevant to today's business considerations may not be relevant to tomorrow's. And most of all, institutions should make all data accessible to those making decisions.

In addition to internal data, institutions can buy a tremendous amount of supporting data to provide a "fuller" picture. Organizations have begun to take existing operating CIFs and add a great deal of marketing information in order to begin understanding their customer base for targeting purposes. The end result of this new database is known as Marketing Customer Information Files or MCIFs.

MCIFs can contain a wealth of data useful for product positioning and design, including gender, lifestyle, consumption patterns, education, income, occupation, and more. Ideally, the MCIF should be fully integrated with the CIF, enabling analysts to request information and get responses without knowing whether the data originated internally or externally. As the financial industry gains access to more and better information, it can deliver more targeted products and services to customers, using a variety of delivery channels.

USING THE INFORMATION

Pricing and Competitive Practices—An Overview

Having gathered the data necessary for analysis, the next challenge is defining their uses. The first and most common use is in pricing products and services. Because pricing is such a broad topic, with unique implications across industries and subindustries, this text will focus on the commercial banking industry.

Competition in the commercial banking business is sometimes defined by price; at other times price is the least important factor. In these cases, the key is the product or service's ability to be unique in the marketplace. In this regard, a service is more likely to be unique than a product. Products, particularly in this industry, are very similar. Only in a few instances does one bank offer a product others do not have.

Traditional Pricing Practices

Historically, banks' regulated environment created a culture that fostered many of the pricing strategies still in place today. Regulation created a stable, sheltered environment. Product offerings were limited, and they were defined and controlled by the regulators. In addition, various state laws established protected geographic areas. Financial institutions within these areas knew each other's prospective behavior and did not have to worry about intrusion by institutions from outside; regulation prevented it. Regulation further ensured that commercial banks had to face direct competition only from other commercial banks—not from other kinds of financial institutions. Because all competitors operated with the same restrictions, there was an even playing field for all who were allowed to play.

This environment led to pricing practices that evolved with little or no active consideration of factors other than the regulations and the limitations they imposed. Following are discussions of a few such practices.

Market-Based Pricing or "Me Too" Pricing

Because regulators set pricing limits through such devices as Regulation Q, many institutions followed a "me too" approach to pricing. For example, under the guise of following established market prices, all commercial banks offered the same interest rate on savings accounts, charged the same for checking accounts, established the same base rate, and so on. If one bank raised or lowered prices, chances were that all in the same protected territory would follow suit. If the market prices were below the bank's costs, assuming costs were known, the loss would be written off to the "relationship" or to the need to maintain market share. Many commercial banks continue to follow this approach even when they have sufficient information to determine whether a relationship is profitable.

However, the availability of performance information should give banks valuable insight as to whether market-based pricing is indeed healthy. Deviations from market-based pricing can be made if the overall profitability drivers can be predicted by following the practice. Banks can price more aggressively than the market if the increase in relationships is known to be favorable, and price less aggressively when it is unfavorable. Examples include banks that continually set market-based prices on a product when each new relationship drains profits.

Cost-Based Pricing

Under cost-based pricing, an institution would assess its costs and then determine prices by multiplying the costs by a certain factor, such as 1.5 or 2.0. The factor was designed to offset the inaccuracies of cost data, cover estimated overhead, and produce a profit. However, if the cost-based price proved higher than the market price, the "me too" price frequently prevailed, because management believed it could not charge more than its competitors.

Although cost-based pricing is not common today, understanding the relationships of cost to price is important in developing pricing decisions.

Punitive Pricing

This type of pricing has no direct relation to costs or markets, but was intended as a disincentive for using a particular product. A classic example is the charge for insufficient funds (NSF): if the penalty was high enough, institutions reasoned, customers would stop writing NSF checks. NSFs became such a fertile source of noninterest revenue that many institutions kept increasing the fees—until the initial punitive intent of the fee finally took effect and NSF revenues declined.

Geographic Pricing

Knowing the profitability of providing certain core products and services can drive a bank to become more aggressive in pricing, especially if the bank has a strong hold on market share. It has been demonstrated that markets in which one bank dominates, can become price leaders. Customers are willing to pay for convenience. Knowing profitability should be as important as determining price in these environments because banks have the opportunity to be price leaders.

Tiered Pricing

Banks have begun to master the art of tiered pricing, which sets different price levels based on balance levels or transaction volumes. Examples include rates applied to money market accounts with increasing balance levels. Profitability information can be a vital link to determining the appropriate tiered levels. Simply stated, why price competitively at balance or transaction levels that are below the break-even point? And why price aggressively at levels where real economic value is not being created?

Relationship Pricing

A bank may offer services and products at a low margin or even a loss when it can improve overall profit from a relationship through cross-selling high-margin services and products. The bank willingly accepts the low margin or loss on a particular product in favor of optimizing return on the total relationship. Without knowing this profitability relationship and when relationship pricing truly adds value, banks can often end up with two or more undesirable relationships. Relationship pricing has several advantages including:

- Providing the ability to cross-sell.

- Building the customer's psychological commitment.

- Attracting relationship customers who are less sensitive to price than transaction customers.

- Increasing the perceived "switching costs" as the customer uses more products and services.

Relationship pricing often can be confused with bundling products. Relationship pricing generally offers incentives or discounts on any second product purchased. Bundled pricing offers incentives/discounts on a distinct package of products.

PRICING ELASTICITY

Pricing elasticity refers to the change in customer demand for a product in relation to the increase or decrease in the price of that product. Elasticity is an important dimension of bank pricing strategy, volume strategy, and profit maximization.

An "elasticity of demand" model can be built to assess the potential effects of price changes. The first step is to gather historical data of past price changes and the resulting volume movements. Next, customers can be surveyed on their perceptions of current pricing. The goal is to assemble information to support more empirical data on actual price/volume movements in the past.

As Figure 17-1 demonstrates, an inelastic product can provide far greater return to the bank in price movements than an elastic product. Buyers of the inelastic product are not as sensitive to price changes, and therefore pricing changes can have a more positive affect on profitability.

Incremental Pricing

The concept of incremental pricing is based on price, cost, and volume relationships and on the fact that fixed costs will remain constant within a relevant range of volumes. At any level of volume, price must exceed average cost to produce profit. Assuming that profit margins and the resulting profitability are acceptable at current volume levels, current price covers the average costs by an appropriate amount, and total costs are covered as well. The pricing for any future product volume does not need to consider the fixed cost component, because fixed costs are already covered and will remain constant.

Incremental pricing often comes into play when a bank is contemplating additional volume, for example when a pricing objective is to increase market share. Incremental pricing analysis lets management assess the impact of additional volume on the overall profitability of the product.

The incremental pricing concept assumes that prices for future volumes can be set at any level above the variable product cost, even if the price of the new volume is below total average cost. Two distinct prices are being used, as shown in Figure 17-2. There, the cost curve is separated into fixed and variable components, indicating how the "old" price of the current volume adequately covers total costs and provides some level of profitability. Figure 17-2 also shows the incremental profits generated by pricing the new customers at a level higher than the variable cost component.

An example of this concept is the pricing of lockbox services in a bidding situation. Assuming the profitability of the present lockbox product is acceptable, fixed costs—including equipment and support systems—are covered. A new lockbox prod-

Figure 17-1—Pricing Elasticity

	Inelastic Product (ATM Fee)	Elastic Product (Money)
Original Volume of Purchases	1,000 transactions	1,000 units
Original Price	$1/transaction	$1/unit
Total Revenue	**$1,000**	**$1,000**
Price Increase of 50%	$1.50/transaction	$1.50/unit
As a result, sales volume declines	−100 transactions	−800 units
New Volume of Purchases	900 transactions	200 units
New Total Revenue	**$1,350**	**$300**
Change in Volume	10%	80%
Change in Price	50%	50%
Price Elasticity	**0.2**	**1.6**

Figure 17-2—Incremental Profits as Viewed Using Cost Curve

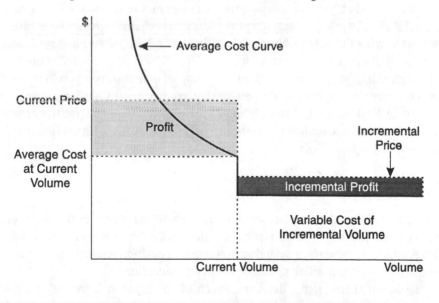

uct, which uses the same equipment management and facilities, can be priced so that its price exceeds only the variable costs, such as check processing and additional clerical time. The original lockbox customers "carry" the fixed costs. This arrangement gives the institution the option of charging a lower fee for the new lockbox volume. In turn, the institution may gain a competitive advantage and increase market share.

A common misconception regarding incremental pricing is that any level of future volume growth will increase profits, as long as the price remains the same. This assumption holds true only within the relevant range of the fixed costs. As volume grows, capacity approaches the limit. When the volume exceeds the relevant range, excess capacity is depleted and significant additional expenditures are required. The step-function nature of the fixed-cost component becomes obvious and average unit costs dramatically increase, as shown in Figure 17-3.

Figure 17-4 illustrates how—in connection with volume growth—incremental pricing affects profitability. As volume increases and approaches the limit of the first range (no excess capacity), there are incremental profits. Once the volume exceeds the relevant range, a significant incremental loss may occur. But if the volume growth is large enough, the new average cost may approach the original level. The required additional volume appears in Figure 17-4 as "equivalent cost volume."

These changes in cost levels can be seen in the lockbox example. As stated, fixed costs such as equipment management and facilities are covered by standard lockbox products. But when product volume grows, changes may be necessary. For example, clerical staff and work space may have to be added. If such cost increases were entirely associated with the new lockbox product, its profitability would be significantly reduced. Will a new average cost be developed for all lockbox products? In that case, the standard lockbox product might unfairly support unnecessary expenditures (e.g., special procedures required for the new lockbox arrangement). Continued growth for the new lockbox product ultimately could create a need for a new facility or other major enhancements, leading to significant cost level increases with a serious impact on profitability.

Pricing Strategy

Today, financial institutions face several major marketing objectives that affect pricing decisions. Among the most important of these objectives are pricing to introduce new products, to increase or defend market share, to position products relative to the competition, and to position products within a product line.

In any of these pricing decisions, much of the input is "revenue" oriented. Management wants to ascertain what the volume will be at a certain price; this estimate translates into expected revenue. The cost side of such decisions provides management with the opportunity to study the margin effects of a particular pricing decision. Before examining product costs and their impact on pricing, however, banks should note a number of factors affecting pricing decisions.

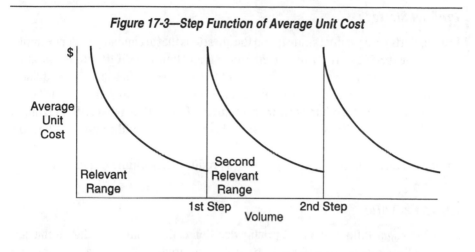

Figure 17-3—Step Function of Average Unit Cost

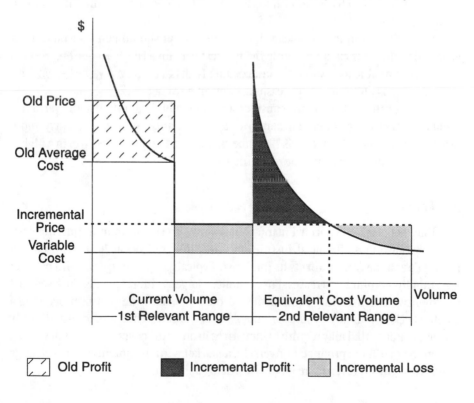

Figure 17-4—Potential Effect of Incremental Pricing on Profitability

Product Strategy

Pricing starts with product strategy and the questions that accompany it. For example, what is the specific purpose of a given product, and how does it fit into the product mix for selected markets? Is the product intended to be a loss leader to establish a customer relationship, or is it expected to be profitable on a stand-alone basis? Does management see the product as a low-cost source of funds? If so, what is the maximum allowable cost? All of these questions, and others, represent valid strategies. The most important point, however, is that the product's purpose should determine its pricing strategy, rather than the "market price" of a product determining its purpose.

Customer Value

A second major influence on the pricing decision is the product's value to the customer. All too often, financial institutions develop products and use either a market or cost-based price, with little or no regard for the product's customer value. The product can be a dismal failure if the price is either higher or lower than the customer is willing to pay. Too high a price loses business. Too low a price brings in less-than-optimal profits.

When determining customer value, an institution should consider more than economic value. For example, while the interest paid on a NOW account represents real economic value to customers, the account also has a perceived value—it enables customers to pay bills and access cash through an ATM network.

An institution also should consider any intangible value that will warrant a higher product price. Premium bank cards, for instance, presumably carry more prestige than standard bank cards. To some customers, that prestige is worth a higher price, even if the value cannot be quantified.

Market Size

Total market size and expected market share provide critical input for pricing decisions. Because most financial institution costs are fixed or, at best, semifixed, a product's volume greatly affects its final cost. Typically, the average cost of a product falls rapidly as volume increases. For example, a larger volume spreads the fixed cost of expensive check-sorting equipment and thereby makes the cost of processing a single check less than it would be under lower volume. Thus a market with only limited size potential may require higher prices in order to "cover" the costs of serving that market with the product. Conversely, a market with the potential for very large volumes might suggest a more moderate pricing approach.

Competition

Competition plays an obvious part in the pricing decision. But rather than automatically pricing the same way as competitors, an institution should try to identify niches for its products and price accordingly. Even if external competition does heavily influence product pricing, an institution still needs product cost information to evaluate a product's profitability for selection, elimination, and analysis purposes.

Effect on Other Products

The way a product's price affects other products is another component in pricing decisions. Many institutions do not recognize this impact to the extent that they should. Management may not realize, for example, that a pricing decision that changes transit product volume also will affect the lockbox product, because lockbox checks use the same equipment, staff, and resources that the transit product does. Possible ripple effects on other products must be considered in a well-planned, rational pricing strategy.

Costs in Pricing

In the simplest sense, profitability is the difference between the revenue generated by a product and the cost incurred by providing the product. Costs depend on the expenses required to provide every facet of a given product, service, or transaction. These expenses, called the unit cost, are in addition to the costs required to support the volume of each service provided. Revenues, too, depend on the volume of services provided, as well as on the price charged for each unit. Profitability, then, is determined by the interrelation of three factors: cost, price, and volume.

The price in Figure 17-5 illustrates a profitable product, but of course not all products can be represented on such a graph. As product profitability information develops, it is likely that many products will be more accurately represented by Figure 17-6. In this figure, the price (presumed to be the market price) is below the cost. The result is a loss, shown by the shaded area.

Use of Costs in Support of Pricing Analyses

Cost information can be used to support pricing analyses—whether the pricing objective is to increase market share, to introduce a new product, to defend market share, or to position a product. Following are examples of using cost information for various objectives.

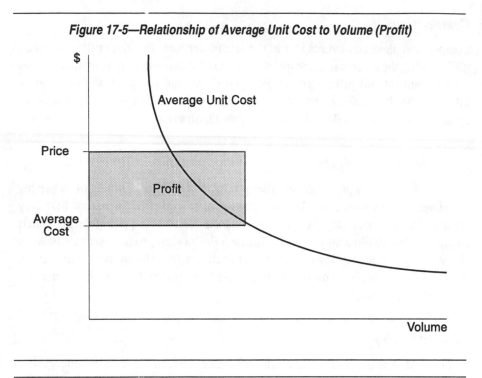

Figure 17-5—Relationship of Average Unit Cost to Volume (Profit)

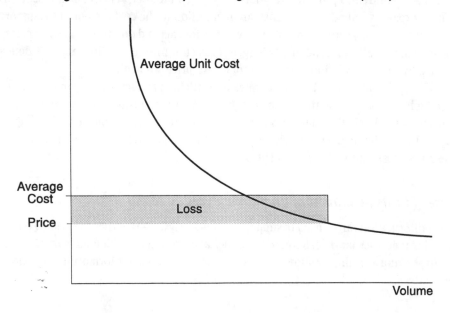

Figure 17-6—Relationship of Average Unit Cost to Volume (Loss)

Break-Even Analysis

Simply stated, break-even analysis examines the relationships among the profitability determinants of price, cost, and volume, to derive the relative profitability of each set of determinants. The break-even point is the level a given determinant must reach in order to produce a profit while all other factors remain at a constant level. For example, given the price and costs (fixed and variable) of a product, the break-even volume is the level at which any lower volume will result in a loss and any greater volume will result in profitability. Figure 17-7 illustrates this relationship. If any one of the three profitability determinants is held constant, a relationship between the remaining two can be established to indicate what the level of one factor, relative to the other factor, must be for the product to realize a profit. If cost remained constant, for example, a relationship could be established between price and volume to indicate what the level of price should be, relative to volume, and volume relative to price, for the product to realize a profit.

Break-even analysis can be particularly useful when introducing a new product. Given a pricing strategy, management can estimate volume levels and, considering costs, determine whether the new product will at least cover those costs. The principles of break-even analysis also can be used in other ways, described in the following three applications.

Lending Rates Based on Loan Characteristics

A loan's dynamics include origination and closing costs, ongoing service costs, and the ensuing stream of revenues. For the most part, only the last of these items depends on the size or balance of the loan. The costs associated with a loan may not vary significantly, and in most cases the levels of those costs may be easily determined. A loan's dynamics can be shown on a rate (price) versus principal balance (volume) curve. This curve can be based on simple profitability for the life of the loan, or it can include the time value of money by discounting the cash flows. It represents the combinations of rate and principal balance that generate a given level of profit.

The primary factor in lending profitability is the cost of funds. By varying the anticipated cost of funds in any given case, a graph consisting of a series of isobars or "parallel" interest rate/loan balance curves can be developed. Each of the isobars represents a different level of anticipated cost of funds, as illustrated in Figure 17-8.

Each curve represents all combinations of rates and balances that result in a given level of profitability for a given cost of funds. Once the anticipated cost of funds is established, the profit margins required to achieve the desired return decrease as the size of the loan increases. Profitability levels, however, are identical for all points

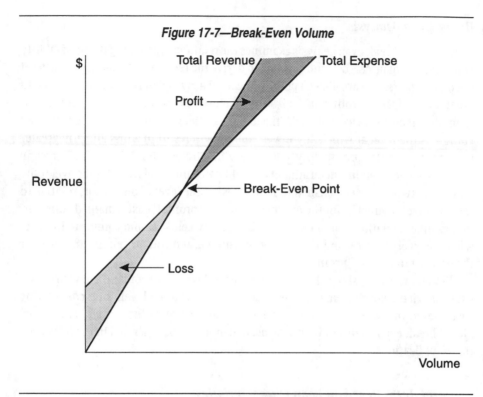

Figure 17-7—Break-Even Volume

along a given curve. When the anticipated cost of funds changes to a higher level, the interest rate/loan balance combinations on the next curve show the required return.

The lending officer can use each curve to price according to the size of the loan. More favorable rates can be offered for higher balance loans without sacrificing profitability. The difficulty of rate setting and the anxiety of losing high balance customers are mitigated by the availability of specific pricing guidelines.

Factors other than the cost of funds can be included in the rate/balance curves. For example, a curve based on inherent risks can be developed for each type of loan. In this way, a loan officer can quickly develop appropriate rates for each risk classification. For riskier loans the officer can shift to the appropriate curve and offer a higher rate. The officer thus has a mechanism for comparing two loans of identical size but of different types and risks.

The same concept can be used for pricing home mortgages and incorporating origination fees: each curve can represent the interest rate/loan balance structure, given the number of points to be paid. The institution then can offer customers the option of paying more initially to receive a more favorable rate, or paying less initially but a higher rate overall.

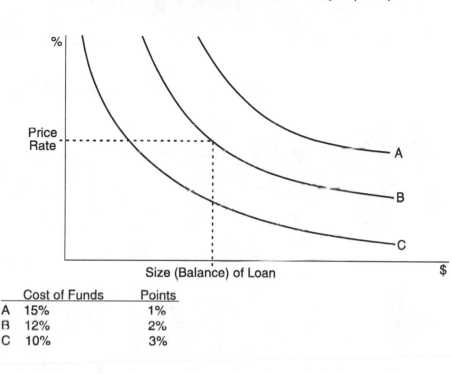

Figure 17-8—Use of Cost Curve in Break-Even Analysis (Loans)

	Cost of Funds	Points
A	15%	1%
B	12%	2%
C	10%	3%

Liability Pricing Based on Maturities or Balances

Applying break-even analysis to the pricing of time deposits is illustrated in Figure 17-9. From the interest rate/deposit balance curves, the institution can determine the minimum balance required at each interest rate to achieve the desired level of profit. As the minimum balance increases, the profit margin required to achieve the profit-ability objective decreases. As a result, the institution can offer more favorable rates without adversely affecting profitability.

The time to maturity for the deposit can be treated the same as the estimated average life of the loan—and with greater certainty, because of early withdrawal penalties. A series of curves can be developed for each level of maturity. The interest rates offered to customers for deposits can be based on the time-to-maturity and on the balance size of the account. The effect will be to induce longer-term and larger deposits (if deemed advantageous to the institution) and to discourage unwanted deposit terms. Flexibility is maximized because rates are tailored to customers' needs.

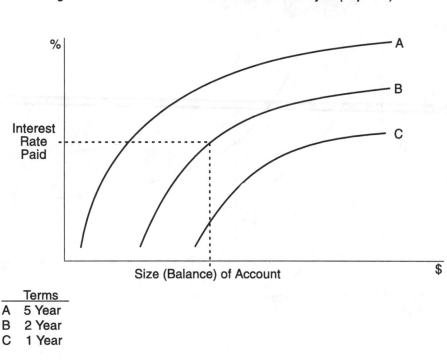

Figure 17-9—Use of Cost Curve in Break-Even Analysis (Deposits)

Terms
A   5 Year
B   2 Year
C   1 Year

Minimum Balance Requirements for Liabilities

The same concepts can be applied to establishing the minimum balance requirements associated with interest-bearing demand deposit accounts. Here the service costs associated with the product determine each interest rate/account balance curve. The rate of interest offered, or the minimum balance required, depend on the amount needed to cover the service costs of the account and provide the desired profit.

The same concepts can be applied to establishing the minimum balance. The application of rate/balance curves on an individual account basis is a powerful tool for establishing compensating balance relationships with commercial customers. The cost associated with various services provided to commercial customers can be incorporated into the individual rate/balance curves. Institutions can then price services to allow flexibility in determining each account's price/balance relationship. They also can include a combination of fee and balance-related revenues in assessing the profitability of the customer relationship.

U-Curve Positioning

Cost information can be helpful in assessing a product's positioning and how that position might be changed. Figure 17-10 illustrates a product positioning "U" curve that accounts for several product factors. The horizontal axis represents a range of positioning approaches in terms of price, average cost, and associated volume. The vertical axis indicates the extent of profitability potential. The theory behind this curve is that profit potential will be higher at either end of the "U" than at the middle. Effective product management, then, will seek to position the product at either end.

Figure 17-10 represents a classic example of U-curve positioning. Over the years, Mercedes-Benz has positioned itself as a supplier of high-priced, luxurious automobiles, thus appealing to a low-volume but price insensitive market segment. Volkswagen, in the days of the "Bug," represented the opposite strategy: appeal to the price conscious, high-volume market segment.

The manufacturing costs of each automobile, though not identical, were much closer than the relative prices. Mercedes looked to high profit margins on each sale, while Volkswagen preferred to "make it up" on volume. Despite considerably different strategies, both companies were highly profitable.

The point is that an institution may position a product on either end of the "U." In an effort to increase the market share of a particular product without reducing profitability, an institution might offer a product of lower quality and lower price. Alternatively, the institution might choose to restructure the product for a different market segment by adding cost. Through this added cost, the institution might provide better-quality service in the form of special account officers, premium funds availability, and so forth. The additional cost would require higher prices, but a premium could be charged—assuming that the added cost provided additional value to the customer. The premium probably would be feasible for a smaller market than the original one, so volume would be lower. However, the overall profitability of the product could be superior to that of its predecessor.

Product positioning has had a dramatic impact on securities and brokerage firms. Discount brokers have penetrated the low price segment of the market by performing basic buy and sell orders at favorable prices and offering no investment advice. Full-service brokers have had to differentiate their product by offering quality service, in the form of advice and peripheral products, or else take the route of competing with the discount brokers on price.

Commercial banks, too, are now positioning themselves at either end of the "U." On the retail side of their business, they have been reasonably successful at differentiating themselves from the competition by using ATM networks, branch automation, customer service units, bank by phone, home banking, and other services. On the commercial side, a similar approach has produced evaluations of customer to loan

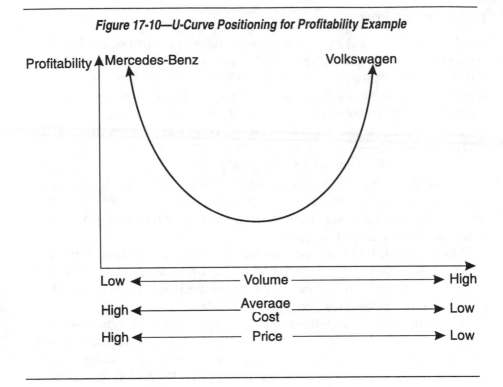

Figure 17-10—U-Curve Positioning for Profitability Example

officer ratios, cash management services, check cashing, and other support services with customer appeal. Where most financial institutions have fallen short is in pricing their products to correspond to the level of service quality they provide. Unless the pricing strategy is matched to the cost of providing the product and the ensuing volume, the potential profits will not be realized.

The concept of product positioning should be used at every level of a financial institution. At the broadest level, an institution itself may be strategically positioned to appeal to retail or commercial customers, to high-net-worth individuals only, or to all customers. It also can position itself by assuming a regional, national, or international scope or a posture as a community bank. These positions do not have to be mutually exclusive, but they do provide some direction.

Once the institution's intent has been established, organizational, product, and customer profitability analyses provide the required information for positioning among and within market segments. Target markets can be selected on the basis of geographic location, customer size, or other criteria. For example, analysis might indicate that expansion within certain geographic areas would yield a higher return than in other geographic areas. Branch relocations might be recommended. Another analysis might suggest allocating resources to expand the commercial lending activities to small businesses, where profit potential is stronger and competition less intense than in the larger corporate market. As the number of states allowing interstate banking increases, this type of profitability information is vital.

Product profitability information allows the institution to tailor each of its products and services to appeal to specific characteristics of targeted markets. Where appropriate, new product development should focus on cultivating specific markets that will give the institution the most help in achieving its strategic objectives. Within the institution, product profitability provides a mechanism for motivating sales representatives and all customer contact personnel to focus on the products that are best for the institution, not just for the individual unit.

It is most important to position products to appeal to each customer segment within each market, and to price products in a manner that maximizes profitability or otherwise best achieves the institution's overall goals.

SYNOPSIS

Product and customer management consists of many phases, and profitability information is useful to each of them—especially to pricing. Pricing may be done to defend market share, to increase market share, to introduce a new product, or to position a product. However, if these analyses consider revenue aspects only, the impact on profitability remains obscured. Cost information plays an important part in pricing and product/customer management, and several pricing analyses—break-even analysis, incremental pricing, and U-curve positioning—highlight its role.

The key points to remember are these:

- Marketing objectives must be clear.

- Given the marketing projections for volumes, necessary resources must be in place.

- The impact on profitability must be assessed.

CHAPTER 18

Planning and Budgeting

OVERVIEW

In the past, planning and budgeting were seen as distinct processes, with little integration. Planning was the domain of corporate staff working with senior management to review various strategic investment proposals. Budgeting was primarily a staff function with the dual purpose of satisfying corporate requirements and providing a control mechanism for mid-level managers.

Leading banks are beginning to link the strategic planning process with the annual budgeting process so that short-term performance goals support the institution's long-term initiatives. Planning and budgeting are key elements of the performance measurement process, incorporating everything from determining what measures to use to achieve the desired objectives to setting the levels of performance against the measures chosen. Further, many banks are putting less emphasis on reporting past results and are stressing prospective views of business performance in their key decision processes. The budgeting process is beginning to include the development of key internal, external, and customer-driven measures, as discussed in the opening chapters of this book.

This chapter addresses these planning and budgeting roles. After an overview of the different methodologies for planning and budgeting, the most widely used budgeting elements and techniques are discussed. The chapter concludes with a brief review of other issues that arise in the planning and budgeting process.

METHODOLOGIES FOR PLANNING AND BUDGETING

Planning, Budgeting, Forecasting

Planning can be broadly defined as all managerial activities that lead to:

- The definition of strategic and operational goals.

- The appraisal of the internal and external environments.

- The determination of appropriate means to achieve the desired goals.

- The specific definition of markets, businesses, and customers.

- Key business processes and products and the reasons for their organizational, geographic, and technological distribution.

- The measurement of progress relative to the desired goals.

Budgeting is the process by which planning is made operational. It is the establishment of specific quantitative objectives and the measurement of performance relative to those objectives.

The budgeting of various responsibility line items usually is based on a prediction of future events. Developed from historical and current information, this prediction can range from the informal (e.g., intuitive) to the formal (e.g., operations research techniques). Once an expected level of activity is projected, the budgeting process quantifies these related measures.

Forecasting is revising budgets based on current information. Forecasts often are calculated by adding year-to-date actual data to the balance-of-year budget data. Alternately, forecasts consist of year-to-date actual data plus revised budget data for the balance of the year. The original budget data is recast, given the current results and economic environment.

Financial institutions approach the budgeting process with many different methodologies. The most common are the bottom-up approach, the top-down approach, and the U-planning approach. These three methodologies are summarized in Figure 18-1 and discussed in detail below.

Bottom-Up

The bottom-up budgeting methodology concentrates on relatively low levels of management, including responsibility center managers. To develop the overall organizational budget or plan, the institution aggregates the budgets and plans of such specific responsibility units as responsibility centers, summary centers, departments, divi-

Figure 18-1—Budgeting Methodologies

Methodology	Characteristics	Disadvantages	Advantages
Bottom-Up	Responsibility unit management focus	May not reflect organizational goals and plans	May be more realistic/attainable
	Developed by aggregation of unit budgets	May ignore unit interdependencies	
Top-Down	High-level management focus	May be viewed as unattainable by lower levels	Budget reflects organizational goals
	Middle management develops budget to support organizational goals/objectives	Lower levels do not perceive ownership of budget	
U-Planning	Both high/low level management focus	Long complex process	More aggressive yet realistic/ attainable
	Budgets are prepared within context of organizational goals		

sions, and groups. Each organizational level bases its budget on available information and on what its manager considers attainable.

The bottom-up approach can produce a more realistic plan than one developed under other methodologies, because managers with line responsibilities create the budgets. The budget also can be more attainable, because it receives input from individuals throughout the organization. The resultant pride of authorship helps to ensure that a wide variety of managers buy into the targeted measures and goals.

The main disadvantage of the bottom-up approach is that an aggregate of individual plans often does not result in common goals or overall organizational objectives. Depending on the degree to which these objectives and the aggregate plans differ, numerous budget iterations may be required to align the plans with the institution's goals. Furthermore, the bottom-up approach may ignore interunit dependencies: different organizational units may not start the planning process with the same goals, assumptions, and other considerations.

Top-Down

The top-down approach focuses on higher organizational management levels than does the bottom-up approach. Under this approach, senior management determines long-term objectives. Based on these objectives, senior management develops—and provides to middle and lower management—strategies and guidelines to support the attainment of the stated aims. Middle and lower management then develop specific plans and budgets to implement the strategies and achieve the goals.

The major advantage of the top-down approach is that all operating and profit budgets and measures are developed within the context of organizational goals and are established at levels designed to attain those goals. From a practical standpoint, the top-down approach is relatively straightforward and easily coordinated, and typically requires relatively few budget iterations.

On the negative side, however, the top-down approach may produce unrealistic corporate goals. Management-established guidelines can force the development of unattainable budgets at lower organizational levels. Such goals may not be readily accepted by the lower levels or by the organization, thereby inhibiting motivation throughout the institution.

U-Planning

The U-planning budgeting methodology is a hybrid of the bottom-up and top-down approaches. Like the top-down approach, it calls for senior management to develop broad organizational objectives and strategies and to communicate these ideas downward through the organization. Like the bottom-up approach, it calls for personnel at lower organizational levels to prepare detailed budgets they consider realistic and attainable. These budgets, however, are prepared within the context of overall organizational objectives and strategies. Detailed budgets are aggregated, and the total budget is reviewed by senior management. As appropriate, senior management adjusts organizational objectives to be more realistic, or requires middle and lower management to reconsider the budgets that have been submitted. It repeats the process until the organizational objectives are deemed realistic, attainable, and clearly supported by the detailed budgets.

The U-planning approach fosters dual benefits by requiring negotiation between lower- and upper-level management. It not only produces a realistic and attainable budget that is "bought into" at all organizational levels; it also increases institution-wide communication of the measures deemed important to management. This communication process also helps communicate the real measures on which management places value. Unfortunately, it also may require exhaustive iterations and a long and complex budgeting process. Furthermore, the negotiation inherent in the U-planning approach may lead to a final plan that is less aggressive than a plan created under the top-down approach as regards its attempts to meet organizational objectives.

ELEMENTS OF BUDGETING

Traditionally, budgets consisted of financial elements. Expenses are relatively easy to project, especially given the fixed nature of many banks' expense bases. People, space, and equipment can be costed and projected based upon recent historical trends and inflation assumptions. However, the planning process has been expanded to include many nontraditional elements.

Financial versus Statistical Elements

Many nonfinancial elements are now included in the planning process. Internal measures of cycle time (e.g., loan response time), efficiency measures, and market penetration measures are being discussed, reviewed, and "budgeted." Customer measures are being included, for instance, customer retention rates, relationships per customer, and satisfaction levels. Volume numbers and other statistical elements are a part of many banks' budgets. These statistics can include number of accounts and new accounts to be opened, volumes charged on credit cards and new cards to be issued, assets under management and number of trades executed, and other key volumes.

Quality measures are entering into the planning process. These can include error rates on transactions processes, number of customer telephone inquiries answered within a given period of waiting time, and department turnover.

Drivers of Business

The use of statistical elements in the budget process is an outgrowth of the use of the budget as a dynamic strategic as well as operational business model. Indeed, in some institutions, a primary use of the annual budget is to require the business managers to rethink, refine, and defend the model of their business implied in the budget. Rather than just a profit and loss statement, the budget in this instance is a dynamic model of how macroeconomics and microeconomics variables influence the business results. Modeling a business means understanding the drivers of the business and the sensitivity of the bottom line to changes in driver assumptions. With a detailed business model, a manager can project business volumes and then calculate projected financial and operational results.

Balance Sheet Budgeting

More and more banks are budgeting balance sheet items at the responsibility unit level. Typically the domain of the Treasury function, balance sheet budgeting is part of business modeling referred to above. With the move toward calculating return on equity by line of business, managers are now accustomed to understanding and managing their balance sheet components as well as income and expense items. To the extent that interest-bearing assets and interest-paying liabilities drive the net interest margin, budgeting for these items is an important part of the planning process.

Capital Budgeting

Another fundamental part of the planning process is budgeting for capital items. Long-term investments in buildings, leasehold improvements, computers, applications software, and other capital items often are handled separately from the annual budget process, or planned for centrally within the organization. Capital budgeting also includes underwriting new business and product development. Leading institutions are incorporating capital budgeting within the annual process, and requiring business line managers to request and justify capital expenditures as part of their annual plan.

Level of Detail

Deciding a budget's level of detail is important for general ledger accounts as well as for responsibility units. General ledger accounts can be budgeted individually, or as ranges of accounts or account categories. Likewise, responsibility units can be budgeted at the center level or at more summary levels. For either general ledger accounts or responsibility units, the tradeoff is the same: the more detail needed, the more time and resources required.

FORMS OF BUDGETING

A financial institution can combine various budgeting techniques with any of the three planning approaches. Following are discussions of the most widely used budgeting techniques—static, moving, and rolling budgets—as illustrated in Figure 18-2.

Figure 18-2—Comparison of Static, Moving, and Rolling Budgets

Type of Expense	January Actual	January Budget	Var.	February Actual	February Budget	Var.	June Actual	June Budget	Var.	July Actual	July Budget	Var.
Static Budget												
Product Expense	185,000	178,000	-7,000	190,000	178,000	-12,000	189,000	178,000	-11,000		178,000	
Selling & Admin.	80,000	83,000	3,000	78,000	83,000	5,000	77,000	83,000	6,000		83,000	
Moving Budget												
Product Expense	185,000	178,000	-7,000	190,000	178,000	-12,000	189,000	178,000	-11,000		188,000	
Selling & Admin.	80,000	83,000	3,000	78,000	83,000	5,000	77,000	83,000	6,000		78,000	
Rolling Budget												
Product Expense	185,000	178,000	-7,000	190,000	178,000	-12,000	189,000	178,000	-11,000		188,000	
Selling & Admin.	80,000	83,000	3,000	78,000	83,000	5,000	77,000	83,000	6,000		78,000	

Type of Expense	December Actual	December Budget	Var.	January Actual	January Budget	Var.	June Actual	June Budget	Var.	July Actual	July Budget	Var.
Static Budget												
Product Expense		178,000										
Selling & Admin.		83,000										
Moving Budget												
Product Expense		188,000										
Selling & Admin.		78,000										
Rolling Budget												
Product Expense		188,000			188,000			188,000				
Selling & Admin.		78,000			78,000			78,000				

Static Budgets

Management develops static budgets from assumptions regarding expected levels of activity, required resource utilization, and resulting profits or losses. Once established, the assumptions remain unchanged for the duration of the budget—which always is a specified period, normally a year. Comparing actual performance to the static budget identifies variances in both volume and rate. Part of Figure 18-2 is an example of a static profit and loss budget.

Static budgeting offers the advantage of being relatively easy to develop, understand, and use. However, it does not automatically provide information necessary to review the causes of the resulting variances. For example, a static budget does not isolate the effect of differences in activity (i.e., product volume). Variances reported as negative could be caused by increased activity and could, in fact, represent a very positive situation. In a period of rapidly expanding activity, a static budget could be of limited value in performance measurement, without additional research.

Moving Budgets

Like static budgets, moving budgets are prepared for a fixed period, usually a year. However, they are updated to reflect more current information and changing assumptions.

The revision process is the main advantage of a moving budget. Including updated data on a continuing basis theoretically enables an institution to reflect current trends and conditions in its budget. If, for example, an institution updates a moving budget semiannually, it can make revisions at the end of six months to reflect business changes. Consider the situation in Figure 18-2, where product expenses are consistently above budget and selling and administrative expenses are consistently below budget. With a moving budget, the budget for the remaining six months can be adjusted to address the variance between budgeted and actual expenses. In Figure 18-2, for instance, the $178,000 per month budgeted for product expenses could be adjusted to $188,000 per month.

This process, however, points to the primary disadvantage of moving budgets: The periodic reexamination and updating requires considerable time and resources. The process also invites controversy by creating a moving target for performance measurement. For example, a manager could meet or exceed the original budget while failing to meet the revised budget, in which case potential disagreements could arise regarding his or her performance. Furthermore, because managers can revise budgets, they may have less motivation to meet challenging targets than they would under static budgets.

Rolling Budgets

Rolling budgets are prepared for *constant* periods as opposed to the fixed periods common to static and moving budgets. A 12-month fixed budget could be a calendar-year budget, while a 12-month rolling budget would always cover the next 12 months, regardless of the month in which it starts (see Figure 18-3).

Rolling budgets offer the advantage of keeping management's attention on a fixed period in the future, no matter what the time of year. Management can factor changing assumptions into the planning process on a continuing basis, producing a plan that always concentrates on the next predetermined period. Rolling budgets, however, fall prey to the same problems that plague moving budgets: exhaustive revisions and increased controversy in evaluating performance, extensive time and resource requirements, and the possibility of being less motivational.

Figure 18-3—Comparison of Static and Flexible Budgets

Static Budget	Actual	January Budget	Var.	Flexible Budget	Actual	January Budget	Var.
Product Expense	185,000	178,000	−7,000	Product Expense	186,900	178,000	8,900
Selling & Admin	80,000	83,000	3,000	Selling & Admin	80,000	83,000	3,000

Product Expense

Per Unit Budget = Budget Expense/Budget Volume
$178,000/20,000 = $8.90 per Unit

Flexible Budget = Per Unit Budget × Actual Volume
$8.90 × 21,000 = $186,900

Flexible Budgets

Under the flexible budgeting approach, management plans expenses and revenues at varying levels of resource utilization and activity, recognizing the fixed and variable aspects of costs, revenues, and profits. This method has the advantages of providing a high degree of control and of increasing performance measurement capability through the ability to measure actual costs, revenues, and profits against what they should be at various levels of activity. Because the impact of changing volumes is isolated, variance analysis can be enhanced by addressing rate and efficiency variances separately.

The flexible budgeting method is not as straightforward as the other methodologies. It can be more difficult to understand and more time-consuming to implement and maintain. It also provides a moving target for individuals and organizational units as volumes change.

Unlike the other three approaches, a flexible budget does not make use of forecasts. Instead, it applies an established rate to actual volumes. If, as shown in Figure 18-3, the $178,000 budgeted for monthly product expense were based on 20,000 units, the per-unit budget would be $8.90. If the actual volume in January were 21,000 units, the flexible budget would adjust to $186,900. Thus instead of the unfavorable variance that exists with a static budget, the variance with the flexible budget is favorable. This type of budget is particularly useful for an operations manager who evaluates expenses relative to volumes processed.

Zero-Based Budgets

Zero-based budgets require management to justify, in each budgeting cycle, all expenditures—as opposed to new expenditures only. Each program or expenditure is treated as if it were new and must be evaluated accordingly. Figure 18-4 further illustrates this process.

The major advantage of zero-based budgeting is that all proposed resource usage can be judged consistently. Management can assess and allocate resources on a quantitative basis such as cost/benefit analysis or net present value analysis. Optional and discretionary operations and expenses can be more closely scrutinized. Ranking and judging each and every program and expense, however, can be an overwhelming task. The required detail and number crunching can make the process itself more important than the outcome. Discretionary programs and programs obligated by legal, regulatory, and operational issues can be difficult to separate for analysis. Assigning relative importance to dissimilar activities may be resisted by individuals and organizational units that fear the elimination of favorite projects. Finally, while

Figure 18-4—Zero-Based Budgeting

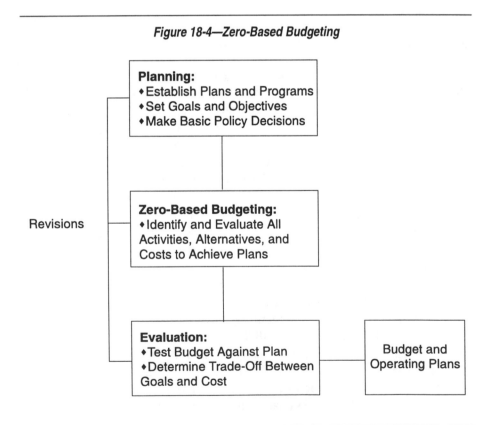

zero-based budgets deal effectively with the management of controllable or discretionary actions, they fail to address the management of interest spreads and production activities.

VALUE-ADDED BUDGETING COMPONENTS

Forecasting and Modeling

Several institutions have implemented sophisticated line-of-business forecasting models. Conceptually, these models project a run rate of the business based upon recent history (current quarter vs. last quarter, current quarter vs. same quarter last year, actual vs. plan, etc.). Run rates are then adjusted for nonrecurring items, special assumptions, acquisitions, new investments, and other incremental additions to the steady state book of business. The advantage of these models is that they automate the more mechanical aspects of forecasting and allow attention to focus on understanding, calculating, and justifying change items. Forecasting models facilitate a continuous forecasting mode, where revised projections are calculated quarterly, or even monthly.

Long-Range Planning

Long-range planning is by nature more high-level than budgeting and forecasting. Most institutions lack a direct active link between the formulation of their long-term strategic plans and their annual budgets. This link is critically important. Without it, day-to-day management of individual businesses can be at odds with overall corporate goals. Short-term considerations can achieve priority over the need to manage a portfolio of businesses to maximize shareholder value.

One way to create a linkage between budgeting and planning is through the use of the strategic scorecard. As discussed in Chapter 3, a strategic scorecard contains those key performance measures and external benchmarks selected as being important for measuring the performance of the business in the context of the bank's long-term strategy. During the annual planning process, each business line manager has a dialogue with senior bank management about the business objectives and key measures. This dialogue revolves around the past year's results against last year's scorecard. The dialogue ends with all parties agreeing on the set of measures which will comprise the scorecard for the following year. Managers understand that their performance-based compensation will be driven by the results measured by the strategic scorecard.

SYNOPSIS

Strategic, tactical, and operational plans differ in time frame, priority, risk, and level of detail, but they are essentially interrelated: operational plans are the first segments of tactical plans, which in turn are the near-term segments of strategic plans. All levels of planning share the need to be ongoing processes—not just once-a-year events. Each process must involve various levels of management.

Of the three types of plans, operational plans—or budgets—are of the shortest term and have the most immediate priority. An institution can base its budgets on any of several methodologies, the most common of which are the bottom-up approach, the top-down approach, and the U-planning approach. All have advantages and disadvantages and vary in their respective levels of management participation, goal attainability, and complexity.

These methodologies can be implemented though various budgeting techniques. Static budgets, moving budgets, rolling budgets, flexible budgets, and zero-based budgets are among the most widely used. As with the budgeting methodologies, these techniques all have their benefits and drawbacks. Selection of one over another should depend on an institution's specific needs and goals.

Budgeting is a tool to support the control of expense and other components of the profitability measurement formula, and it can play an important performance measurement role as well. Tying the success of a budget to the effectiveness of a manager, however, can provide valid conclusions only when the areas measured are those over which the manager clearly has control, and when the manager's decisions can be directly linked to results. By addressing both concerns, an institution can establish an effective planning environment that will assist management in improving the institution's profits.

CHAPTER 19

Cost/Expense Management

OVERVIEW

In the previous chapters we discussed developing cost and profitability information. However, the development of more accurate and credible profitability information is not an end in itself, and it does not automatically result in improved profitability and performance for the financial institution. Business line and product managers must incorporate this information into both their tactical and strategic decision making and act on the information to improve the institution's bottom line.

This chapter will focus on how cost and profitability information can be used to support analysis and decision making throughout the institution. We will begin by discussing some of the more traditional ways that managers have used cost and profitability information to support their business and operational analyses. This discussion will include an overview of such concepts as performing fixed and variable analysis, capacity analysis, acquisition cost analysis, and new product analysis, including life-cycle and target costing.

We will conclude with presenting the concepts and methodologies incorporated in Total Cost Management, which we introduced in Chapter 8. As previously described, fundamental to the concept of Total Cost Management[1] is its use of Activity Based Costing and Business Process Analysis, as well as a concept called Continuous Improvement. These concepts can help an institution improve the value of its products and services and ultimately its financial performance. We will discuss each concept in more detail here in order to show how the information gathered and developed as part of the costing and profitability measurement efforts also can be used

---

1 Terminology and definitions in this chapter draw from and are consistent with Ernst & Young LLP methodologies and *The Ernst and Young Guide to Total Cost Management* by Michael Ostrenga with Terrence R. Ozan, Marcus D. Harwood, Robert D. McIlhattan (1992).

in the day-to-day analysis of the business and in ongoing, institution-wide improvement efforts.

TRADITIONAL USES OF COST AND PROFITABILITY INFORMATION

Once cost and profitability information have been developed for any unit, product, customer or other cost object, the most immediate opportunity for using the results of this information centers on implementing both near-term actions and long-term strategic improvements for those cost objects that are the most unprofitable or out of line with their intended goals and performance requirements. Comparing actual results to plan, creating trended performance data, and ranking data are some of the more common ways of analyzing cost and profitability results and prioritizing areas for improvement.

A more innovative way of viewing the results of the profitability information is to array or plot the profitability results of products, services, markets, etc., against the institution's perceived competency to deliver the products or services or compete in particular markets. An example of this type of mapping or ranking of results is shown in Figure 19-1.

Figure 19-1—Acting on ABC

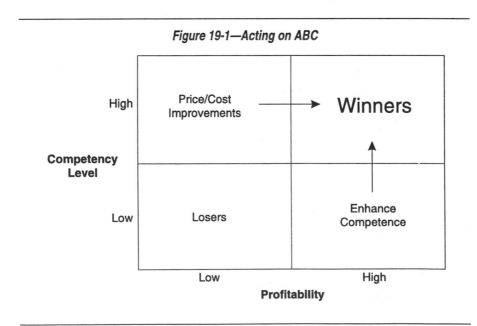

The competency indicator used can be a judgment resulting from competitor analyses of the institution's competency in a particular area vis a vis the competency of its competition. Results are plotted and the implications assessed in order to focus on and prioritize the candidates for action that will gain the most benefit for the institution. Institutions also can perform this type of mapping by plotting the information showing dollar amounts of profit or loss by cost object within each quadrant. This provides a graphical view with dollar impact, and aids in prioritizing action plans by potential dollar impact.

As shown in Figure 19-1, this type of analysis might show that there is an opportunity to take a product where the organization has high competency but lower-than-expected profitability and make cost or pricing improvements to move the product into the high-performing "winner quadrant." On the other hand, a product in the lower left quadrant, where the institution lacks a high level of competence or competitive advantage and also is a loser from a profitability standpoint, may be a candidate for deemphasis or discontinuance. Overall profitability could be enhanced by eliminating this product or limiting the amount of resources, such as marketing dollars, people, and capital that are allocated to it. An analysis such as this mapping exercise shows that profitability results should not be viewed in a vacuum. Many insights and benefits can be gained by analyzing the results of profitability information in conjunction with other factors, whether financial or nonfinancial.

Additional day-to-day tactical and longer-term strategic situations in which institutions can use cost and profitability information include the following:

- Support for pricing decisions and market analysis
- Justification for marketing expenditures
- Analyzing the impact of product mix changes
- Exit or entry decisions relating to products, markets, or delivery channels
- Resource allocation decisions, including staffing and capital allocations, etc.
- Process improvement and cost reduction initiatives
- Organizational infrastructure changes
- Activity based budgeting and planning support
- Target costing analysis
- Marginal costing analysis, addition/deletion of products, customers, etc.
- New account/customer acquisition cost and payback analysis
- Fixed/variable cost analysis
- Capacity analysis

- Investment justification
- Sourcing decisions, including insourcing and outsourcing
- Life-cycle costing
- Product, pricing, market, and distribution channel strategy decisions

This is only a partial list of the decisions and analyses that can be supported by cost and profitability information. The information derived from data developed during an Activity Based Costing effort can be especially useful in supporting these types of analyses and decisions, due to its focus on business process, customer requirement, and activity level costing data. The following section provides a brief discussion of some of the analyses listed above.

FIXED AND VARIABLE COST ANALYSIS

Most financial institutions' cost accounting systems do not distinguish between fixed and variable costs. However, users of the information may from time to time need to understand the impact of a particular action on the institution's cost structure. This section will explain the concepts of fixed, variable, and semivariable costs and discuss relevant uses of the information.

As shown in Figure 19-2, fixed costs are costs that do not fluctuate as product volumes change, although they can change as a result of managerial or strategic decisions. Variable costs change in direct correlation to changes in product volume. Semivariable costs vary over a range of volumes, but do not change in a linear relationship.

For profitability reporting purposes, it is not necessary to classify all costs as fixed, semivariable, or variable. However, for tactical and strategic decisions such as pricing decisions, volume fluctuations, and outsourcing, an ad hoc analysis can be performed to determine how the organization's cost structure may change as a result of the action. This classification requires a careful analysis of the impacted areas to identify which cost components will change due to incremental changes in volumes. Capacity constraints, resource requirements, operating expenses, and the impact on indirect areas must also be considered.

In the short run, financial organizations have a high degree of fixed costs relative to variable costs. For example, most costs to originate a commercial loan are already in place. Loan officers are on the payroll, equipment is in place, and the process has been developed. The only variable costs may be approval forms, credit inquiry charges, minor transportation charges, etc. However, over time, all costs are variable

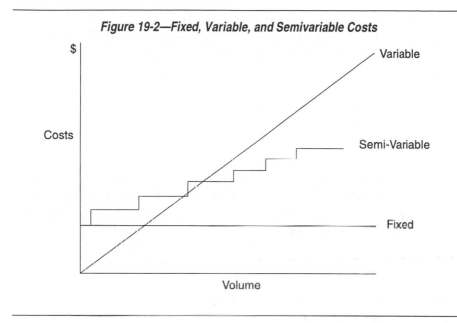

Figure 19-2—Fixed, Variable, and Semivariable Costs

because all cost components can be modified to meet projected demand. Management can strategically respond to such issues as rethinking business lines, buying versus leasing facilities, and outsourcing operations.

Many leading authors on the subject suggest that fully absorbed costing leads to better pricing decisions than does incremental costing. They consider fully absorbed costing analogous to long-term variable costing. New customers result in long-run implications, they believe, and thus should carry a share of fixed costs.

ACQUISITION COST ANALYSIS

The costs associated with acquiring new accounts can often be high. This section will address some costs associated with the acquisition of new accounts and their implications in performance measurement.

Acquisition-related costs refer to all costs associated with selling and originating new accounts. For example, the cost to acquire a commercial loan may include sales calls, the loan origination and approval process, loan closings, collateral processing, etc. It is important to understand acquisition costs in order to position products in the marketplace to maximize profit opportunities. For instance, institutions may choose to not advertise 30-day certificates of deposit if the cost of acquiring them exceeds potential profits.

Acquisition costs vary by product type and it is not unusual for many products to have payback periods in excess of one year. Implementation of a product profitability system can enable institutions to identify both the costs associated with acquiring accounts and the projected profits resulting from them. This information can then be used to determine the payback period associated with each product. Many institutions have been surprised to learn how high the acquisition costs of certain accounts can be. For example, the origination process associated with commercial loans can be complex and time consuming. Certain commercial loans with low balances and short average lives may never achieve a profitable payback period.

Payback periods also demonstrate the need to retain customers. New accounts tend to turn over more quickly than seasoned accounts. One recent study published by the Council on Financial Competitiveness found that almost 25 percent of new demand deposit accounts turned over in the first year, compared to less than 15 percent of accounts at least five years old (see Figure 19-3).[2] As a result, many new customers may not remain with the organization long enough to pay back start-up costs.

Finally, by implementing a performance measurement system an institution can pinpoint the source of product acquisition costs, which is often the branch network system. As a result, it may uncover performance improvement opportunities to improve the efficiency of the origination process. For instance, many institutions have turned to platform automation systems to expedite the process of originating new account relationships.

CAPACITY ANALYSIS

In many nonfinancial organizations, managers have recognized the need to identify and understand capacity-related costs. However, financial institutions have been slow to realize the financial implications associated with under capacity or excess capacity situations.

Unlike manufacturing companies, institutions cannot easily adjust their staffing levels to meet demand requirements. Thus, they generally have developed their staffing levels to absorb peak periods of demand and are experiencing excess capacity within many departments. By identifying capacity-related costs, managers can improve their decision-making abilities.

Capacity costs can include personnel, CPU time, personal computers, floor space, etc. In fully absorbed profitability reporting, the costs associated with overcapacity are allocated to organizational units, products, and business lines. Products with low

---

2   Source: *Retail Customer Retention*, Volume 1, page 42, Council on Financial Competition, 1991.

Figure 19-3—"Young" Accounts Less Stable than "Seasoned" Accounts

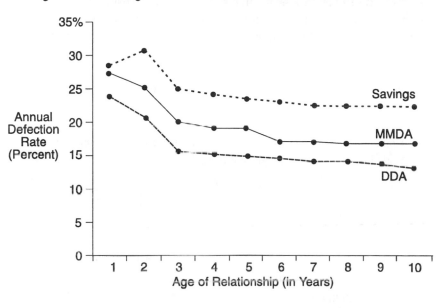

capacity utilization will have a high unit cost structure. It is important to avoid the "death spiral," in which prices are increased to cover excess capacity costs, resulting in lower volumes and more excess capacity. Instead, volumes should be increased to reduce unit costs and make the product more competitive in the marketplace.

Capacity costs can also be linked to the semivariable costing issues discussed earlier in this chapter. As volumes fluctuate over a given output range, certain areas may need to add or delete capacity.

LIFE-CYCLE COSTING

Originally a concept used in the manufacturing industry, life-cycle costing groups cost information into the stages of a product or service's life cycle and then uses the resulting information to make decisions about the product or service. The greatest benefit of life-cycle costing is its ability to identify the costs associated with each stage of product or service development, delivery, and after-sales customer support. Today institutions are faced with increasing competition and more new products being developed as well as shorter product life cycles and an emphasis on shortening the time it takes to get new products to market without sacrificing quality and customer satisfaction. It is important that they know what it will cost to develop a new product or product feature and how long it will take to recoup that cost.

In management accounting, a new product's profitability may be projected by capturing the cost of development separately and amortizing it over the product's life expectancy. The product or service is considered profitable when all of its development costs are recovered.

Another way to organize cost information and cost and profitability projections is in the traditional marketing view of life-cycle: new product introduction, growth product, mature product, declining product, etc. Costs, volume, and profitability information can be organized in this way to support product and market sales forecast, annual budgeting, and strategic planning.

TARGET COSTING

Target costing is another concept that has been primarily used in manufacturing but is being discussed more frequently in the service industry. Like life-cycle costing, it deals with developing the costs of new products and services. It attempts to target a cost to produce and deliver a product and service. The analysis is focused on the following:

- Determining the market share that the new product or service will capture.

- Determining what features and services the product must have to satisfy customer requirements and induce them to purchase it.

- Determining what profit margin is necessary, the overall costs of delivering the product across all the departments, and the processes that will be impacted, across its entire value chain.

- Determining how the product or service can be delivered at a profitable cost.

After these analyses are performed, a "go or no go" decision is made—whether or not the product or service can be delivered with the specified product features, at the specified cost, and with the ability to achieve the desired volume of sales to be profitable over time.

These types of analyses are not new to financial institutions, although they may be called by such new terms as target costing, versus new product cost or profitability costing. What may be new for many institutions is the ability to support these types of sophisticated costing, investment, and profitability analysis because the institution has more complete, accurate, and timely cost information. Also the ability to produce these analyses is supported by cost information that is available at an activity and business process level, not by the old functional unit view of cost and profitability information. Many analyses such as new product investment decisions and life-cycle or target costing, sourcing, etc., need to view the entire value chain. They thus incorporate all the activities and business processes involved in order to make a fully informed decision for the financial institution as a whole.

The next section provides an overview of the Total Cost Management approach to developing and using Activity Based Cost information and business process analysis and the decision support tools offered by Continuous Improvement to improve the bottom line. We will begin by defining the concepts, including revisiting why business process analysis is important. We will then briefly discuss some of the more traditional approaches to cost reduction and profitability improvement that are still used as quick fixes today—and explain why these don't work over the long run.

Next we will focus on the concept of business process analysis and the use of Activity Based Cost analysis to support cost reduction and process improvement efforts, using root cause analysis and process value analysis. Finally, we will discuss the concept of Continuous Improvement, including improving decision support, establishing and monitoring critical success factors, and developing improved performance measurement information.

A detailed review and presentation of the full complement of tools and methodologies within Total Cost Management cannot be presented in one or two chapters of this text. This chapter and Chapter 8 are designed to provide an overview of the Total Cost Management concepts and methodologies for use in financial institutions. A more complete presentation of this topic is provided in the book *The Ernst & Young Guide to Total Cost Management.*

TOTAL COST MANAGEMENT OVERVIEW

Total Cost Management (TCM) is a comprehensive set of approaches and techniques used to proactively manage total corporate resources (e.g., human resources, equipment and supplies, capital, etc.) and the activities that consume those resources. Figure 19-4 shows the approaches and techniques which comprise TCM. Fundamental to TCM is the belief that in-depth understanding and continuous improvement of an institution's business processes and management of activities—and their associated costs—provide the keys to improved business and financial performance.

The power of TCM is that each of its techniques builds on the previous ones. The depth of analysis that these techniques allow offers significant opportunities to manage an institution's business processes and ultimately influence and improve

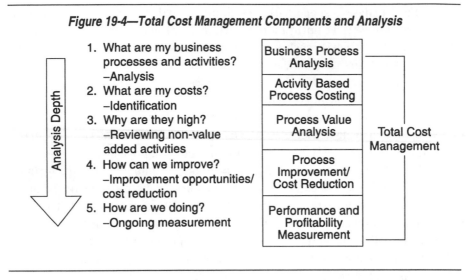

Figure 19-4—Total Cost Management Components and Analysis

1. What are my business processes and activities?
   –Analysis
2. What are my costs?
   –Identification
3. Why are they high?
   –Reviewing non-value added activities
4. How can we improve?
   –Improvement opportunities/ cost reduction
5. How are we doing?
   –Ongoing measurement

Analysis Depth

Business Process Analysis	
Activity Based Process Costing	
Process Value Analysis	Total Cost Management
Process Improvement/ Cost Reduction	
Performance and Profitability Measurement	

profitability. To recap on a high level: In the initial step, known as Business Process Analysis, all of the institution's business processes and activities are identified and analyzed. Next, costs are identified for those processes and activities through Activity Based Costing. Once an institution has begun to view and calculate costs on a process/activity basis, it can use the data generated to improve the business process, reduce costs, and improve management decisions. The final step is to develop Profitability Reporting and Strategic Performance Measures. These support tactical and strategic objectives in order to monitor the impact of changes and the institution's progress toward established goals.

TCM is based on the theory that it is not the organizational units, products, or customers within an institution that consume resources and incur cost, but the business processes/activities which make up them up. The various products, customers, organizational units are comprised of different levels of business processes and activities, and therefore have different cost structures.

Thus, it is important to understand that all of the TCM tools and techniques, including Activity Based Costing, are most effective if based on a process/activity view of the organization, rather than following the traditional organizational and accounting method of developing, analyzing, and acting on management accounting information. As stated in Chapter 8, the process and activity view of the organizations and cost development is the foundation of the new approach to cost management. TCM promotes the concept that an institution cannot manage costs themselves, but must manage instead the underlying processes and activities that result in those costs.

A few years ago, the popular approach to cost management and cost reduction was to cut expenses out of budgets, review actual line item expenses at a departmental level, and impose percent reductions in expense levels, headcount reductions, and so on. This across-the-board broad-brush approach often was unsuccessful in the long run because it did not focus on the underlying causes of the costs. It did not take into consideration the processes and activities necessary to deliver products and services and meet customer requirements. Often, because the underlying activities that caused the costs were not eliminated, the costs returned.

The new philosophy of cost management recognizes that an institution must manage the processes and activities that consume costs. Only by changing, reducing, or eliminating the cause of the activity and its associated costs, can the institution have a sustainable impact on reducing costs and improving profitability. This new approach also focuses on customer requirements as a key to determining which cost producing processes and activities are truly necessary.

WHY THE PROCESS ANALYSIS IS IMPORTANT IN TOTAL COST MANAGEMENT

As explained in our discussion of Activity Based Costing in Chapter 8, the traditional approaches to cost reduction were based on the premise that institutions were not made up of processes and activities, but rather were merely collections of individual activities taking place within various departments. Activities were targeted for elimination or redesign based solely on their importance to the objectives of the departments where they occurred. If the cause of the activity or task in one department was the result of an activity or underlying objective of another department, and the study did not follow the process flow, the underlying root cause may have been missed and inappropriate action taken. As a result an eliminated activity or task may have to be reinstated. Getting at these underlying root causes requires viewing an institution as a network of linked business processes. Each process is a series of related activities, and several departments share responsibility for the entire process.

Processes and activities flow horizontally across departments. A single department can perform many activities related to a number of distinct processes, and all of the components of a single process may be performed by a number of unrelated departments throughout the institution.

Taking the process approach should enable an institution to realign tasks around a management objective or a customer requirement, without necessarily changing the organizational structure. Customers are defined in this context as both internal and external. External customers purchase the product or service and have requirements for features, price, quality, and after-purchase service or support. Internal customers depend on the output of others as the input for their own work, and likewise have requirements that must be met (e.g., timing and quality). Instead of focusing on organizational structures and independent departments TCM focuses on defining customer requirements, identifies what is needed to accomplish those requirements, and identifies the most efficient and cost-effective way of doing so.

A general outline of the steps of a business process analysis includes:

- Defining relevant activities.

- Identifying and validating input requirements from other areas.

- Estimating cycle times. Cycle time is simply the time it takes to perform an activity or task.

- Identifying the root cause of the activity and the customer for the activity.

- Determining the value of each task or activity relative to customer requirements.

ROOT CAUSE IDENTIFICATION

Root cause analysis means finding out what causes a cost to be incurred or an activity to be performed. Within the context of business process analysis and improvement, when a problem in the process is identified the root cause of the problem also is identified. Some examples of root causes are incompatible systems, redundant processes such as redundant data entry, incomplete or poorly designed data collection vehicles such as poorly designed forms, poorly designed work areas impeding work flow, inadequate controls, or too many controls—the list goes on.

PROCESS VALUE ANALYSIS

Every process or activity requires input in the form of resources, capital, materials, technology, etc., and converts that input to an output needed by an internal or external customer. If an activity is not being performed to meet a customer requirement it should not be performed. All too often when performing a process analysis, one discovers that an activity or process is being performed because "it has always been done," or work is done in a particular manner because "we've always done it that way." A fundamental part of business process analysis is a technique called process value analysis.

Process value analysis is a technique whereby each activity or task is reviewed and classified as to whether it meets the criteria of being value-added or non-value-added from a customers point of view. Within the value-added classification there are generally two further breakdowns, real-value-added and business-value-added.

The definition of these three classifications are as follows:[3]

- *Real-value-added*—A task or activity is classified as real-value-added if it exists to meet a customer requirement, or if a customer would deem it important to be performed in order to produce the expected end output.

- *Business-value-added*—These are activities and tasks that, while not adding value from a customer's point of view, are required to run the business. Examples may be producing the annual report, completing forms to meet regulatory requirements, or performing credit checks and filing documents with the IRS.

- *Non-value-added*—These are activities and tasks that are not required to achieve the desired output and which customers would not consider important and might not be willing to pay for. Possible examples of non-value-added activities are storage of inventory or processing rework.

After root cause and process value analysis are completed, the financial institution will be armed with sufficient information to perform cost reductions and business process improvements that will be sustainable in the long run. The cost reduction and process improvement efforts will take the form of eliminating unnecessary activities and process steps, combining or resequencing activities to make a more efficient and smooth process, simplifying processes or product options, moving locations and layouts to improve workflow and reduce wait and transfer time, or automating processes.

Figure 19-5 shows an example of the "drill down" capabilities of TCM techniques for the customer service area of a financial institution. Starting with the Activity Based Cost phase, the customer service area's process and activity costs were studied. One of the processes, called customer service inquiries, was determined to be a high-cost area that needed further analysis for cost reduction and process improvement. The next step was to "drill down" to the activity components of the customer service inquiry process, identify the costs of the activities, and perform a process value analysis on them.

The process value analysis and root cause analysis identified two problem areas within the research area relating to payment options. The problem areas were (1) confusing account statements, and (2) too many payment options. Poorly designed and confusing customer account statements were causing additional work to be

---

3   H. James Harrington, *Business Process Improvement: the Breakthrough Strategy for Total Quality, Productivity, and Competitiveness,* McGraw-Hill, Inc., New York (1991).

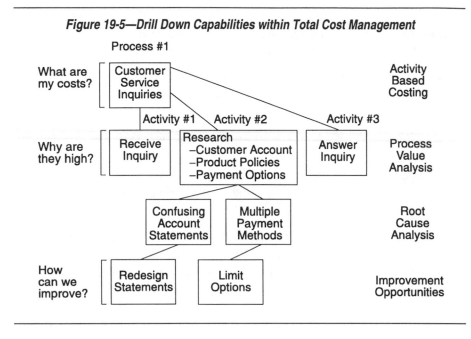

Figure 19-5—Drill Down Capabilities within Total Cost Management

incurred in answering and researching information. These statements were also negatively impacting customer satisfaction. And the proliferation of payment options was adding to processing costs. The research staff had to be trained on all of the various payment options. The improvement opportunities identified were to redesign and simplify the account statements and reduce the number of payment options available. These actions resulted in an improved process, sustainable cost reductions, and increased customer satisfaction.

The solutions undertaken using TCM methodologies will have sustained results because they are based on an understanding of the business process input, conversions, and outputs. They also take into consideration customer requirements: both internal and external customer needs as activities flow within and across departments, and the requirements of the external customers who purchase the end products and services. Root causes and value are assessed as well as cost data, in order to make informed and sustainable changes to the institution's processes and cost structures.

VALUE-ADDED VERSUS NON-VALUE-ADDED COST ANALYSIS

Another use of cost information that combines the results of Activity Based Costing and Process Value Analysis results is shown in Figure 19-6. Being able to analyze

Figure 19-6—Activity Based Costing—the Insight

| | Traditional | ABC | | |
		VA	NVA	Total
Salaries	$11	$ 9	$ 2	$11
Equipment	2	1	1	2
Occupancy	4	3.5	.5	4
Imputed Interest	1		1	1
Overhead	6	2	4	6
Total	$24	$15.5	$8.5	$24

Activity Based Cost information and decompose total cost information into its value-added and non-value-added components provide more insights and actionable information than what is available from the more traditional cost view of total costs. Using a combination of Activity Based Costing and value analysis, action can be taken to reduce or preferably eliminate the non-value-added cost components to improve profitability. This approach also provides information on which cost elements can be eliminated without the danger of reoccurrence and without impacting customer requirements. Under the traditional view of cost information, all an institution knows is that overhead costs are a large component of the cost, but not that 66 percent of that cost is non-value-added and can be safely eliminated.

CONTINUOUS IMPROVEMENT

The final component of TCM is a concept called Continuous Improvement. In today's increasingly competitive environment, in order to gain and maintain competitive advantage and indeed survive, a financial institution must continually change and improve itself relative to past performance. Continuous Improvement is that process of continual betterment.

The principles of Continuous Improvement, improved performance measurement, and improved decision making were touched on earlier in this book. The first principle, of establishing critical success factors and improved performance measurement systems, was discussed in Chapter 3. Under Continuous Improvement, a financial institution must not simply develop cost, profitability, and performance information. It must establish critical success factors that the organization as a whole, each business and operational unit and product, market, etc., must achieve and surpass in order to achieve its desired performance and profitability.

Also, a process must be put in place to monitor and track performance against goals. As discussed in Chapter 3, this performance measurement should encompass both financial and nonfinancial measures. Under Continuous Improvement, it is important to continually measure progress towards achieving a desire objective and to measure improvements against past results. Each performance measure established should support the achievement of critical success factors.

The second principle of Continuous Improvement is to use the information developed through Business Process Analysis and Activity Based Costing for improved decision support throughout the institution. The primary tenet of this approach is that when information is organized around business processes and activities, it provides a depth and breadth of information that supports better and more informed business decisions. For example, the process and activity view provides the right information to develop product and service cost information over their full process life cycles. The Activity Based Costing view, along with value analysis, provides insightful cost information for cost reduction decisions. Other decision support approaches include the ability to estimate and track the impact of process improvements and capital investments.

SYNOPSIS

Continuous Improvement efforts are therefore rooted in improved capability for analysis and decision making and in enhanced ability to develop and track performance measures against customer requirements and critical success factors.

In summary, Total Cost Management concepts and methodologies, along with the other cost analysis approaches presented in this chapter, represent traditional as well as newer and more sophisticated uses of cost and profitability information to support decision making and improve performance. Developing good cost information is not the end goal—the goal is using that information to make informed decisions and continuously improve performance. This will result in sustainable competitive advantage and improved profitability and performance for the institution and its shareholders.

Index

T–U–V–W